Bakery Science and Cereal Technology

The Authors

Dr. (Mrs.) Neelam Khetarpaul presently working as Professor and Head, Department of Foods and Nutrition at CCS Haryana Agricultural University, Hisar is the recipient of many awards viz., Distinguished teacher Award-2000, Young Investigator Award, Ms. Manju Utreja Gold Medal and cash award for doing the best research work in the University and Best research Paper Award by AFST (I), Hisar Chapter. She is the recipient of various Visiting Fellowships abroad funded by different national and international agencies and visited USA, Australia, UK, Hungary and Netherlands for academic pursuits. She has published more than 150 research papers in various journals of national and international repute and 12 books in the discipline of Food Science and Human Nutrition.

Dr. (Mrs.) Raj Bala Grewal is presently as Associate Professor in Centre of Food Science and Technology, CCS Haryana Agricultural University, Hisar. She has an excellent academic record and was recipient of the All Round Best Student Award of the College and also of International Women Year Gold Medal. She was nominated as FAO Fellow for undertaking training in 'Recent Methods in Food Science and Technology at Michigan State University, USA. She has published 4 books and 40 research papers in national and international journals.

Dr. (Mrs.) Sudesh Jood is presently working as Associate Professor in the Department of Foods and Nutrition at CCS Haryana Agricultural University, Hisar. She has a brilliant academic record. She has been awarded Indian National Science Academy (INSA) Young Scientist Award 1993 for doing the best research work. She has been a visiting Research Scientist to the University of Reading, Department of Food Science and technology, UK from 1997-1998 on the Academic Commonwealth Staff Fellowship. She has published 50 research papers in various journals of national and international repute and one book.

Bakery Science and Cereal Technology

by

Neelam Khetarpaul

Professor & Head, Department of Foods & Nutrition,

CCS Haryana Agricultural University, Hisar

Raj Bala Grewal

Associate Professor, Centre of Food Science & Technology

CCS Haryana Agricultural University, Hisar

Sudesh Jood

Associate Professor, Department of Foods & Nutrition

CCS Haryana Agricultural University, Hisar

Daya Publishing House®

A Division of

Astral International Pvt. Ltd.

New Delhi – 110 002

ISBN 978-81-7035-763-6 (PB)

Published by : **Daya Publishing House®**
A Division of
Astral International Pvt. Ltd.
– ISO 9001:2015 Certified Company –
4736/23, Ansari Road, Darya Ganj
New Delhi-110 002
Ph. 011-43549197, 23278134
E-mail: info@astralint.com
Website: www.astralint.com

Laser Typesetting : **Classic Computer Services**
Delhi - 110 035

Printed at : **Replika Press Pvt. Ltd.**

PRINTED IN INDIA

Preface

Bakery science and cereal technology is one of the important courses being offered to undergraduate students as a professional elective. Through this course the students shall acquire adequate knowledge of structure, nutrient composition and processing of various cereals particularly those which are used in bakery industry, milling of wheat, physico-chemical and functional properties of cereals, role and storage of ingredients used in baking, types and grades of flour, baked products prepared by hard and soft wheat *viz.* bread, cakes, crackers, cookies, wafers etc, losses in baking, quality evaluation, standards, packaging and sale of bakery products, and prospects and problems of bakery industry. This book containing the above information can also be used as a technical guide and reference book to personnel engaged in bakeries.

We sincerely feel that this ready reference study material shall prove to be very useful and handy to the students.

Neelam Khetarpaul
Raj Bala Grewal
Sudesh Jood

Contents

Preface *v*

1. Importance of Cereals 1
2. Nutrient Composition of Cereal Grains 10
3. Structure of Cereal Grains 26
4. Milling of Wheat 40
5. Types and Grades of Flour 52
6. Processing and Parboiling of Rice 59
7. Processing of Maize 77
8. Processing of Sorghum 84
9. Processing of Barley 90
10. Processing of Oats 96
11. Quality Evaluation and Functional Properties Used in Baking 101
12. Characterization and Importance of Wheat Gluten Protein in Baking 126
13. Role of Bakery Ingredients 133
14. Bread Making 151
15. Quality Control of Bread Making 170

16.	Baked Products from Soft Wheat	186
17.	Macaroni Products	218
18.	Storage of Bakery Ingredients	222
19.	Bakery Norms and Setting of Bakery Unit	228
20.	Specification for Raw Material Used in Bakery	236
21.	Losses in Baking	246
22.	Packaging and Sale of Baked Products	251
23.	Bakery Sanitation and Personal Hygiene	258
24.	Prospects and Problems in Bakery	271
	Appendix I: Cake Faults	278
	Glossary of Baking Terms	286
	References	293
	Index	298

Chapter 1
Importance of Cereals

The cereals comprise a group of plants from the grass family, Gramineae whose seeds are valuable for food for both man and domestic animals. Cereal grains are among the first crops to be planted and harvested by mankind. Long before the beginning of the historic period, man learnt to use cereals (Fig. 1.1). Ancient civilizations flourished partly due to their abilities to produce, store and distribute these cereal grains. In the Western hemisphere, maize was the cereal domesticated in America by the early Indians, even before the arrival of Europeans. When Columbus discovered America, maize was growing in most of the region by the inhibitants. Afterwards, it was introduced into Europe. In ancient Mexico, the harvest festival was held in honour of the goddess of Maize, or the 'long-haired mother' as she was called. The festival began at the time when the plant had attained its full growth and the tassel at the top of the cob indicated that the grain was full formed. At this festival, the women and men wore their hair long to imitate maize tassels and they danced tossing their hair to encourage the tassels to grow large and in profusion so that the grain might be correspondingly large and fat, that the people might have abundance.

Rice and wheat were the important early cereals developed in Asia Minor and Asia. These cereals had important place in the great Asian civilizations. Records show that from about 2300 to 1750 BC, wheat, barley and rice were grown by the inhabitants of northern India. In all these ancient societies, cereals continued to be among the preferred crops right through to the Egyptians and to the modern farms of our time. Since wheat was grown in the prehistoric times, geneticists as yet are not aware of the fact what wild seeds were the parents of today's high yielding varieties of wheat. Barley had its origin in Ethiopia and northeast Africa. The use of barley in both ancient Hindu and ancient Greek religious rites suggests that barley cultivation is ancient. This has been confirmed by remains found at Stone Age lake-dweller sites in Europe.

Cereals form the main bulk of the food supply consumed by mankind especially in developing countries as they are the inexpensive source of food energy and protein. They are used directly or in modified form. Cereals are also used as animal feed and hence, converted into meat, milk and eggs. They are also used for industrial purposes.

The principal cereal grains grown in the world are corn, rice, wheat, sorghum, barley, oats, rye and millets. A new cereal of considerable interest is triticale which is a cross hybrid of wheat and rye. Different cereals grow under different agro-climatic conditions *e.g.* sorghum and millets grow well in semi-arid conditions, deep water rice in arid regions while rye and oats require cold climates. Cereal plants range in height from 30 cm (*e.g.*, teff) to 300 cm (pearl millet and sorghum). Most cereals are thin-stemmed grassy plants, but maize, sorghum and pearl millet have thick stems more similar to sugarcane than grass. Cereal crops provide the farmer with straw for fodder and thatch, as well as grain for the family and the market.

Each cereal grain is a seed and hence, a living entity. If not damaged, it is viable and has all the characteristics expected of a living organism. The grain has genetic information, all the complex biochemical substances required for biosynthetic machinery and energy stores which help the grain to germinate under optimum condition.

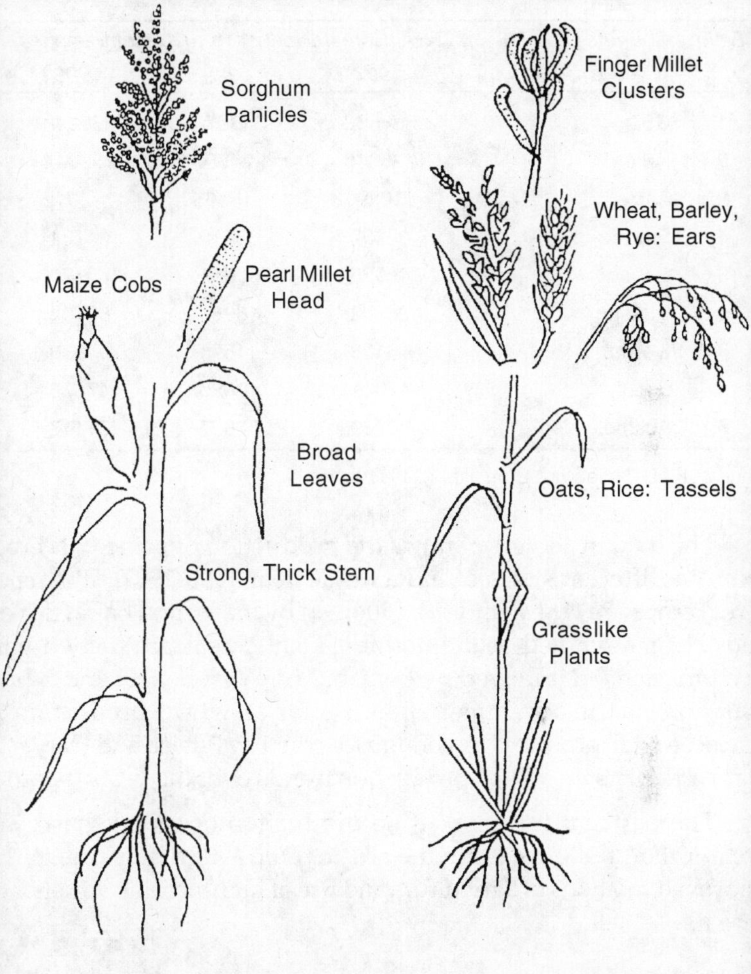

Fig. 1.1: The Principal Types of Cereal Plants

Cereal Production and Importance

The world production of major cereals has improved over the years. The data in Table 1.1 represents the major cereal producing countries in the world during 1997-1999. The cereal production was maximum in USA followed by India and Africa.

Table 1.1: Major Cereal Producing Countries of the World

S.No.	Countries	Total Cereal Production (000 metric tonnes) 1997	1998	1999
1.	USA	336502	349570	336028
2.	India	226646	224707	230042
3.	Africa	110891	115165	112912
4.	France	63432	68419	64761
5.	Canada	49526	50851	53776
6.	Russia	86802	46969	53783
7.	Germany	45486	44575	44333
8.	Brazil	47321	40625	47635
9.	Australia	30829	31667	31117

Source: FAO Bulletin of Statistics (2000) 1: 15-17.

The data in Table 1.2 shows the production of principal cereal crops in different states of India in the year 1996-1997. The major cereal crops are wheat and rice followed by maize and bajra. Barley and jawar remained at the bottom. Total cereal production was maximum in UP followed by Punjab, MP, West Bengal and Bihar. Haryana stands at number eight. As far as wheat production is concerned, UP produced maximum followed by Punjab and Haryana. Fig. 1.2 depicts the wheat production trends over the years in India.

The per cent increase in the production of cereals has been greater than the increase in the area of cultivation. It is due to the improved methods of agriculture and use of high yielding varieties of cereals.

Energy

Cereals are the staple food for majority of the global population. They supply the bulk of the food consumed by the humans, as they are the cheapest and excellent source of food energy especially in developing nations. In the infants' diet, cereal is the first food to be added. In adult's diet, most of the calories are recommended to be derived from complex carbohydrates present in cereals. Whole grains provide about 350 Kcals per 100 g. Cereals provide 70-80 per cent of the daily energy intake of large section of the population in India.

Table 1.2: Production of Cereal Crops in India (1996-1997)

S. No.	States	Cereals (000 tonnes)							
		Rice	*Jawar*	*Bajra*	*Maize*	*Wheat*	*Barley*	*Other Cereals*	*Total Cereals*
1.	Uttar Pradesh	11773.4	361.8	1017.3	1550.9	24331.6	668.8	325	40028.8
2.	Punjab	7338	2.2	4.0	352	13679	108	—	21483.2
3.	Madhya Pradesh	6200.9	828.2	125.8	947.9	7383.5	95.9	265.6	15847.8
4.	West Bengal	12636.8	0.4	0.1	83.5	839.0	5.0	18.4	13583.2
5.	Bihar	7236.4	2.9	3.8	1510.8	4610.5	49.6	106.8	13520.8
6.	Maharashtra	2614.4	6240.5	1831.1	490.2	1167.0	1.2	208.6	12553.0
7.	Andhra Pradesh	9900.2	627.8	117.1	1075.8	6.3	—	188.8	11916.0
8.	Haryana	2466.0	30.0	652.0	44.0	7832.0	88.0	—	1112.0
9.	Rajasthan	174.2	290.8	2313.0	1022.7	6776.1	378.0	7.8	10962.6
	All India	81312.3	11088.0	7905.1	10611.5	69274.7	1435.8	3234.0	184861.4

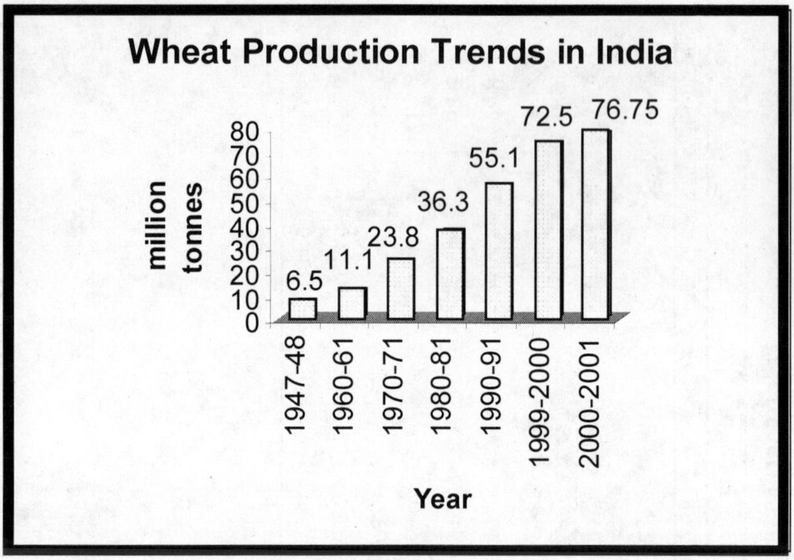

Fig. 1.2: Wheat Production Trends over the years in India

Protein

The protein content of cereals varies as they contain 6-12 g protein per 100 g (Table 2.1) and can easily meet more than 50 per cent of the daily protein requirement of an adult. Cereal protein consists of albumin, globulin, prolamin and glutelins. The quality of cereal protein is not very good as that of the animal protein because cereal proteins lack the essential amino acid lysine. Among cereals, rice protein is of better quality than others. Hence cereals should be taken in combination with the legumes or milk and milk products.

Almost all the tissues of cereal grains contain protein. Embryo, scutellum and aleurone layers contain higher concentration of protein than the starchy endosperm, pericarp and testa. In the embryo also protein concentration increases from the central part to the periphery. The quality of protein present in germ and aleurone layer is better as compared to that of endosperm.

Carbohydrates

Carbohydrates constitute 80 per cent of the dry matter of cereals. Cereal grains are largely composed of starch, a complex carbohydrate. Other carbohydrate constituents present are cellulose, hemicellulose and pentosans which constitute dietary fibre. Due to high fibre content, whole cereals are considered important for the maintenance of good health. Small amount of dextrin, sucrose, raffinose, glucose and galactose are also present.

Fat

Cereals are generally considered to have low fat content as determined by ether extraction which represents only free fat. Recent studies have shown that cereals contain much more fats if bound fat is also taken into account. The total fat thus may vary from 2 to 5 per cent per 100g. Cereals like wheat, rice and barley contain 1 to 1.7 per cent fat. The fat content is higher in maize (3.6 per cent), oats (4 to 6 per cent) and bajra (5.0 per cent). Germ and bran of the grain contain higher concentration of fat than other parts. For example, wheat germ contains 7.4 per cent fat while the bran and endosperm contain 3 to 5 and 0.8 to 1.5 per cent fat, respectively. Rice bran contains 16.2 per cent fat while in maize, it is mainly present in germ *i.e.* 35 per cent. Therefore, upon separation and removal of germ from the endosperm as in milling of cereals, keeping quality of milled products is improved. In general, cereals contain triglycerides of palmitic, oleic and linoleic acids. They also have some amount of phospholipids and lecithin.

Recent researches suggest that for reducing calories from fat, people should be encouraged to replace fat with cereals, as they are low in fat and high in fibre content. Moreover, cereals contain the polyunsaturated fatty acids which are healthier. Considering the amount of cereals consumed, it is estimated that fat content in cereals in our diet can meet more than 50 per cent of our essential fatty acid requirement.

Minerals

The ash content of cereals varies from 0.6 to 3.3 per cent. The husk of cereal grains is rich in minerals. Rice husk contains about 22.5 per cent ash content which is 96 per cent silica.

In cereals, calcium and iron are not present in good amount but the grains contribute significantly due to fairly large amounts of cereals consumed daily. Among cereals, rice is poorer in these two minerals as these are lost during milling and polishing. Millets contain good amount of minerals and fibre. Rye, oats and ragi are very good sources of calcium. As the main storage form of phosphorus present in cereals is phytin, hence it affects adversely the bioavailability of minerals especially calcium, magnesium phosphorus, zinc and iron. Some trace minerals *i.e.* copper, zinc and manganese are present in small amounts in cereals.

Vitamins

Whole cereal grains are important sources of B-vitamins. Removal of bran from cereals, polishing and refining of these grains especially rice reduce B-vitamin content to varying degrees depending upon the extent of refining and polishing. Therefore, high extraction wheat flour (maida) and pearled millets also contain less amount of B-vitamins.

Vitamin A and C are not present in cereals except yellow maize and some varieties of sorghum which do contain β-carotene. Oil from cereal grains is rich in Vitamin E. Distribution of vitamins in different parts of the grain is not uniform.

Enzymes

A number of enzymes *viz.* amylases, proteases, lipases and oxidoreductases present in cereals are important from the point of view of processing. During germination and fermentation, these enzymes become active and influence the digestibility and availability of nutrients.

Utilization of Cereals

The main uses of cereals are depicted in Table 1.3. They are put to many uses in our diet depending upon the taste preferences and cultural influences. Cereals are ground into coarse flour (meal) and made into porridges and puddings. Fine flour is used for the preparation of leavened and unleavened bread, cakes, biscuits, cookies, pasta and noodles and breakfast foods. Table 1.4 depicts the Indian wheat varieties suitable for preparing various industrial and traditional end products. Alcoholic beverages can also made from all kind of cereals.

Table 1.3: Utilization of Cereals

Cereal	*Whole*	*Porridge*	*Leavened Bread*	*Unleavened Bread*	*Beer Spirits*	*Snacks Breakfast*	*Starch Glucose*
Wheat	✓	✓	✓	✓	✓	✓	✓
Rye		✓	✓		✓		
Rice	✓				✓	✓	
Maize	✓			✓	✓	✓	✓
Sorghum		✓	✓	✓	✓		
Pearl millet		✓		✓	✓		
Small millet		✓		✓	✓		
Oats		✓		✓	✓	✓	
Barley	✓	✓		✓	✓		

Source: Dendy, D.A.V. and Dobraszezyk, B.J. 2001. Cereals and Cereal Products: Chemistry and Technology. An Aspen Publication, Maryland, USA.

Table 1.4: Suitable Indian Wheat Varieties for Development of Industrial and Traditional End Products

Chapati	All cultivars make good to very good *chapati* but few like C306, Raj 1482, WH147, HD2402, UP262, WH216, Sujata, GW496, PBW226 are the best.
Bread	HI977, PBW226, K9107, HD2285, GW120, GW190, DWR195 and NI5439
Biscuit	Sonalika
Pasta products	PDW233, WH896, Raj1555, HI8498, GW1139, HI8381 and MACS2846
Khapli products	DDK1001, DDK1009 and NP200

Chapter 2
Nutrient Composition of Cereal Grains

In general, cereal grains contain about 10-14 per cent moisture, 58-72 per cent carbohydrates, 8-13 per cent protein, 2-5 per cent fat and 2-11 per cent indigestible fibre (Table 2.1). They contain 300 to 350 Kcal per 100 g of grain.

Table 2.1: Nutrient Composition of Cereal Grains (per cent on dry matter basis)

Cereal Grains	*Moisture*	*Carbo-hydrate*	*Protein*	*Fat*	*Crude fibre*	*Energy (Kcal/100 g)*
Wheat	12.8	77.2	11.8	1.5	1.2	346
Pearl millet	12.4	67.5	11.6	5.0	1.2	361
Corn	14.9	66.2	11.1	3.6	2.7	348
Sorghum	11.9	72.6	10.4	1.9	1.6	349
Barley	12.5	69.6	11.5	1.3	3.9	336
Rice	13.7	78.2	6.8	0.5	0.2	345

Nutrient composition of cereals varies depending upon varieties of particular grain, geographical and weather conditions and other factors. Chemical composition of individual cereal grains is discussed as below:

I. Wheat

Various factors including soil, environment and variety influence the chemical composition of wheat kernel. Chemical composition of different parts of wheat kernel is given in Table 2.2.

Table 2.2: Chemical Composition of Whole Wheat Grain and its Various parts (per cent on dry matter basis)

Nutrients	*Whole Grain*	*Endosperm*	*Bran*	*Germ*
Protein	16	13	16	22
Fat	2	1.5	5	7
Carbohydrates	68	82	16	40
Dietary fibre	11	1.5	53	25
Minerals	1.8	0.5	7.2	4.5
Other components	1.2	1.5	2.8	1.5
Total	**100**	**100**	**100**	**100**

Moisture

The moisture content of wheat may vary between 12 and 18 per cent depending on the weather during harvest. If moisture content is high, chances of mold growth during storage are more and hence, before processing, wheat grains must be dried.

Protein

Variety, geographical and environments factors influence the protein content of wheat. Wheat protein consists of the following fractions:

1. Albumin–5-10 per cent of total protein
2. Globulin–5-10 per cent of total protein
3. Prolamin–40-50 per cent of total protein
4. Glutelin–40-50 per cent of total protein

The distribution of proteins in different parts of wheat kernel is as under:

1. Pericarp–8 per cent
2. Endosperm–82.5 per cent
3. Embryo–1.0 per cent
4. Scutellum–1.5 per cent

Bran and germ proteins have a higher content of essential amino acids than the inner endosperm. That is the reason why biological value of whole protein is higher than that of endosperm proteins. In the wheat endosperm, a prolamine (called gliadin) and a glutelin (called glutenin) are present in approximately the same concentrations; in the bran a prolamin is most abundant with fair amounts of an albumin and globulin. The unique presence of glutenin and gliadin in the wheat endosperm is important to the baking operation. In the presence of water and with mechanical agitation, these protein fractions form a tough, elastic complex termed gluten which is capable of retaining gases and by doing so makes a leavened product possible. Cereals other than wheat cannot form a large light loaf since gluten is not developed.

The properties of gliadin, glutenin and gluten are briefly discussed below:

Gluten

Gluten is a mixture of gliadin and glutenin. It forms 90 per cent of the total proteins of wheat. It is the main component of wheat flour responsible for the rheological properties of dough. Gluten can be readily prepared by adding 60 to 65 per cent water to a hard wheat flour, allowing the dough to stand approximately 30 minutes, and then washing out the starch granules and soluble compounds under a stream of water. A tough, elastic, gummy product is obtained which is known as gluten. The wet gluten contains about 66 per cent water. On dry basis, crude gluten contains about 75 to 85 per cent proteins, 5 to 10 per cent lipids, 6 per cent starch and 0.7 per cent ash. The lipid is held strongly to the protein and cannot be extracted with organic solvent.

Hard wheat gives gluten of good strength while soft wheat forms gluten of low strength. Earlier it was thought that the total protein content of wheat flour is a measure of gluten strength but it is not true. Flours with the same percentage of protein may have widely different gluten strengths. However, it is true that hard wheat flours which form the strongest gluten, have the highest percentage of protein.

Gluten proteins are denatured when heated to over 90°C in the wet condition. The denatured gluten loses its elastic property and does not form a dough.

Lipids

The lipid content of Indian wheat varies from about 0.97 to 2.28 per cent. Wheat flour contains about 1.88 per cent lipids. Different structural components of wheat kernel are as given under:

1. Endosperm–1 to 2 per cent
2. Bran–5 to 6 per cent
3. Germ–8 to 15 per cent

The lipids of wheat are concentrated in the germ but this does not mean, however, that all the lipids are held in the germ. The proportion of compound lipids in the endosperm is much higher. Crude gluten prepared from flour contains about 8-10 per cent lipids on dry basis. About 70 per cent of the lipid present in the flour is found in the isolated crude gluten.

The lipids present in wheat include neutral glycerides as well as phospholipids and sterols. Wheat germ oil is a particularly rich source of vitamin E and essential fatty acids. Wheat germ oil is produced commercially.

Carbohydrates

The principal carbohydrate of wheat kernel is starch and practically all of the starch is present in the endosperm. Germ contains almost all the soluble sugars. The water soluble carbohydrate *i.e.* sucrose is more abundant in the germ than in the endosperm or bran. Bran mainly contains complex carbohydrates *i.e.* cellulose and hemicellulose. Some cellulose is present in all parts of the seeds since it is the chief component of cell walls. There are small amounts of lignins and pentosans present in the bran. The distribution of carbohydrates in wheat fractions is presented in Table 2.3.

Table 2.3: Distribution of carbohydrates in wheat fractions (per cent)

Carbohydrate	*Fractions of Wheat*		
	Endosperm	*Germ*	*Bran*
Starch	95.8	31.5	14.1
Sugars	1.5	36.4	7.6
Cellulose	0.3	16.8	35.2
Hemicellulose	2.4	15.3	43.1

Source: Wealth of India, Vol. X, CSIR, New Delhi, 1976. p. 364.

Vitamins

Whole wheat is a good source of thiamine and niacin but is relatively poor in riboflavin. Other B-vitamins are present in small amounts. In general, the bran layer is rich in the B-complex vitamins. When wheat is milled, a large part of aleurone layer is lost as bran and the resulting flour is devoid of a major part of B-vitamins. Table 2.4. depicts the distribution of B-vitamins in wheat kernel. Wheat also contains carotenoids, principally xanthophyll which has no vitamin A activity in man or other animals. Wheat germ is particularly rich in vitamin E. Ascorbic acid is completely lacking in seed or flour. Vitamins A and D are absent.

Table 2.4: Distribution of B-Vitamins in the Wheat Kernel

Structural Parts	*Vitamins (% of Total)*			
	Thiamine	*Riboflavin*	*Niacin*	*Pantothenic Acid*
Pericarp, testa and hyaline	1	5	4	8
Aleurone	31	37	84	39
Endosperm	3	32	11.5	41
Scutellum	62.5	14	1	4
Embryo	2	12	1	3.5

Source: Wealth of India, Vol. X, CSIR, New Delhi, 1976, p. 361.

Minerals

A significant amount of minerals including iron, phosphorus, magnesium, manganese, copper and zinc are present in wheat (Table 2.5).

Table 2.5: Mineral Composition of Wheat (mg/100 g)

Minerals	*Whole wheat*	*Wheat flour*
Calcium	41	48
Phosphorus	306	355
Iron	5.3	4.9
Magnesium	138	132
Copper	0.68	0.51
Manganese	2.29	2.29
Zinc	2.70	2.2

Source: Nutritive Value of Indian Foods, NIN, Hyderabad (1995).

These minerals are mainly present in the outer layers and embryo of the kernel and when wheat is milled for the white flour, these minerals are passed on to the byproducts of milling.

Enzymes

Wheat flour contains the following enzymes:

1. Amylases
2. Proteases
3. Lipases
4. Phenol and aromatic amine oxidase
5. Peroxidase

Amylase (Diastase)

Flour contains two enzymes which are essential to bread production. These enzymes are:

1. Beta-amylase
2. Alpha-amylase

These enzymes develop in the wheat during the initial stages of sprouting. β-amylase converts dextrins and a portions of soluble starch to maltose which is essential for an active yeast fermentation.

This enzyme is susceptible to heat. Its activity occurs during fermentation.

α-amylase converts soluble starch to dextrins. During fermentation it acts on soluble starch and broken granules. It can survive at temperatures as high as 75-80°C and hence is more stable to heat than β-amylase. A considerable degradation of starch by α-amylase hydrolysis occurs during the initial phase of baking. Hydrolysis is a chemical process of decomposition involving addition of water. Some baking technologists consider this stage of degradation to be the most important aspect of the proper malting of flour. Malt flour is prepared from barley or wheat, which have been sprouted under controlled conditions, dried and then ground into flour. Malt supplements are added to flours and doughs in order to increase gas production by furnishing fermentable sugars for the yeast.

Proteases

These enzymes are present in the dormant stage in the wheat flour. High activity of this enzyme has an adverse effect on the quality of dough by acting on gluten. Its activity can be inhibited by potassium bromate.

Lipase

This enzyme acts on lipid content of the dough and produces free fatty acids if the flour is stored for a longer period.

Lipoxidase

It is present in small amounts in flour. It acts on polyunsaturated fatty acids and catalyses their peroxidation.

Phenol and Aromatic Amine Oxidases

Discolouration of the dough is caused by these enzymes.

Peoxidases

These enzymes catalyse the oxidation caused by phenol and aromatic amine oxidases resulting ultimately in discolouration of the dough.

II. Rice

Rice is consumed all over the world as the intact grain, minus hull, bran and germ. Its chemical composition is influenced by genetic and environmental factors. Table 2.6 depicts the nutrient composition of Indian rice.

Table 2.6: Nutrient Composition of Rice

Nutrients	*Amount*
Moisture (per cent)	13.7
Protein (per cent)	6.8
Fat (per cent)	0.5
Ash (per cent)	0.6
Fibre (per cent)	0.2
Carbohydrates (per cent)	78.2
Energy (Kcal/100g)	345
Calcium (mg/100g)	10
Phosphorus (mg/100g)	160
Iron (mg/100g)	0.7
Thiamine (mg/100g)	0.06
Riboflavin (mg/100g)	0.06
Niacin (mg/100g)	1.9

Source: Nutritive Value of Indian Foods, NIN, Hyderabad (1995).

Moisture

Moisture content of rice varies from 10.9-13.8 per cent.

Protein

Rice contains 5.5-9.3 per cent protein. Rice contains less amount of protein than that present in wheat but its protein quality is superior as compared to that of wheat and other cereals. Different protein fractions present in rice are:

1. Glutelin (Oryzenin)
2. Albumin
3. Globulin
4. Prolamine

Glutelin is the major protein of rice whereas albumin, globulin and prolamins are present in small amounts. Rice proteins contain more amount of arginine as compared to other cereal proteins but are deficient in lysine and threonine. The proteins of the husked and polished rice have a lower biological value but a higher digestibility than those of rice bran and rice polishings.

Germ, the aleurone layer and a layers of cells beneath it contain about one-fourth of the protein present in whole rice.

Carbohydrate

Major carbohydrate in rice is starch (72-75 per cent). Amylose content of starch varies according to grain type, the long superior grains contain about 17.5 per cent amylose while coarse type are completely devoid of it. Glutinous rice mainly contains amylopectin. Some free sugars like glucose, sucrose and dextrin are also present in rice. Rice bran consists of hemicelluloses which are made up of the pentoses, arabinose and xylose.

Minerals

Mineral composition of rice is almost the same as that of other cereals. Pericarp and germ portions of the rice mainly contain the mineral matter. Polished rice is poor in calcium and iron.

Enzymes

Enzymes present in rice are:

1. Amylases
2. Proteases
3. Lipases
4. Oxidases
5. Peroxidases
6. Phenolase

Upon storage of rice, the activities of enzymes *viz.* amylase remains constant. α-amylase activity in fresh rice is responsible for its sticky consistency after cooking.

Pigments

Anthocyanins and carotenoids are present in coloured rice. Some varieties of rice possess a characteristic sweet aroma which is recognized upon rice cooking. 'Basmati' rice is highly esteemed for its peculiar aroma.

III. Corn

The nutrient composition of corn is discussed as follows:

1. Moisture
2. Protein
3. Fat
4. Fibre
5. Carbohydrates
5. Minerals

Protein

The predominant maize protein in endosperm is the prolamine known as zein. Maize starch granules are embedded in protein. The protein–starch bond is much stronger in maize than in other cereals such as wheat. Maize germ is rich in glutelin accounting for 49-54 per cent of the total protein of germ. Major protein fractions of maize are:

1. Albumin (16.3 per cent)
2. Globulin (6.5 per cent)
3. Prolamine (3.5 per cent)
4. Glutelin (23.5 per cent)
5. Insolubles (21.3 per cent)

Maize protein is of low biological value when compared to wheat and rice as zein is deficient in some of the essential amino acids like lysine, methionine and tryptophan. Some modern hybrid varieties *e.g.* opaque-2 are nutritionally superior because they contain higher lysine. The concentration of lysine and tryptophan also increases in most maize varieties during germination.

Carbohydrates

Starch is the major carbohydrate (66-74 per cent) on dry matter basis present in maize. Maize starch is normally 30 per cent amylose and 70 per cent amylopectin. High amylose corn contains upto 55-80 per cent amylose. Waxy maize varieties that have a waxy appearance especially when broken, consist of very little amylose and is effectively 100 per cent amylopectin. Sweet corn has a large proportion of carbohydrates as dextrin and sugar in the unripe kernels.

In popcorn variety, major part of the endosperm is hard starch on all sides, with a very small core of soft starch. Sugars like glucose, fructose, sucrose and raffinose are present in small quantities. Hemicelluloses are mainly present in the maize hulls.

Lipids

Maize germs are relatively large compared with other cereals and mainly rich in unsaturated oils. About 84 per cent of total fat of the kernel is found in germ and 1.5 per cent in the endosperm. On an average, 25 per cent of the weight of the kernel is maize oil and its major lipids are triglycerides. Phospholipids and glycolipids are present in small amounts.

Vitamins

Maize is generally a poor source of B-vitamins. Niacin is deficient in maize. The grain does contain niacin but 50-80 per cent of it occurs in the bound form as niacytin which is biologically unavailable and makes the grain deficient in niacin. The niacin deficiency disease (pellagra) is common in populations dependent on maize, especially where the people do not use alkaline treatments in their food preparation and who are also unable to include other food sources in the diet.

Minerals

Maize lacks many essential minerals but is a fairly good source of phosphorus and iron. Phosphorus is mainly present as phytin. Calcium is present in low amounts.

IV. Barley

The average nutrient composition of barley is as follows:

Component	*Per cent (Dry Weight)*
Moisture	
Protein	10-24
Total lipids	3-5
Crude fibre	3-5
Mineral matter	2-3

Contd...

Component	Per cent (Dry Weight)
Starch	58-65
Soluble sugars	1-2
Hemicellulose and gums	10-17
Pentosans	7-11
β-glucans	3-6
Neutral lipids	2-3
Phosphorus	0.3-0.6
Potassium	0.3-0.6
Silicon	0.3-0.4
Calcium	0.03-0.07
Magnesium	0.1-0.2

Protein

Barley proteins consist of:

1. Albumin (2.9 per cent)
2. Globulin (18.5 per cent)
3. Prolamin (37.4 per cent)
4. Glutelin (41.4 per cent)

Barley protein is lacking in essential amino acid lysine. Its biological value is low as compared to that of wheat.

Lipids

The total lipid content of barley is usually about 3.5 per cent, 2.5 per cent being neutral lipids that are concentrated in the embryo and the aleurone layer.

Carbohydrates

The grain contains significant amounts of soluble sugars, sucrose predominating, but the most abundant carbohydrates are polysaccharides, which in plump grains may be starch, 58 to 65 per cent, β-glucan, 3 to 6 per cent, pentosans 7 to 11 per cent, with minor amounts of others. The amylase contents of barley starches are often 25-30 per cent and 70-75 per cent amylopectin. Barley with waxy starches are 100 per cent amylopectin.

Minerals

Barley contains 2-3 per cent ash content. Amongst minerals, iron is in high proportion.

Vitamins

Table 2.7 depicts the vitamin content of barley grains.

Table 2.7: Vitamin Contents of Barley Grains (reported values differ widely)

Vitamin	*Concentration (mg/g)*
Thiamine	2-16
Riboflavin	0.8-3.7
Niacin	47-147
Pantothenic acid	3-11
Vitamin B_6	3-12
Vitamin E	2-5
Biotin	0.1-0.2
Vitamin C	Probably present
Vitamin B_{12}	Possibly present

Source: Dendy and Dobraszezyk, 2001. Cereals and cereal products: Chemistry and Technology. An ASPEN Publication, USA, p. 328.

V. Sorghum

Generally, the chemical composition of sorghum (Table 2.8) is similar to that of maize.

Table 2.8: Nutrient composition of sorghum

Nutrients	*Amount (% Dry Matter Basis)*
Moisture	11.9
Protein	10.4
Fat	1.9
Carbohydrates	72.6
Crude fibre	1.6
Minerals	1.6

Protein

Protein content varies depending upon the genetic and environmental factors. Sorghum has more protein than maize. Different protein fractions of sorghum are:

1. Albumin (5 per cent)
2. Globulin (6.3 per cent)
3. Prolamine (46.4 per cent)
4. Glutelin (30.4 per cent)

Endosperm mainly contains prolamine and glutelin fractions. The digestibility and biological value of sorghum protein is superior to wheat protein.

Carbohydrates

Like other cereals, the major carbohydrate present in sorghum is starch. The amylase content of sorghum starch is 21 to 28.7 per cent but the waxy varieties contain little amylose. Free sugars like sucrose, glucose and fructose to the extent of 1.2 per cent are present.

Lipids

Sorghum lipids are mainly triglycerides. Triglycerides are rich in unsaturated fatty acids like oleic and linoleic fatty acids. Phospholipids constitute about 5 per cent of the total lipids of sorghum. About half of the phospholipid present in sorghum is lecithin. Sorghum also contains some wax.

Vitamins and Minerals

Unlike maize, niacin present in sorghum is in the available form. Germ contains higher proportion of the vitamins than the endosperm or bran. Riboflavin content of germ and bran are similar.

Table 2.9: Vitamin Content of Sorghum

Vitamins	*Amount (mg/100g)*
Thiamine	0.37
Riboflavin	0.13
Niacin	3.1

Minerals present in sorghum are mainly calcium, magnesium, potassium and iron (Table 2.10).

Table 2.10: Mineral Content of Sorghum

Minerals	*Amount (mg/100g)*
Calcium	25
Phosphorus	222
Iron	4.1
Potassium	131
Magnesium	171
Zinc	1.6

VI. Pearl Millet

Pearl millet is the most important millet and is staple food of many in lower rainfall areas of Africa and Central India. It forms a major source of dietary nutrients to a large section of Indian population. Pearl millet is equal or superior to corn, sorghum and rice in protein and oil contents.

Pearl millet is eaten as porridge and chibuku beers in Africa, as fermented flat breads in Sudan and Ethiopia and as *khichri* and *chapati* in India. Table 2.11 depicts the nutrient composition of pearl millet.

Lipids

Lipids are mostly in the germ and in composition similar to those of sorghum.

Protein and Amino Acid

The protein content of pearl millet ranges from 8 per cent to 19 per cent. It is a typical cereal grain, being low in lysine, tryptophan, threonine and sulphur containing amino acids.

Carbohydrates

Carbohydrates of pearl millet consist of starch and small amounts of soluble sugars including pentoses and hexoses. Amylopectin (67.9 per cent) is the major constituent of pearl millet starch.

Table 2.11: Nutrient Composition of Pearl Millet

Nutrients	*Amount*
Moisture (per cent)	12.4
Protein (per cent)	11.6
Fat (per cent)	5.0
Fibre (per cent)	1.2
Carbohydrates (per cent)	67.5
Energy (Kcal/100g)	361
Calcium (mg/100g)	42
Phosphorus (mg/100g)	296
Iron (mg/100g)	8.0
Magnesium (mg/100g)	137
Potassium (mg/100g)	307
Zinc (mg/100g)	3.1
Thiamine (mg/100g)	0.33-0.41
Riboflavin (mg/100g)	0.19-0.24
Niacin (mg/100g)	1.54-3.88
Lysine (mg/g N)	109-297
Tryptophan (mg/g N)	69-130
Methionine (mg/g N)	93-163

Source: Nutritive Value of Indian Foods, NIN, Hyderabad (1995)
Post-harvest Biotechnology of Cereals (1990).

Vitamins

Pearl millet contains only marginal amounts of essential vitamins, thus prolonged consumption of this millet based diet may lead to deficiency of niacin, B_{12} and riboflavin etc.

Minerals

Pearl millet has a relatively better mineral profile but owing to certain inherent factors the bioavailability of these minerals to human system is low. More than half of the phosphorus in pearl millet is present in the phytate form which is not available to the human system.

Chapter 3
Structure of Cereal Grains

Cereals are members of the grass family (Gramineae) which produce dry, one seeded fruits. This type of fruit is a caryopsis but is commonly called a kernel or grain. The grain consists of a fruit coat or pericarp, which surrounds the seed and adheres tightly to a seed coat. Fruit wall (pericarp) and seed coat are united as a result the seed and fruit cannot be separated. This type of fruit, which is characteristic for all grasses, including cereals, is known as caryopsis in botanical term.

The caryopsis of all cereals develops within floral envelopes, which are actually modified leaves, called lemma and palea. During threshing of wheat, rye, maize and some varieties of sorghum and barley, the lemma and palea get separated from the grain and form chaff or glumes. As during threshing, hull and grain separate readily, these grains are said to be naked grains because they have uncovered caryopsis. In rice, oats and some varieties of barley and sorghum, the floral envelops cover the caryopsis so closely and completely that they remain attached to the caryopsis when the grain is threshed and constitute the hull or husk of those grains. Therefore, these grains are covered or coated caryopsis. The threshed rice along with husk is known as paddy.

The overall structure of all cereal grains is basically similar with slight variations when studied in detail. The structures of different cereals are discussed as below:

I. Wheat

Wheat belongs to the genus Triticum of the grass family Gramineae. It has more than 30,000 species and varieties. It is one of the most important cereal crops in the world. It is cultivated from prehistoric times (5000 BC). The longitudinal section of the caryopsis or grain of wheat is diagrammatically shown in Fig 3.1. The length of a whole wheat grain is about 8mm. and weighs about 35 mg. The kernel has a somewhat vaulted or ovoid shape with the germ or embryo at one end, and a bundle of hairs, which is referred to as the beard or brush at the other end. Along one side of the grain, there is a furrow or crease which is due to infolding of the aleurone and all covering layers. Wheat grains have either a dark, orange-brown appearance or a light, yellowish colour. Colour of the grain is related to pigment in the seed coat. The wheat grain or kernel can be divided into three distinct morphological parts:

Endosperm

It makes up most of the grain. It is the storage portion of the seed which supplies the sprouting embryo with food in the period before the root and leaf begin to function.

Bran Layer

It surrounds the grain, hence forms the covering or protecting layers.

Germ

It includes the embryo and the scutellum. From it the root and leaf of the new plant are formed when it sprouts. It is small and is attached to the base of the seed.

Pericarp

Entire seed is surrounded by pericarp which is composed of several layers. The outer pericarp is what millers call the beeswing or epidermis. Next to the epidermis is the hypoderm of varying

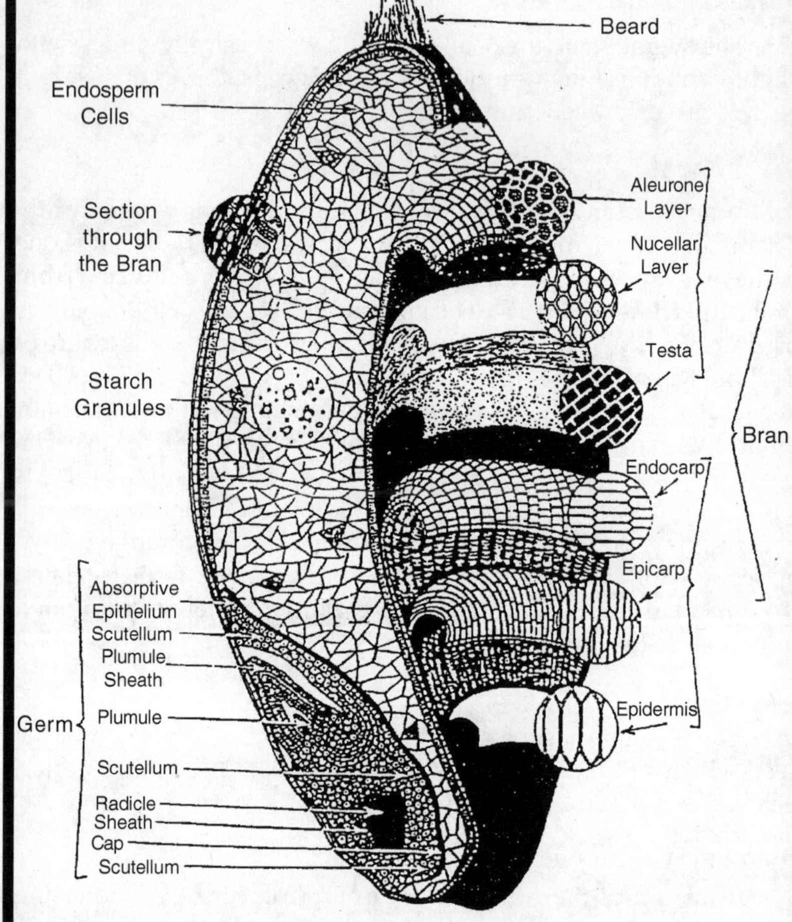

Fig. 3.1: Morphology of the Wheat Grain

thickness. The innermost portion of the outer pericarp consists of the remnants of the thin- walled cells. This innermost layer tears during ripening of the seed and in mature grains, they are represented by branching hypha-like cells known as tube cells. The total pericarp has been reported to comprise about 5 per cent of the kernel and consist of about 6 per cent protein, 2 per cent ash, 20 per cent cellulose and 0.5 per cent fat, with the remainder being non-starch polysaccharides.

Seed Coat and Nucellar Epidermis

The seed coat or testa consists of three layers, a thick outer cuticle, a layer that contains pigment which gives the grain its characteristic colour and a thin inner cuticle. The seed coat of white wheat has two compressed cell layers of cellulose containing little or no pigment. Thickness of seed coat varies from 5-8 µm. Next to testa in hyaline layer or nucellar epidermis and it is about 7 µm thick. It is closely attached to both the seed coat and the aleurone layer. It is colourless and devoid of any obvious cellular structure.

Aleurone Layer

It is the outermost layer of endosperm. It is generally a single layer of thick-walled cubical cells and completely covers both the starchy endosperm and germ. The average size of the cells is about 50 µm. The cell walls are 3-4 µm thick. Aleurone cells have a large nuclears and a large number of aleurone granules (grains of phytic acid with some protein). The cells contain about 20 per cent each of protein, oil and mineral matter, and 10 per cent of sugar, principally sucrose, neo-ketose and raffinose. Hence, the aleurone layer is relatively high in ash, protein, total phosphorus, phytate phosphorus, fat and niacin. Thiamine and riboflavin are also higher in the aleurone than in other parts of the bran and enzyme activity is high. Over the embryo, the aleurone cells are modified, becoming thin-walled cells that may not contain aleurone granules. The thickness of the aleurone layers over the embryo averages about 13 µm or less than one third the thickness found elsewhere.

Germ or Embryo

The germ is composed of two major parts:

1. Embryonic axis (rudimentary root and shoot).
2. Scutellum

Scutellum functions as a storage organ. When the seed germinates, scutellum mobilizes the stored food reserves in the endosperm to embryo. The germ is rich in protein (25 per cent), sugar mainly sucrose and raffinose (18 per cent), oil (16 per cent of the embryonic axis and 32 per cent of the scutellum are oil) and ash (5 per cent). It contains no starch but is rather high in B-vitamins and contains many enzymes. The germ is quite high in Vitamin E (upto 500 ppm).

Endosperm

The starchy endosperm, excluding the aleurone layer, is composed of three types of cells which vary in size, shape and location within the kernel:

Peripheral

These cells are the first row of cells inside the aleurone layer and are usually small, being equal in diameter in all directions or slightly elongated towards the centre of the kernel.

Prismatic

Several rows of elongated prismatic cells are found interior of the peripheral cells.

Central

These cells are interior of the prismatic cells. They are irregular in size and shape than are the other cells.

The endosperm cell walls are composed of pentosans, other hemicelluloses, and β-glucan but not cellulose. The thickness of the cell wall varies with location in kernel; they are thicker near the aleurone. Cell wall thickness also varies among cultivars and between hard and soft wheat types. In hard wheats, hemicellulose of cell walls absorbs large amounts of water.

The endosperm cells are packed with starch granules embedded in protein matrix. The protein in mostly, but not entirely, gluten, the storage protein of wheat. In hard wheats, there is a tight adherence of the protein and starch. The strength of the protein-starch bond explains the kernel hardness. In soft wheat, the protein-starch bond ruptures easily and the kernel get crushed with minimal force. In harder wheats, the protein starch bond is progressively stronger.

Another important characteristic of wheat endosperm is its appearance. Some wheats are vitreous, hornlike, or translucent in appearance while others are opaque, mealy or floury. Traditionally, vitreousness has been associated with hardness and high protein content and opacity with softness and low protein. However, vitreousness and hardness are not the result of the same fundamental cause, and it is possible to have hard wheats that are opaque and soft wheats that are vitreous, although these are somewhat unusual.

II. Corn

The ripe ear of corn contains approximately 300-1000 single kernels depending on the number of rows, diameter and length of the cob. Kernel weight may be quite variable, ranging from 19 to 40 g per 100 kernels. The kernels are attached to the cob by structure called pedicel. The maize kernel is botanically known as caryopsis.

There are four major parts of the kernel (Table 3.1, Fig. 3.2).

1. Hull or bran (Pericarp and seed coat)
2. Germ
3. Endosperm
4. Tip cap

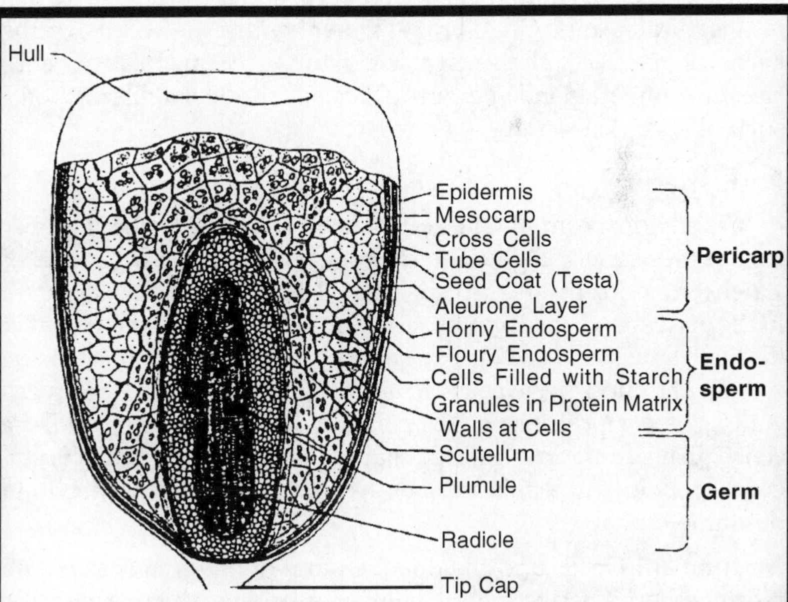

Fig. 3.2: Longitudinal Section of Corn Grain

Table 3.1: Weight Distribution of Main Parts of the Kernel

Structure	*Percentage Weight Distribution*
Pericarp	5-6
Aleurone	2-3
Endosperm	80-85
Germ	10-12

Hull

Hull or pericarp constitutes 5-6 per cent of the kernel. The hull surrounds the endosperm and germ but not pedicel. The pericarp is characterized by a high crude fibre content of about 87 per cent which is constituted mainly of hemicellulose (67.1 per cent), cellulose (23 per cent) and lignin (0.1 per cent).

Germ

Maize germs are relatively large compared with other cereals as its average weight is around 11 per cent and are particularly rich in unsaturated oils. On average 25 per cent of the weight of the kernel is maize oil. The germ also contains protein (18.4 per cent), enzymes, minerals and vitamins, especially the oil-soluble nutrients such as tocopherols.

Endosperm

The endosperm, the largest structure, provides about 83 per cent of the kernel weight. The endosperm contains a high level of starch (87.6 per cent) and protein levels (8 per cent). Crude fat content in the endosperm is relatively less. Corn is different from wheat in that both translucent and opaque endosperm are found within a single kernel. The endosperm cells are large with relatively very thin cell walls. The composition of their contents varies in density, and as a consequence, the kernel can appear to be either opaque, translucent, or more commonly a mixture of both opaque and translucent within the same kernel.

Immature cells and the opaque parts of mature cells contain mostly spherical starch granules, whereas polygonal starch granules are found in the more dense translucent regions of mature endosperms. As the kernels ripen and lose water, they collapse and in some varieties a dent forms on the top of the kernel, hence the term dent corn.

The translucent endosperm in tightly compact with few or no air spaces. The starch granules, polygonal in shape, are held together by a matrix protein. In opaque endosperm the starch granules are spherical and are covered with matrix protein that does not contain protein bodies. The many air spaces are to be expected from its opacity.

Tip Cap

The tip cap, the attachment point of the cob, may or may not stay with the kernel during shelling (removal from the cob).

III. Rice

The caryopsis of rice is harvested with the hull or husk attached. This is called paddy. The structure of rice consists of (Fig. 3.3):

1. Hull
2. Aleurone layer
3. Endosperm
4. Germ

The composition of paddy is given in Table 3.2.

Table 3.2: The Composition of the Paddy Grain

Structural Parts	*Range (per cent DWB)*
Endosperm	66-76
Husk (Hulls glumes)	18-25
Seed coat, aleurone layer, pericarp	4-6
Germ (Embryo)	1.5-3

Hull

The husk which generally forms about 20 per cent weight of the paddy, is made up of the floral envelopes *i.e.* lemma and palea, two specialized leaves that respectively cover the back and front of the seed. These are loosely joined by an interlocking fold on each side and are therefore, easily separated. The hulls are high in cellulose (25 per cent), lignin (30 per cent), pentosans (15 per cent) and ash

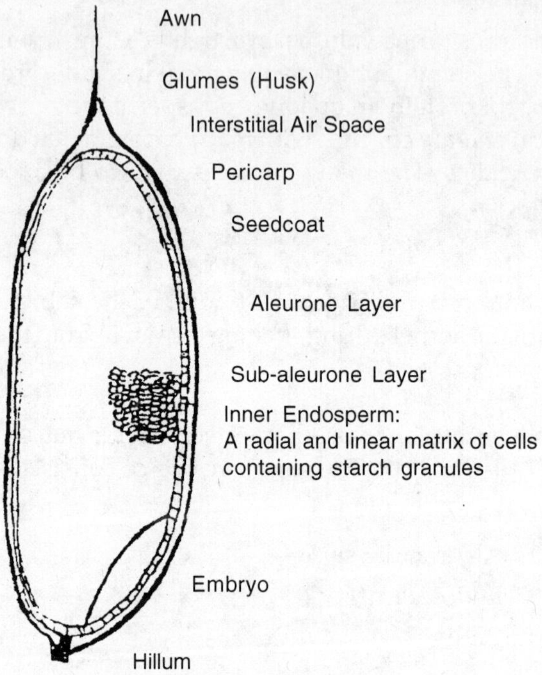

Fig. 3.3: Paddy Caryopsis

(21 per cent) which is 95 per cent silica. Due to high amounts to silica and lignin, rice hull is of low value both commercially and nutritionally.

Aleurone Layer

The nearest layer to the endosperm is the aleurone layer which is rich in protein lipids, vitamins and phytic acid. This layer is removed with the pericarp and seed coat during milling.

Endosperm

Endosperm forms 89-93 per cent of the dehusked rice. Endosperm, the rice we eat is rich in starch with some protein, although less than most other cereals. The endosperm is of two types:

1. Hard (Non-glutinous)
2. Vitreous (Glutinous)

Endosperm has compound starch granules *i.e.* large granules made up of many small granules. The individual rice starch granules are small (2-4 μm).

Germ

Attached in an indent is the germ or embryo. Rice has a much smaller embryo than most other cereals. This is rich in lipids, protein and B-vitamins. The germ is covered by the aleurone layer, the seed coat and pericarp, with the husk forming the final outer layer. The removal of husk and of the combined germ and pericarp layers is important to have a white palatable rice grain that can be stored for longer periods.

IV. Barley

Like rice and oats, barley is harvested with the hull or husk intact. Medium sized kernels weigh approximately 35 mg. The husked barleys of commerce usually have thousand corn (dry) weights of 30-45 g. Most barleys grown for commerce are husked, that is the palea and lemma of the floret adhere to the outside of the grain. Huskless barleys are not suitable for malting, but they are used for human food in the East and have higher digestibility than the hulled types (Fig. 3.4):

Barley caryopsis consists of:

1. Pericarp
2. Seed coat
3. Germ
4. Endosperm

The aleurone layer of some cultivars is blue whereas in others it is white. Grains of some barley varieties appear green because they have blue aleurone layers that are seen through the yellow husk. Unusual forms, not grown commercially, may be red, blue or black. The endosperm cells are packed with starch embedded in a protein matrix. Barley starch has both tenlicular granules and small spherical granules.

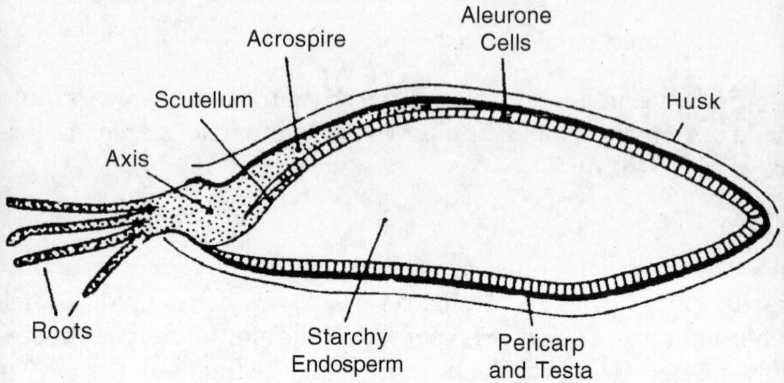

Fig. 3.4: Longitudinal Section of Germinated Barley Kernel

Table 3.3 depicts the proportion of various parts of barley grain.

Table 3.3: The Proportions of the Tissues in Barley Grains

Grain Part	*Proportion (% Dry basis)*
Embryo (Soluble sugars, 20-25 per cent, lipids, 14-17 per cent; protein, about 34 per cent)	2-5
Husk and pericarp (fibrous and largely inert)	7-15
Testa (double culticularized layer, with wax)	1-3
Aleurone layer [lipids, minerals and vitamins are concentrated in this layer + Nucellar tissue (triacyl glycerols 20 per cent; protein 17-20 per cent]	7-12
Starchy endosperm (Starch 85-89 per cent; protein about 10 per cent)	About 75 per cent

Source: Dendy, D.A.V. and Dobraszczyk, B.J. Cereals and Cereal Products: Chemistry Technology. An ASPEN Publication, USA.

V. Sorghum

The sorghum grain is small and rounded weighing 20 to 30 mg and may be red, yellow or brown. Fig. 3.5 shows the various parts of the sorghum kernel. Sorghum grain has a similar structure to the other cereals in having germ (9.8 per cent), a relatively large scutellum

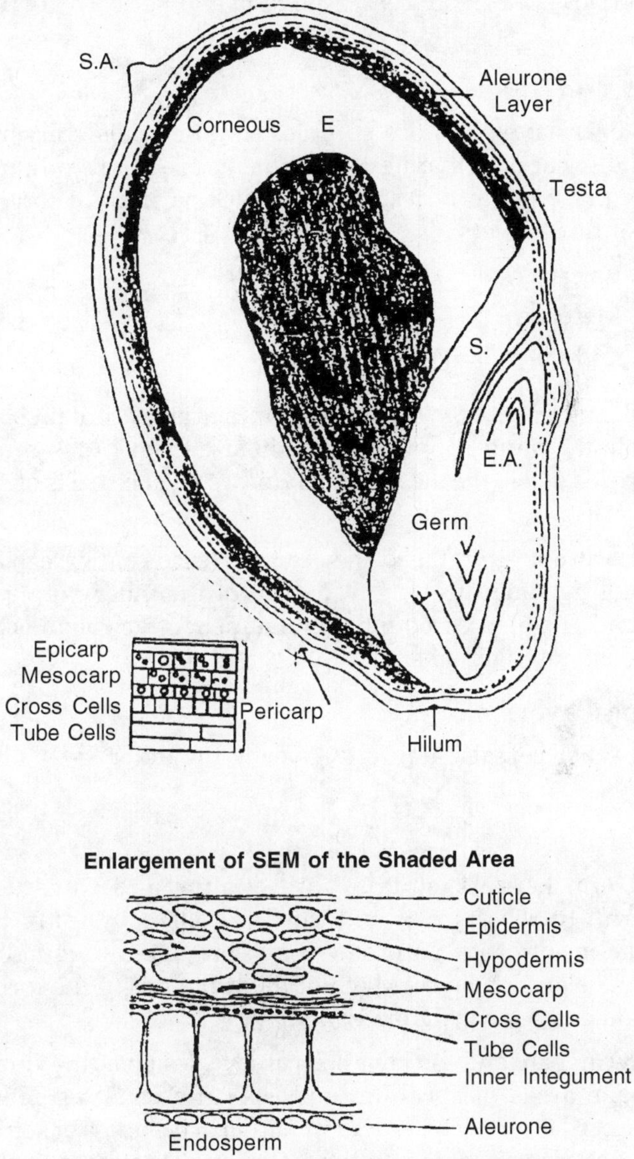

Fig. 3.5: Longitudinal Section of Sorghum Structure

and endosperm (82.3 per cent), enclosed in a seed coat (testa) and a fruit coat (pericarp 7.9 per cent). The testa and pericarp are fused together.

Pericarp and Testa

The bran layer is more complex, having cells containing polyphenols that may manifest as pigments. The hulls or glumes are rarely present after threshing. The thick pericarp of sorghum consists of three layers:

1. Epicarp
2. Mesocarp
3. Endocarp

Unlike other cereals, many sorghum varieties contain starch granules in the pericarp which range in size from 1 to 4 μm and mainly are located in the mesocarp. Endocarp layer consists of cross and tube cells.

All mature sorghum seeds have a testa (seed coat) which may or may not be joined to the other edge of the inner pigmented integument. The pigmented inner integument often contains high levels of condensed tannins.

Aleurone Layer

Like other cereals, aleurone layer is the outer layer of the endosperm.

Endosperm

Sorghum kernels contain both opaque and translucent endosperm. In the starchy endosperm, cells containing high concentrations of protein and few-starch granules are found just beneath the aleurone layer. Much of the protein is in the form of protein bodies 2-3 μm in diameter.

The terms hard and soft have been used to designate the vitreous and opaque areas of sorghum endosperm as well as general appearance of kernels. Visual determination of hardness or softness in sorghum kernels is based on the assumption that hardness and vitreousness are the same. This appears to be an unwarranted assumption.

VI. Pearl Millet

Pearl millet consists of small (average about 9 mg), tear-shaped kernels that are threshed clean of their hulls. Pearl millet kernels are about one third the size of sorghum kernels (20-30mg). The most common colour is a slate grey, giving the grain a pearly look- hence its name, but colours from creamy white through yellow to black are known. Different parts of pearl millet are:

Pericarp

The caryopsis of pearl millet is similar to those of other cereals. The coarse grain contains 8-10 per cent husk. The pericarp does not contain starch, as the pericarp of sorghum does, nor does pearl millet contain a pigmented inner integument.

Germ

The germ of pearl millet is a much larger percentage of the total kernel than is the germ of sorghum (17.4 per cent compared with 9.8 per cent in sorghum). This difference explains in part the higher protein and oil contents of pearl millet compared with sorghum.

Endosperm

Like sorghum and corn, the endosperm of pearl millet is both opaque and translucent. The opaque endosperm contains many air spaces and spherical void of air spaces and contains polygonal starch granules embedded in a protein matrix.

Chapter 4
Milling of Wheat

Most cereal grains are used either for the production of animal feed or for the milling of flour for human consumption. The grinding of wheat for human consumption, has to meet higher standards and is called milling. Milling is an ancient art. In simple terms, its objective is to make cereals more palatable and thus more desirable as food. The aim of milling is twofold:

1. To grind cleaned and tempered cereal
2. To completely separate the bran and germ from the mealy endosperm and to thoroughly pulverize the mealy endosperm into middlings, semolina and flour in case of wheat.

The bran and germ are relatively rich in protein, B-vitamins, minerals and fat and hence the milled product is lower in these entities than was the original grain. Thus, as a result of milling, the palatability is increased but the nutritional value of the product is decreased.

In addition to making the product more palatable and increasing its ability to store longer, milling often involves some type of constraint with regard to particle size. For example, the endosperm of rice or barley must remain in one large piece; from wheat and rye, fine flour is necessary; large grit is desirable from maize. Thus, a miller uses a number of procedures to produce the desired product.

Milling of Wheat

Wheat grain contains 85 per cent endosperm, 3 per cent germ and 12 per cent bran, all three nutritious in their own way (Table 4.1).

Table 4.1: Composition of Endosperm, Germ and Bran of Wheat

Parameters	*Endosperm (%)*	*Germ (%)*	*Bran (%)*
Moisture	14.0	11.7	13.2
Protein	9.6	28.5	14.4
Fat	1.4	10.4	4.7
Ash	0.7	4.5	6.3
Carbohydrate	74.3	44.9	61.4
Starch	71.0	14.0	8.6
Hemicellulose	1.8	6.8	26.2
Sugars	1.1	16.2	4.6
Cellulose	0.2	7.2	21.4
Total carbohydrate	74.1	44.5	60.8
Recovery of fraction	99.8	99.6	99.4

Table 4.1 shows the increasing gradients from endosperm to germ or bran or to bran or germ of protein, fat, ash, hemicellulose, sugars and cellulose. Endosperm is relatively carbohydrate rich. All these are commercially important in flour milling. Whole meal, for example, is flour made out of the whole wheat kernel, also known as 100 per cent extraction flour. White flour generally has an extraction of upto 78 per cent with bran sold separately or together.

The relationship between the physiological and technological parts of the wheat kernel is shown in Fig. 4.1.

Milling Process

Wheat is commonly consumed in the form of flour obtained by milling the grain while a small quantity is converted into breakfast foods, such as wheat flakes, puffed wheat and shredded wheat.

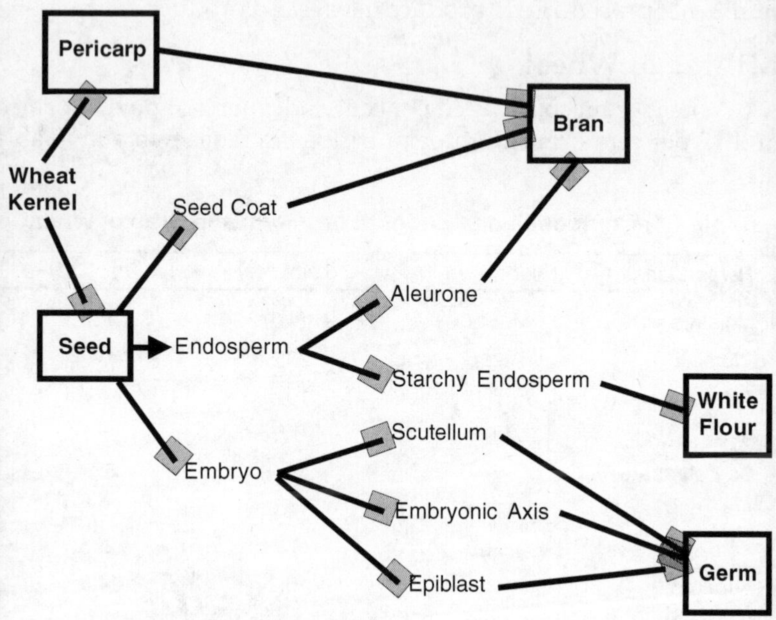

Fig. 4.1: Relationship Between the Physiological and Technological Parts of the Wheat Kernel

Traditional Milling

The traditional procedure for milling wheat in India has been stone grinding (*chakki*) to obtain whole meal flour (*atta*). This method results in 90-95 per cent extraction rate flour which retains almost all the nutrients of the grain while simultaneously eliminating that part of the grain which is most indigestible like cellulose, and phytic acid which binds and carries away minerals. Therefore, Indian style flour is not technically 'whole wheat' but it is superior to the usual whole grain flour that is produced by simply grinding everything to a fine powder. Stone grinding is gradually giving place to power driven small and big *chakkis* and to modern flour mills.

Modern Milling

Modern milling process consists of the following steps:

1. Grain cleaning
2. Tempering or conditioning
3. Roller milling

Graining Cleaning

Grain is removed of various types of impurities together with damaged, shrunken and broken kernels which are collectively known as 'screenings'. A magnetic separator removes any tramp metal. Also early in cleaning system, a milling separator removes sticks, stones and other foreign material that is either larger or smaller than the grain being cleaned. Basically, this machine removes chaff, small pieces of straw etc. by aspiration, that is, air is pulled through the grain as it is fed into the machine. The grain is then fed into a sieve larger than the desired grain. This removes large material, including larger grains. The next sieve retains the desired grain but removes smaller grains, by allowing them to pass through. The sieves are reciprocating *i.e.* they move back and forth. In some machines, disk separators are also used to separate grains of about the same density from the desired grain. The separation is based on the length of the kernels.

Impurities that adhere to the grain are removed by another important piece of cleaning equipment *i.e.* scourer. The design varies, but the basic idea is to scour or rub the grain against itself, a perforated metal screen, or any emery surface to remove adhering dirt. The adhering material loosened by this treatment is removed by aspiration. This machine helps to remove not only mud but also the smut or rust that results from common wheat diseases.

Dry stones are used to remove stones from grain. Specific gravity is used to sort stones, glass, non-ferrous metal and plastic segments.

Overall, there are six different principles of separation normally used in wheat cleaning. These include separation based on differences in size, shape, terminal velocity in air currents, specific gravity, magnetic and electrostatic properties, colour, surface roughness etc. The layout is facilitated by installation of equipment over four to five floors so that gravity can be used for wheat to fall from one machine to the next and then elevated and re-elevated. The total quantity of screenings removed generally amounts to 1-1 ½ per cent of the grain fed to the machine.

Conditioning or Tempering

The term conditioning implies the use of heat in conjunction with water to mellow endosperm. To improve the physical state of grains for milling, conditioning or tempering of wheat precedes the actual milling process. This process involves the addition or removal of moisture for definite period of time to obtain desired moisture content in grain. There are 3 reasons to condition wheat.

1. To toughen the bran so that a longer extraction of low ash content flour can be made.
2. To ensure that moisture migration to endosperm is sufficient to produce flour of approximately 14 per cent to 15 per cent moisture content.
3. To ensure that the endosperm is mellow enough for relative ease of milling.

Moisture content of original grain is between 12 per cent and 14 per cent. If the wheat is too dry (<12 per cent), the wheat be hard and brittle, making it difficult to grind, and the bran will break into small fragments, making it more difficult to separate from the endosperm, resulting in darker flour of higher ash content.

In European mills, grains of soft-kerneled wheats are usually brought to moisture content of 16 per cent and hard-kerneled wheats to 17.5 per cent. Higher moisture levels are required for milling extremely hard wheats. Duration of tempering varies from about 8 hours (soft wheats) to 24 hours (for hard wheats). Generally, temperature greater than 50°C should be avoided.

A tough bran and a friable mealy endosperm are prerequisites for an efficient separation of the two. As the bran becomes progressively tougher and less brittle with increasing moisture content, milling will produce flour that is less contaminated by bran dust, thus being whiter and having a low ash content. The mealy endosperm is rendered mellower and more friable with the addition of correct amount of moisture.

Roller Milling

The grinding of most cereal grains, particularly those grains having a crease, is done with a roller mill. Around 1850 the idea arose, first in Switzerland and later in Hungary, to use porcelain or steel rollers instead of millstones. The diameter of these rollers is 25 or 30 cm and their length may vary between 100 and 150 cm. The rollers are positioned horizontally in pairs and rotate at different speeds in opposite directions; the fast roll going about two and a half times the speed of the slow roll. The distance between the rollers can be adjusted. Porcelain rolls are not used any more.

Roller-mills have certain advantages over traditional stone-mills.

1. The capacity of roller-mill is much larger than that a windmill or water mill.
2. The range of products from a roller mill is larger and better geared to the needs of industrial processing.
3. Roller-miller does not require the laborious and time-consuming sharpening of the furrow edges of the millstones.

In flour milling, the first objective is to remove the bran and germ from the endosperm. This is mainly accomplished by the break-system of the mill. Roller milling comprising several grinding steps, each being followed by a sifting operation. Broadly speaking, the grinding stages may be grouped into two successive systems (Figs. 4.2 and 4.3):

1. The break system
2. The reduction system

The Break System

The breaking system aims to bring about a virtual separation between the bran and the mealy endosperm. It is carried out with the help of corrugated or fluted iron rollers, called break rollers. They operate in pairs, revolving in opposite directions and at different speeds (the speed differential is approximately 1:2).

The break system consists of four or five breaks (set of rolls). After each grinding, the ground stock is separated on sieves and purifiers (by air aspiration); the small particles are saved as flour and the large particles are sent on for further grinding. In early breaks, the endosperm is taken off in rather large pieces, and in later breaks, the action is more like a scraping of the bran.

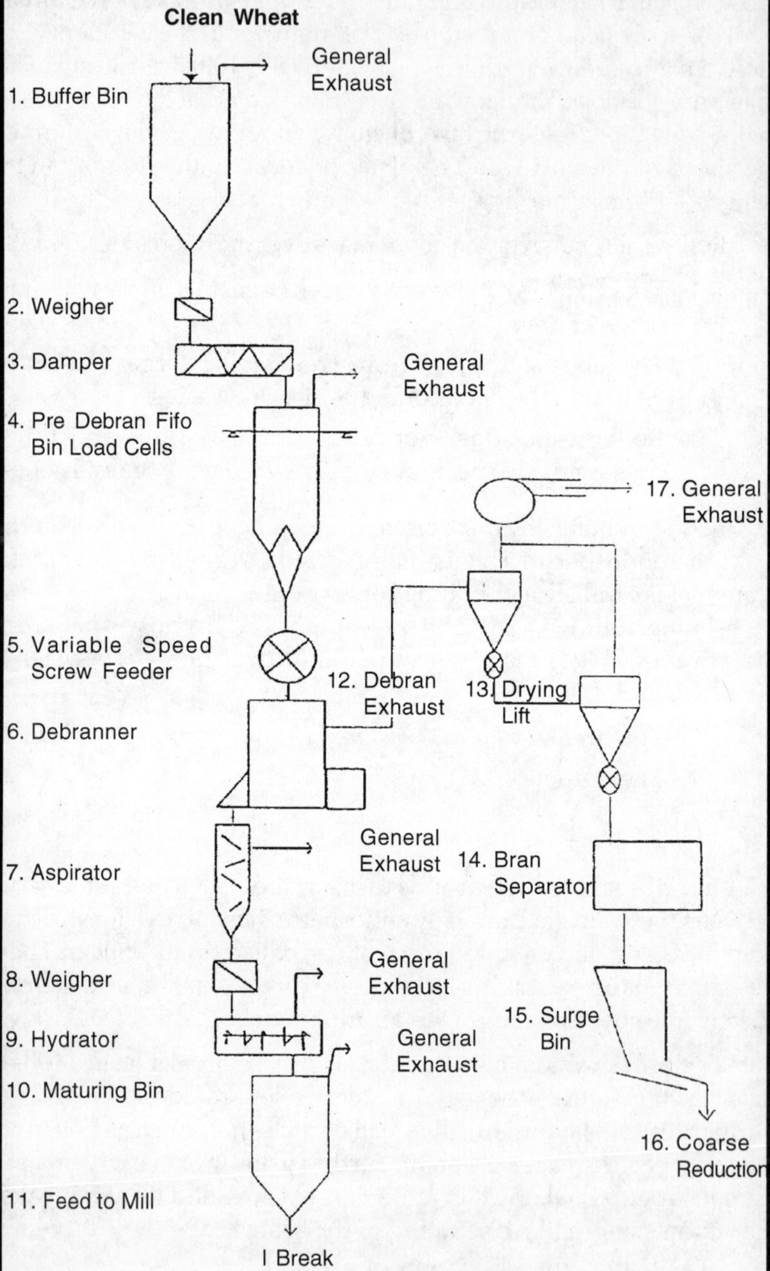

Fig. 4.2: Debranning Diagram Between Clean Wheat and First Break

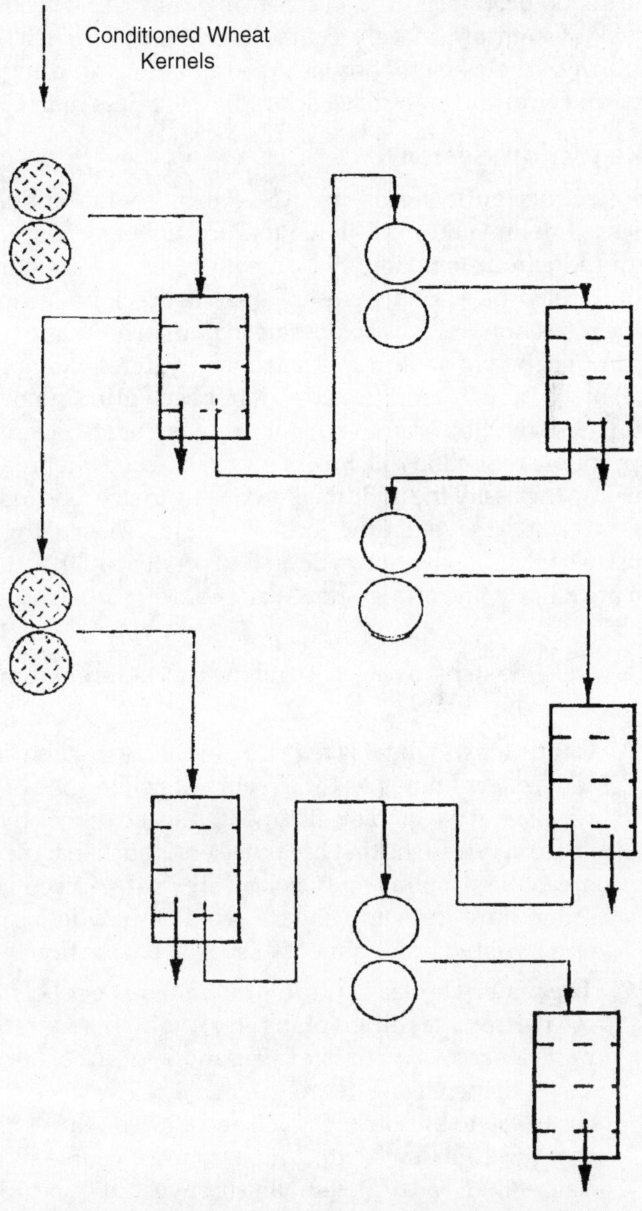

Fig. 4.3: A Milling Diagram Showing Two Parts of Break Rolls and Three Pairs of Reduction Rolls Together with Sifters

Under each pair of rollers, a set of horizontal sieves is placed so that the milled product is graded according to size. End products of the break system are mainly coarse offals (bran), germ, coarse endosperm particles (semolina, 300-750 μm and middlings, 125-300 μm) and a certain amount of flour (diameter less than 125 μm).

The Reduction System

The reduction system aims to reduce coarse endosperm particles (semolina and middlings) to flour fineness. It involves a series of reduction steps, in which, as in the case of breaking, the rollers are set progressively closer at each successive processing step. The reduction rollers also operate in pairs. They have smooth, slightly roughened (mat) surfaces and speed differentials are 4:5 (in Europe) or 2:3 (in USA and Canada). After each grinding pass, the stock is sifted, the flour removed, and the coarser particles sent to the appropriate reduction roll. Purifiers are also used after reduction rolls, mainly to classify the middlings according to size. The reduction process is repeated several times until ultimately most of the mealy endosperm has been converted to flour. End products of the reduction system are mainly fine offals (shorts) and fine endosperm particles (flour).

Overall, the steps involved in milling process are summarized as under:

1. Conditioned wheat is fed to a pair of corrugated chilled-iron rollers known as the first break-rollers, one of which revolves at two and a half times the speed of the other. The space between the first break-rollers is such that the grains are broken mainly into relatively coarse pieces with a minimum of crushing, so as to avoid the powdering of bran as powdered bran cannot be separated from flour.
2. The material released from the first break-rollers passes to a sifter machine (plansifter), which separates the particles according to size by means of a stack of horizontal sieves of increasing degree of fineness. The sieve sizes are (from top to bottom) 750, 300 and 125 μm, thus, dividing the grinding stock into four fractions: coarse materials (larger than 750 μm), semolina (between 300 and 750 μm), middlings (between 125 and 300 μm) and the flour (smaller than 125 μm).

3. The finest material (flour) leaves the mill and passes directly to the flour bag. Intermediate-sized particles, those larger than flour particles, are sent to the first reduction rollers (semolina) or (the smaller particles, middlings) to the third reduction rollers.

End Products of Milling and Their Application

1. Semolina is a milling product consisting of coarse particles of mealy endosperm with a diameter of 300-750 μm.
2. Middlings are a product consisting of intermediate-sized endosperm particles with a diameter of 125-300 μm. Both semolina and middlings are used as ingredients in porridge and for the production of pastas.
3. Flour consists of fine endosperm particles of less than 125 μm diameter. It is used for making white bread, confectionery products and certain pasta products.
4. Besides fine endosperm particles or flour, meal contains a certain amount of flaky bran and, sometimes, germ. Bran represents 11 per cent of the total products and shorts about 15 per cent. Germ can be an additional product, usually recovered at about 0.5 per cent. Bran is used for making light and dark types of brown bread.

Milling Quality

In commercial mill, the aim is to obtain a maximum yield of flour with a 'healthy' white colour. Lower the ash content, the whiter the flour. The milling quality of wheat is determined by successively measuring the following characteristics in a standard milling experiment:

1. the amount of grain that can be milled per unit time.
2. the flour yield of each milling passage and
3. the moisture and ash content of each milling passage.

The values of (2) and (3) need to be converted to a standard moisture content (approx. 14 per cent). The successive flour fractions are combined till an extraction rate of 70 per cent has been reached. If an extraction rate of 70 per cent cannot be reached, a small quantity of shorts is added. Finally, the ash content of this mixture is determined. The ash content of flour at a standard milling or extraction rate (*e.g.* 70 per cent) is a liable indication of the milling quality of wheat. The lower the ash content, the higher the flour yield in a commercial mill will be. The ash content of flour may vary between 0.45 per cent and 0.60 per cent. In other words, the flour yield at a standard ash content (*e.g.* 0.45 per cent) is taken as a measure for milling quality. Thus the determined extraction rates vary from 67-75 per cent. This method is generally used in commercial milling practice.

Milling of Soft Wheat vs Hard Wheat

In the milling of soft wheats, the mealy endosperm is fragmented indiscriminately. Therefore, the flour particles consist mainly of fragments of single cells or fragments of clusters of two or three neighbouring cells. The interior of the cells more or less bulges. When rubbed between thumb and forefinger, the flour has a soft, 'woolly' feel. The flour of soft wheat contains many loose starch granules and protein particles due to the low degree of cohesion between starch and proteins. The flour easily sticks together and sifts with difficulty, tending to close the apertures of sieves.

In the milling of hard wheats, fracturing of the grain follows the middle lamellas of the mealy endosperm cells. As a consequence, flour particles consist of one or more intact cells, some with and some without adhering wall material. As the cohesion between starch and protein is much stronger in hard than in soft endosperm wheat, the flour contains hardly any loose starch granules and protein particles. Hard wheats yield a coarse, gritty flour which is free flowing and easily sifted. When rubbed between thumb and forefinger, a more or less 'sandy' structure can be felt. The flour yield of a hard wheat is generally a few per cent higher than that of a soft wheat.

Flour Treatments

Bleaching

Flour may receive a number of treatments at the mill. Bleaching is very common. Flour contains a yellow pigment xanthophyll which is not desired in the making of white bread. When the flour is exposed to air, the colour of the flour is bleached by oxidation. When the flour is stored in bulk, this change is slow. The bleaching process is accelerated by treating the flour with chemicals. For bread and all-purpose flours, the most common bleaching agent is benzoyl peroxide, which is added as a dry powder and whitens flour over a two-day period. It only bleaches flour pigments and has no effect on the baking properties. Chlorine is detrimental to bread flours but beneficial to cake flours. High-ratio cakes *i.e.* those that contain more sugar than flour cannot be made without treatment with chlorine gas. In cake flours, chlorine is both a bleach and an improving agent. In whole meal *atta* to be used for *chapati* making, no chemical additives for bleaching are used.

Maturing

The breadmaking quality of freshly milled flour improves with storage for 1-2 months. A number of oxidizing agents are used at the mill as maturing agents. These include chlorine dioxide, acetone peroxide and azocarbonamide. Other improvers used are potassium bromate, potassium persulphate, ascorbic acid and L-cysteine hydrochloride. Maturation brings about changes in the physical properties of gluten during fermentation in such a way that results in better bread being obtained. Like bleaching, chemical substances or improvers accelerate maturation.

Chapter 5
Types and Grades of Flour

Different types of flours are used for different types of end products. Figure 5.1 depicts the different uses of wheat flour in UK.

White flour

This is made from the starchy endosperm only, bran and germ are rejected as co-products. Composition of white flour and co-products is given below:

Composition	*White Flour*	*Separated Flour*	*Coarse Bran*	*Fine Wheat Feed*
Moisture	14.4	12.7	12.6	12.7
Protein (Nx5.7 per cent)	12.0	23.0	13.6	14.2
Ash per cent	0.45	4.7	9.2	4.8
Fat per cent	1.0	10.6	2.8	4.0
Crude fibre per cent	0.1	10.6	2.8	4.0
Sugar per cent	2.0	–	–	–
Starch per cent	70.0	–	–	–

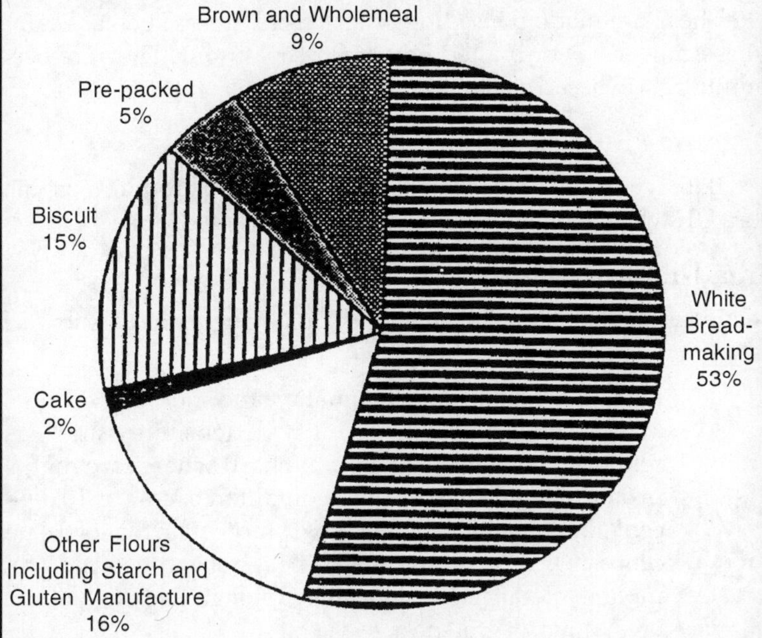

Fig. 5.1: Breakdown of UK flour production (1994-1995)

Brown Flour

This is made by adding selected co-product streams to white flour.

Whole Meal Flour

This contains the entire products of the milling of cleaned wheat, thus, whole meal flour has exactly the same composition as the wheat from which it was milled.

Germ-enriched Flour

These are white flours to which cooked wheat germ has been added. Apart from contributing flavour, vitamins in the germ enrich the flour, giving it additional nutritional value. The quantity of germ added to flour is no less than 10 per cent calculated on a dry matter basis.

Multigrain Flour

These are made by adding other cereal grains such as maize, rye, sesame seeds or malted barley to wheat flour. They are used for multigrain bread, rolls and confectionery.

Organic Flour

Both white and whole meal organic flours are produced usually from UK wheats for either bread-making or domestic use.

Bread-making Flour

Bread-making flour should have the following characteristics such as:

1. Protein should be of good quality, and should give gluten of necessary strength, stability, extensibility and gas-retaining properties. Generally, hard wheats are high in protein. Bread flour should contain in excess of 10.5 per cent good quality protein and not more than that of 0.4 per cent ash. Bread flour should have high absorption and good mixing tolerance which means prolonged mixing without breakdown of gluten.
2. Gassing power must be adequate. Flour should have sufficient damaged starch to provide enough sugar for the yeast to feed on during fermentation and/or proof periods.

Biscuit Flours

There are four main types of biscuits mostly in European countries.

1. Short dough
2. Hard sweet
3. Hard crackers
4. Wafer

Variations can be made by adding chocolate, nuts, cream etc.

The type of wheat used for short dough biscuit flours is not critical as gluten development is not needed.

1. Low protein flours with weak, extensible glutens are normally used for hard dough sweet biscuits. Bakers may add sodium metabisulphite as a source of sulphur dioxide.

2. Cracker flours contain mainly bread making wheats with protein contents in the range of 9 per cent to 10.5 per cent. Flour improvers such as ascorbic acid are rarely used.
3. Low protein soft flours are frequently specified for wafer production, as gluten must not develop in the batter during mixing.

Plain or Self-raising Flour

These are either plain or self-raising and are made of fairly soft wheats. Protein contents range between 8.5 and 10.5 per cent, depending on the harvest. In self-raising flour, baking powder (sodium bicarbonate) is used so that it does not need to be added by the home user. Many mills make self-raising flour on the batch mixing system. This method is popular because it mixes the ingredients accurately.

Cake Flours

Cake flours should contain less than 10 per cent protein and 0.4 per cent ash, and should have water absorption capacity.

Composite and Alternative Flours

Composite flour means blends of wheat and other flours for the production of various types of products such as baked products, leavened or unleavened, pastas etc. The term 'alternative flours' is used to describe a total substitution of one raw material by another. For example, a wheatless 'bread' made from cassava starch and soy flour. Composite flours serve two different functions such as:

1. to lower or remove the use of wheat or other staple by partial or total substitution, for economic reasons.
2. to change the nutritional characteristics of the product, for example, by protein, vitamin, or mineral enrichment for enhancing the nutritional status of the population.

Raw Materials Suitable for Composite Products

Table 5.2 shows the proportion of non-wheat material (as per cent of total flour) that can reasonably be incorporated into conventional leavened bread.

Table 5.2: Proportion of Non-wheat Material (as per cent of total flour) for Blending with Wheat for Breadmaking

Commodity	*Range*	*Realistic Maxima*
Maize (white cvs)	18-30	30
Sorghum (cvs)	15-50	30
Millets	10-30	30
Barley	10-30	30
Rice	10-25	25
Cassava flour (dry weight basis)	13-30	30
Raw cassava	10-25	25
Cassava starch	10-50	40
Yam	10-30	20
Potato	6-30	25
Sweet potato (white)	15-30	30

Quality of Raw Materials

The basic criteria for the quality of raw materials are:

1. For a composite, wheat flour of reasonable strength–preferably more than 12 per cent protein.
2. Clean, fine flour from the non-wheat source. This should be free from specks of coloured bran or, in the case of roots, skin, and of as low a coarse fibre content as is attainable. The colour should be as white as possible and free from any taint or strong odour.
3. The raw materials must be consistent, so as to give a predictable performance.

Some composite flour programs failed because of lack of a regular supply of raw materials. Wheat mills have no difficulty in producing regular supplies of bread flour. However, in most developing countries to arrange for thousands of tonnes a year of an agricultural product to be trade and brought, either processed or not, from many small farms to a central point, requires an extremely high level of planning, good transport infrastructure, suitable storage, and the technological capability to ensure high and consistent quality. In the countries where composite flours was thought of as a means of saving foreign exchange and stimulating local agriculture, these criteria are rare.

Grades of Flour

Different grades of flours can be obtained by milling of wheat. A complete flour is produced by blending some (patent) or all (straight run) of the individual machine flours. The flour streams from the various rollers are named for the roller–'first break stream' etc. They vary in chemical composition because they vary in the amount of bran and germ which they contain as well as in the portion of the endosperm which has been released. Many different flour streams are produced, especially in large mills. These streams are combined and blended to form flours with particular baking characteristics.

Straight Flour

It is a combination of all flour streams. It is seldom produced. Composition of a straight-run flour in terms of proportion, colour grade and protein from three streams are given below:

	Stream 1	*Stream 2*	*Stream 3*	*Straight run*
1. Per cent of total flour produced	65	30	5	100
2. Colour grade	-0.5	4.0	10.5	1.4
3. Protein (per cent)	10.0	11.0	14.0	10.5

Patent Flours

Patent flours are from the more refined streams and vary considerably in the percentage of the total flour represented. In the US flour milling industry, flours are identified as First Patent, Short Patent, Medium Patent and Long Patent. Characteristics of these flours are determined by percentage of separation obtained from a 72 per cent extraction. The manner in which the particles of endosperm are separated is called 'separation' whereas 'extraction' refers to the percentage of flour which has been extracted from wheat kernel.

Following approximate percentages of patent flours:

1. First Patent: 70 per cent total flour
2. Short Patent: 80 per cent total flour
3. Medium Patent: 90 per cent total flour
4. Long or Standard Patent: 95 per cent total flour

First Patent is used as cake flour and is obtained from soft wheats.

Short Patent is used for premium brands of breads.

Medium Patent is used for featured brand of breads. Medium patent flour is also called cut-off flour. It is between short and long patents.

Long Patent is used for competitive brands of breads.

Clear Flours

The flour remaining after the patent is removed, is called clear flour and it may be separated into different grades. It is also called low grade flour. This flour which comes from the tail end of the breaks and reduction system has high ash and dark colour.

Clear flours have more strength and are used especially in the production of rye and other dark breads. Clear flour is derived from the outer portion of endosperm because this portion has more good quality proteins. Flour made from soft wheats is used for cakes, pastries and biscuits. Hard wheat varieties are used for the production of yeast leavened breads. Amber durum wheats are used for the production of noodles, macaroni etc.

Red Dog Flours

The flours from the last reduction is called red-dog because it is dark in colour and contains relatively large amounts of bran and germ. It is usually sold as animal feed.

Bran

Wheat bran is used mainly as poultry and cattle feeds.

Wheat Shorts

This is another fraction obtained in roller milling of wheat. It is found mixed with bran and germ in the mill feed.

Germ

In the process of roller flour milling, germ is eliminated along with mill feeds. It can be separated and used for the production of wheat germ oil. The residual solvent extracted wheat germ is rich in proteins and B-vitamins and can be used in the preparation of weaning foods.

Chapter 6

Processing and Parboiling of Rice

Rice with the hull on is called paddy or rough rice. About 20 per cent of paddy rice is hull. To obtain edible rice, the husk must be removed. The kernel remaining after the hull is removed, is brown rice. Brown rice has a strong flavour and is indigestible. Furthermore, during the dehusking process, some of the cells may be damaged and enzymes (lipo oxygenase) released that cause rapid oxidation of the lipid, leading to rancidity. The bran must, therefore, be polished away to yield desired white rice. Bran, however, contains the water soluble B-vitamins.

The milling of rice consists of the following steps:

Cleaning

Before passing to the husker, the paddy should be clean, free from straw, chaff, sacking, dirt, stones and metal. The cleaned rice is then dehulled in a huller.

Dehusking

Dehulling of rough rice to brown rice can be carried out either manually (hand pounding) or mechanically (Figs. 6.1, 6.2, 6.3 and 6.4).

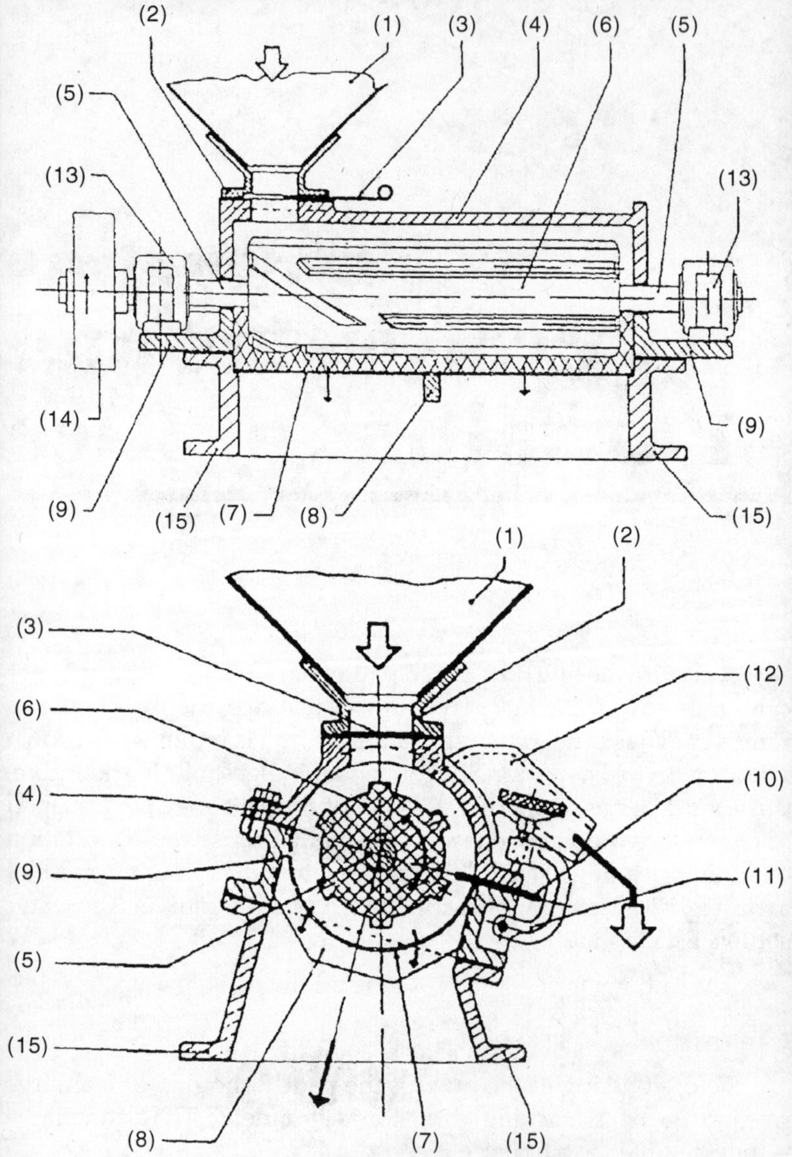

Fig. 6.1: The Engleberg Paddy Huller

Key: (1) Hopper, (2) Hopper seat, (3) Feed-granulation gate, (4) Cover, (5) Cylinder shaft, (6) Cylinder shell, (7) Screen, (8) Screen holder, (9) Frame, (10) Frame, (11) Cover clamp, (12) Outlet clamp, (13) Bearings, (14) Pulley, (15) Frame.

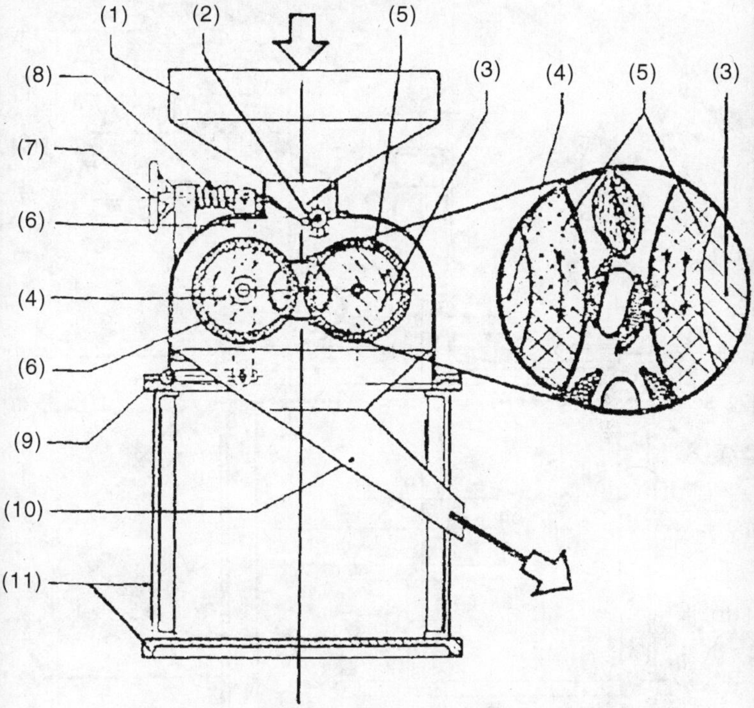

Fig. 6.2: A Rubber-Roller Dehulling Machine

Key: (1) Hopper, (2) Feeding roll, (3) & (4): Drive rolls, (5) Rubber coating, (6-8) Pressure adjustment system, (9) Housing, (10) Delivery spout, (11) Stand.

Hand Pounding

Hand pounding is most commonly done using a pestle and mortar made of wood and worked by hand or foot (*dheki*). The product is winnowed by hand using shallow basket or mats. Winnowing can take place throughout the process, ensuring that rice that is dehusked, atleast partly, debranned, is not unnecessarily broken. The average recovery of rice, including the broken rice, in home pounding is higher than in rice milling. Home pound rice has a short storage life owing to the high content of fat in the bran which develops rancidity.

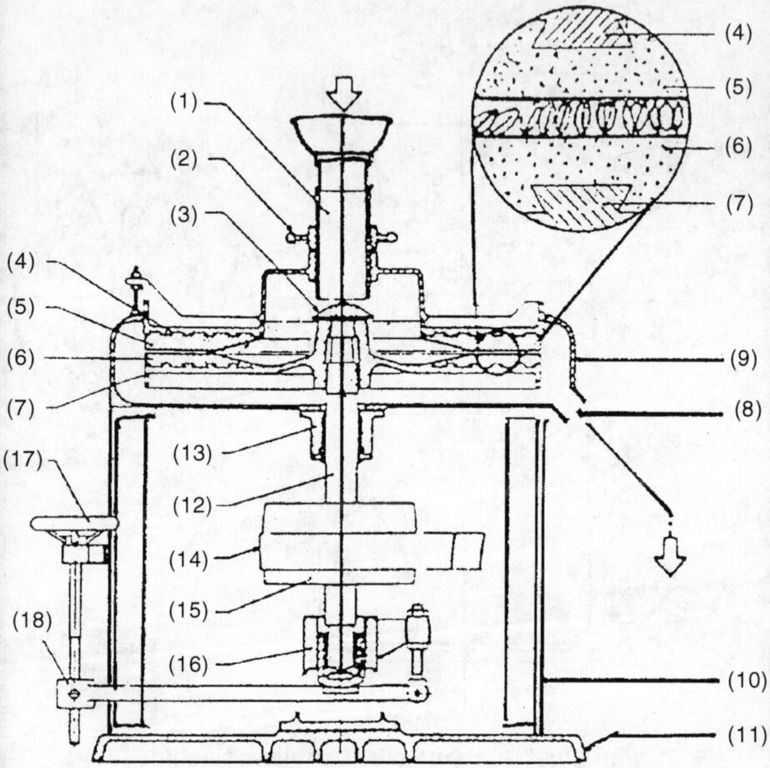

Fig. 6.3: An Abrasive Rice Dehuller

Key: (1) Feed spout, (2) Slide gate, (3) and (7) Rotating abrasive wheels, (4) Fixed wheel, (5) and (6) Abrasive stones, (8) Outflow spout, (9) Housing, (10) and)11) Stands, (12)-(16) Drive mechanism and bearings, (17) and (18) Adjustment system for distance between stones.

Mechanical Hullers

Mechanical hullers are of three main types:

1. Stone dehullers
2. Engleberg mills
3. Rubber dehullers

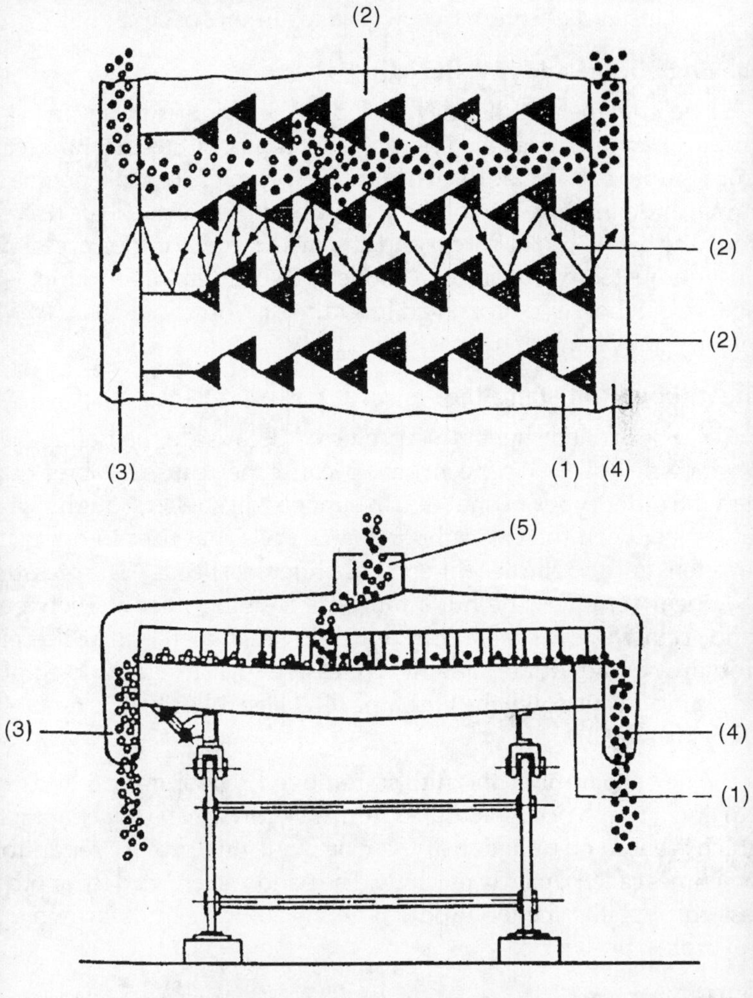

Fig. 6.4: A Paddy Separator

Key: (1) Table, (2) Compartments, (3) Outlet for brown rice, (4) Outlet for paddy, (5) Inlet for mixture of brown rice and paddy.

Stone Dehullers

Stone dehullers are still common in tropical Asia, where surface-bruised brown rice is immediately milled with either an abrasive or friction mill. Rubber rollers are common in Japan, where brown rice is stored instead of rough rice, with a resultant space saving.

The Engleberg Paddy Huller Mill

The Engleberg huller developed in the nineteenth century is a simple machine, easy to operate and repair. One machine can process upto 500 kg paddy an hour. The principle of the machine is simple and basically that of the mortar and pestle; paddy is driven along the barrel by the screw and churned rapidly under pressure. This is adjusted by means of a choke at the outlet. The product is a mixture of whole and broken grain, grain dust, bran and husk. This is winnowed by hand or by machine.

The Rubber Roll Dehuller

Rubber-rolled shellers are preferred because of their efficiency in removing hull (>90 per cent) and because they cause less breakage than the older types of shellers. In rubber-roll sheller, rough rice is passed between the two rubber-coated rolls that turn in opposite directions and are run at a differential (different speeds). The pressure and shear removes the hulls much as rubbing peanuts between hands removes the shells. Different cultivars may require different pressures for adequate shelling. Excessive pressure may discolour the grain and cut down the life of the rolls. The rolls must be replaced every 100-150 hr.

After separation, the hull is removed by aspiration and the remaining rough rice is separated from the brown rice. The separation, which is based on bulk density, can be made on a gravity separator, sometimes called a paddy machine. The paddy is returned for another pass-through the sheller. Products at this point are hulls, brown rice and broken brown rice.

Milling

Brown rice is milled in a machine called pearler to remove coarse outer layers of bran and germ by a process of rubbing, resulting in unpolished milled rice. Most of the breakage of rice occurs in this milling.

In a typical pearler, the brown rice enters through a flow-regulating value and is then conveyed by a screw to the pearling chamber, where the mixing roller causes the grains to rub against each other, abrading off the bran. Most of the bran is removed by the grain rubbing on other grains, although a small amount is also removed by the grain rubbing on the steel screen surrounding the chamber. At the discharge end of the pearling chamber is a plate held in place by a weight. The position of the weight varies the pressure on plate and thus the back pressure on the rice in the pearling chamber. The degree of milling can be controlled by varying the pressure and thereby changing the average residence time in the chamber.

High humidity in the atmosphere during milling improves the yield of head rice (unbroken milled kernels). Increasing the moisture content of the grain to 14 to 16 per cent by steam vapor prior to milling also improves the head rice yield and its taste, since 14 to 16 per cent is the critical moisture content for crack susceptibility for most rice varieties. Breakage is minimized for all varieties by tempering the grain to 16 per cent moisture before milling. However, the milled rice may have to be redried to 14 per cent for safe storage.

After milling, the loose bran is removed by an aspirator. The milled rice is then polished (Fig. 6.5). The term 'polished rice' refers to milled rice that has gone through polishers that remove bran adhering to the surface of milled rice and improve its translucency (Fig. 6.6). The polisher consists of a rotating vertical cylinder to which straps of leather are attached. An additional amount of bran is removed by the polisher. Some rice consumers prefer a very glossy or shiny rice called coated or glazed rice. The rice is prepared by adding dry talc and glucose solution to well milled rice. The old system of 'polishing' using talc (calcium silicate) has been discontinued because the mineral was suspected to causing stomach cancer, although it was subsequently found to have been caused by aesbestos contamination from machinery.

After polishing, the head rice is separated from brokens by screening or by disk separators. The products from the rice mill are:

1. Head rice and Brokens (70 per cent)
2. Rice bran (8 per cent)
3. Rice polish (2 per cent)
4. Hulls (20 per cent)

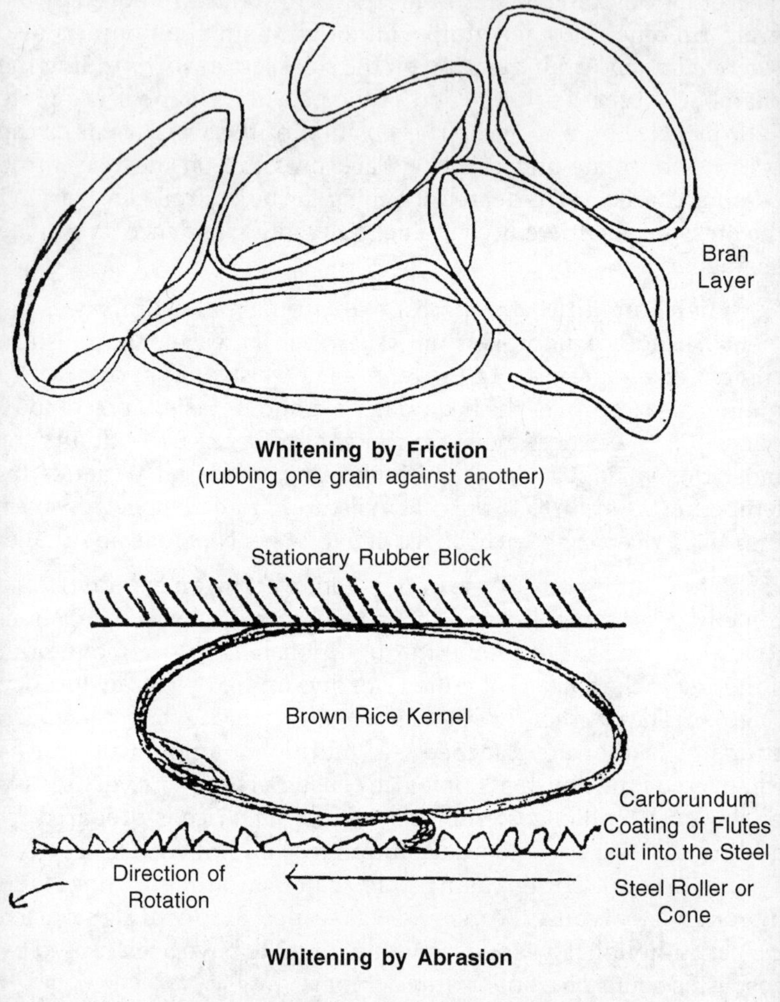

Fig. 6.5: Whitening by Friction and Abrasion

By-products of Rice

These include:

1. Rice hulls
2. Rice bran
3. Rice polishings

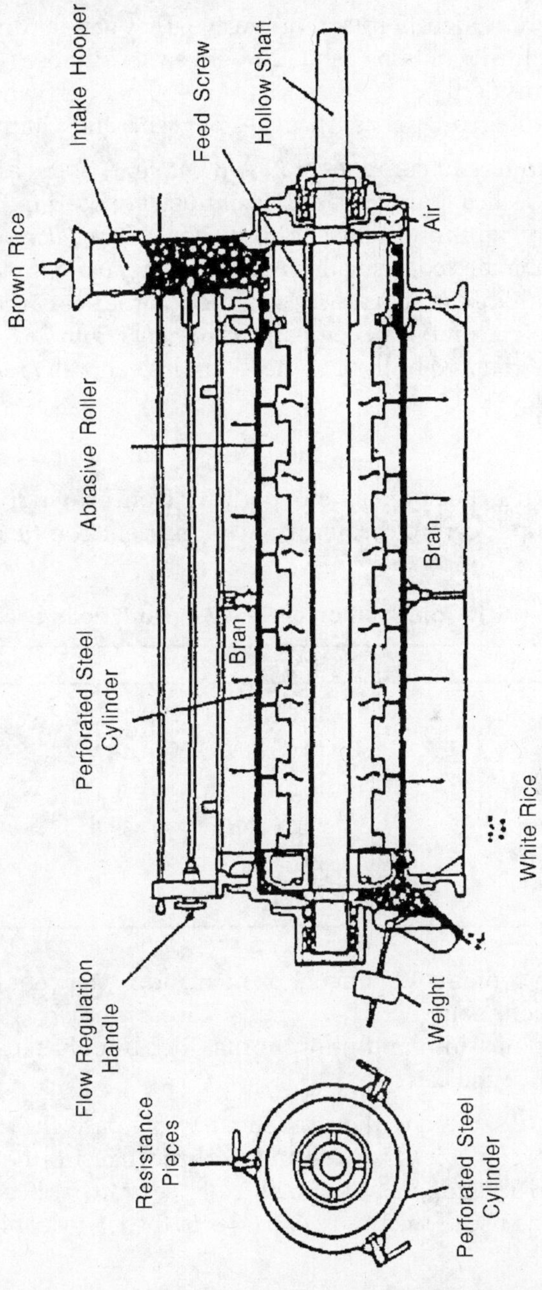

Fig. 6.6: An Abrasive Whitener

Rice Hulls

Rice hulls are tough, fibrous and abrasive. They have low nutritive value. Paddy husk contains ash (~20 per cent), cellulose (~30 per cent), pentosans (~20 per cent) and lignin (~20 per cent) and small amounts of protein (~3 per cent), fat (~2 per cent) and vitamins.

The predominant component (94-96 per cent) of the ash from paddy husk is silica. Large quantities of husk are used in India as fuel for boilers, kilns and household purpose. Other uses include roughage for animal feed, insulating material, paper making etc. Small amounts of hulls are used as abrasives and to produce carbon. The rice hull yield of furfural is low compared to the yield from such sources as oat hulls, cottonseed hulls or corncobs and is generally related to the pentosan level.

Rice Bran

The bran is the outer layer of pericarp from brown rice. Bran is normally 8 per cent of brown rice. Its nutrient composition is given as under:

Table 6.1: Composition of Rice Bran and Polish

Constituent	*Bran*	*Polish*
Protein	12.0	12.0
Fat	13.0	16.0
Ash	10.0	8.0
Nitrogen free extract	40.0	56.0
Crude fibre	12.0	7.3
Pentosans	10.0	—

Rice bran contains 12 per cent protein and 13 per cent fat. It is also an excellent source of B-vitamins. Rice bran ash is high in magnesium, potassium and phosphorus. Rice bran has also been shown to reduce cholestrol.

If rice bran is stored without inactivation of lipase, the fat in the bran rapidly becomes hydrolyzed and oxidized, causing the bran to become rancid and unpalatable. Stabilized rice bran has been made available by the use of the Brady extruder in the US to stabilize the full-fat bran by inactivating its lipase. It is finding application in breakfast cereals, snack foods and bakery products. Stabilized rice bran has been incorporated into whole-wheat bread, muffins, peanut butter cookies and oatmill cookies at levels of upto 20 per cent.

Rice bran is a source of oil which is obtained by the extraction of rice bran with solvents. The oil contains a high percentage of unsaturated fatty acids yet it is quite stable because of the presence of natural antioxidants. After refining, rice bran oil is comparable to other edible oils.

Rice Polishings

Polishings are the inner layers, containing aleurone cells and small amounts of starchy endosperm. The amount of polishings vary widely, depending upon the milling procedure employed, generally it amounts to 2 per cent. Its nutrient composition is given in Table 6.1. They are mostly used as animal feed.

Aging of Rice

Storage changes or aging, occur particularly during the first 3 to 4 months after harvest and are known as 'after harvest ripening'. Rice milled from freshly harvested paddy gives very pasty and sticky kernels after cooking. If the paddy is stored under good storage conditions, within weeks, the milled rice will cook with less tendency to stick together. Storage of milled rice also produces decreased cohesiveness, drier surface, larger volumes and firmer texture in cooked kernels. Cooking time becomes longer with increased storage time. This is due to high α-amylase content of fresh rice, which acts on starch in the kernel but is inactivated during storage.

Parboiling of Rice

Parboiling consists of three steps (Fig. 6.7):

1. Steeping
2. Steaming
3. Drying

The traditional parboiling process involves soaking paddy rice overnight or longer in water at ambient temperature, followed by boiling or steaming the steeped rice at 100°C to gelatinize the starch, while the grain expands until the hulls lemma and palea start to separate.

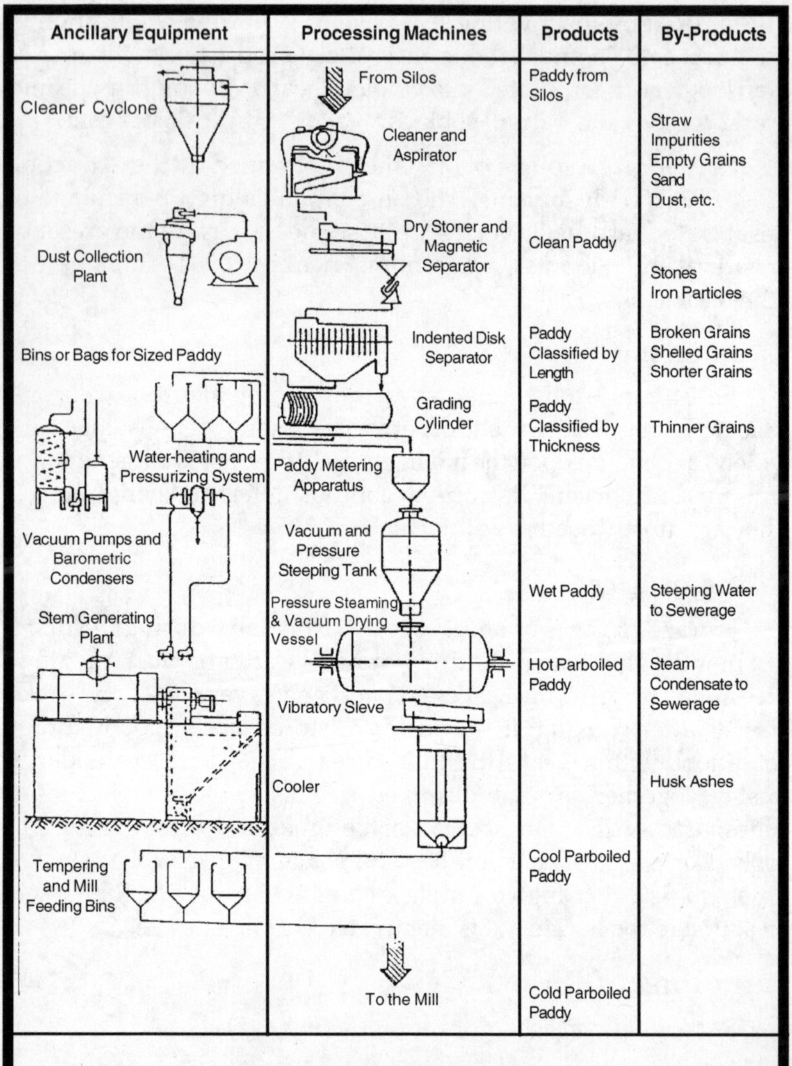

Fig. 6.7: Parboiling of Paddy

The parboiled rice is then cooked and sun-dried before storage or milling.

Modern methods involve the use of a hot water soak at 60°C (below the starch gelatinization temperature) for a few hours to reduce the incidence of aflatoxin contamination during the soaking step. Leaching of nutrients during soaking aggravates the contamination, together with the practice of recycling the soak water.

Vacuum infiltration to de-aerate the grain prior to pressure soaking is applied to obtain good quality product, as is pressure parboiling. The parboiled rice has a cream to yellow colour depending on the intensity of heat treatment. Aged rice may give a grayish parboiled rice, probably because it has a lower pH owing to the presence of free fatty acids.

Parboiling gelatinizes the starch granules and hardens the endosperm, making it translucent. Parboiling results in inward diffusion of water soluble vitamins, in addition to partial degradation of thiamine during heat treatment, except in heated-sand drying. Riboflavin content is not decreased by parboiling. Despite the degradation of thiamine, parboiled rice has a higher vitamin content than raw milled rice in all parboiling procedures tested.

Parboiling of paddy has several advantages (Table 6.2):

1. Dehusking of parboiled rice is easy and the grain becomes tougher resulting in reduced losses during milling.
2. Higher yield of head rice from milling because kernel is more resistant to breakage.
3. Milled parboiled rice has greater resistance to insects and fungus infection.
4. The nutritive value of rice increases after parboiling because the water dissolves the vitamins and minerals present in the hulls and bran coat and carries them into the endosperm.
5. The water soluble B-vitamins, thiamine, riboflavin and niacin, are higher in milled parboiled rice than in milled raw rice.
6. Parboiled rice does not turn into a glutinous mass when cooked.

There are certain disadvantages of parboiling also. The colour change and sometimes, the unpleasant smell of parboiled rice due to increased susceptibility to rancidity are not preferred. These changes are due to defective steeping during parboiling. During steeping, fermentative changes take place which result in the yellowish colour and off flavour of rice. These defects are overcome in modern methods of parboiling.

Table 6.2: Rice: Parboiled versus Raw

Advantages	*Disadvantages*
The process produces a higher value product.	At all scales some extra equipment is needed (capital cost).
The process uses up the waste husk on site.	Husk already has a value as a fuel.
The process creates employment.	Uses scarce labour.
Greatly increased vitamin content.	Inherent and acquired pigments or precursors penetrate from the husk causing discolouration.
Lower losses of substance (solids, proteins) on washing and cooking.	Maillard browning occurs.
Rancidity–causing enzymes are inactivated, bran is already stabilized.	
Biological processes (germination, microorganisms) are prevented.	
Insects are destroyed.	
Parboiled paddy can be rapidly dried in simple dryers.	
Endosperm is harder, resists insect attack in store, gives higher milling out-turn and a lower proportion of broken grains.	
Grains remain firm during cooking.	
More water is absorbed during cooking.	
After cooking, the rice absorbs less oil from the curry.	
After cooking, the rice keeps better and can be used the next day.	
Lipids migrate from endosperm to bran, giving bran of higher oil content.	
Parboiled rice can be used as raw material for products that cannot be made from raw rice, such as flaked, canned, puffed rice.	

Processed Rice Products

The important processed products of rice are:

Precooked and Instant Rice (Quick-cooking Rice)

Quick-cooking rices are those that require significantly less cooking time than raw milled rice (15 to 25 min.). Because of the demand from the modern consumer, many processes have been developed for quick-cooking rice. The most common processes, all starting with milled rice are:

1. Rice is cooked as above but is dried at a low temperature, the rice is then heated rapidly to expand or puff off the grains.
2. Presoaked rice freeze dried. The product reconstitutes very well in hot water.
3. Precooked rice is frozen, thawed, drained and then dried. Much of the water is removed at thawing and this cuts down the cost of drying.

Precooked rice is used for rice-based convenience food products in which non-rice ingredients are packed separately and mixed only during heating. Retort rice in Japan is made by hermetically sealing cooked non-waxy and waxy rice in laminated plastic or aluminium-laminated plastic pouches and pasteurizing at 120°C under pressure. Steamed waxy rice with red beans accounts for 80 per cent of retort rice in Japan. An aluminium-laminated plastic pouch is warmed directly in hot water for 10 to 15 min. while plastic pouches may be punctured and heated in microwave oven for 1 to 2 min.

Canned Rice Products

Various canned products that contain rice include soups, baby foods, milky rice pudding, plain and flavoured cooked rice. The most suitable varieties for most of these are the long grain high-amylase types. The rice should, for preference, have been parboiled. In this way, the grain will retain integrity throughout the canning process.

There are, however, few successful canned rice products on the market because the grain is not stable at retorting and tends to become too soft. In soups or other canned foods, where the rice must remain in suspension, parboiled rice is cooked enough to prevent settling and then added to the mix. The most successful and well known is canned rice pudding. If the rice and milk mixture are prepared separately and combined in the can aseptically, the flavour and texture of the product are preserved. Dry products such as fried rice and 'rice and beans' can also be canned.

Breakfast Foods and Snack Foods

There are many uses of rice and rice flour for culinary preparations. They include puffed/crisp rice breakfast cereals, cakes cookies, snacks, crackers, strained baby foods and precooked baby cereals for weaning.

Puffed rice for snacks and breakfast cereals is made by either the sudden application of heat or the sudden application to heated rice of a drop in pressure. In either case there is rapid expansion of steam inside the precooked grain. Other techniques include 'gun puffing' and extrusion.

Parched Extrusion Paddy/Puffed Rice from Paddy

Paddy is soaked in water to increase the moisture to about 20 per cent. The moist paddy is puffed by subjecting to sudden heat treatment at 250-270°C for 30-40 seconds. The husk splits and the rice is puffed. Puffed rice is mixed with jaggery and made into balls is used as a snack.

Puffed Rice from Parboiled Rice

The rice is soaked in salt water to increase the moisture to about 20 per cent. The moist rice is put into a hot vessel at about 250-270°C for 30-40 seconds. The rice puffs and it is consumed as a snack.

Flaked Rice

Flaked rice is made from parboiled rice. Paddy is soaked in water for 2-3 days (or hot water 70-80°C for 20 min) to soften the kernel, followed by boiling in water for a few minutes. After cooking, the water is drained off and paddy is heated (250-275°C) in a shallow earthen vessel till the husks break open, after which it is pounded by a wooden pestle, heavy iron rollers which flatten the rice kernel and remove the husk. Husk is removed by winnowing. The vitamin content of flaked rice is equal to that of parboiled rice. This precooked product is widely used for the preparation of snacks in India.

Noodles (Rice 'Pasta')

Broken rice is often used to make noodles. With improvements in milling technology, there is shortage of broken grain for noodle manufacture. Whole grain rice of poor quality is, therefore, being used. The first step is to mill the broken rice to flour. This is then processed in much the same way as when Italian pasta is made from durum wheat. The difference is that rice contains no gluten, which in case of pasta, acts as the binding agent, when the dough is extruded. For rice, pregelatinized starch is used.

Traditionally, extruded noodles are prepared from aged high-amylase broken by wet-milling the steeped rice, kneading it into first-sized balls, surface-gelatinizing the flour balls (about 500 g) in a boiling water bath until they float, remixing, extruding through a hydraulic press with a die, subjecting the extruded noodles to heat treatment for surface gelatinization, soaking in cold water and sun-drying in racks. Extruders may also be used to cook and knead premoistened dry-milled flour and then extrude it as noodle at the end of the barrel. Considerable starch degradation occurs during extrusion, such that the gel consistency changes from hard to soft.

Fermented Rice Products

In the East, there are many fermented products, some highly localized, others ubiquitous in large regions and nations. Among the solid products are sour breads such as Indian *Idli*, highly flavoured cheeselike cakes, *dosa*; Japanese *koji*; Chinese red rice; predigested 'yellow rice' of the Andes. Liquid products include opaque and clear beverages such as *sake*, distilled spirits and vinegar. Rice vinegar results from the completion of the rich starch fermentation and is a traditional Japanese and Chinese product. Acetic acid fermentation is carried out by mixing seed vinegar with the rice wine and takes one to three months. The product is ripened, filtered, pasteurized and bottled. Broken rice, together with maize grits, is an adjunct in beer manufacture in the US and Japan. Rice is preferred to maize because of its lower protein content and fat content (<1.5 per cent).

Rice Flours and Starch

High protein rice flours for early childhood feeding may be obtained from cooked milled rice by destraching treatment with

α-amylase. A high-fructose rice syrup and a high-protein rice flour have been produced from broken rice using α-amylase, glucoamylase and glucose isomerase.

Rice starch production involves mainly wet milling of brokens with 0.3 to 0.5 per cent sodium hydroxide to remove protein. Brokens are steeped in alkali solution for 24 hours and are then wet milled with the alkali solution. After the batter is stored for 10-24 hours, fibre is removed by passing it through screens; the starch is collected by centrifugation, washed and dried. Protein in the effluent may be recovered by neutralization and the precipitated protein used as a feed supplement.

Baked Rice Products

For those suffering from celiac disease, a yeast-leavened bread of 100 per cent rice flour has been successfully developed, consisting of 100 parts rice flour, 75 parts water, 7.5 parts sugar, 6 parts oil, 3 parts fresh compressed yeast, 3 parts hydroxypropyl methylcellulose and 2 parts salt. Low amylase and Low-GT rice give a soft textured crumb. A medium-grain low amylase rice flour: waxy rice flour ration of 3:1 in place of wheat flour could produce satisfactory muffins for gluten-sensitive individuals. Non-waxy rice cakes or crackers are prepared from both low and high-amylase rices in China. A similar rice product made in the Phillipines from intermediate-to high-amylase rice is called *puto seko*. These crackers break easily on handling.

Chapter 7
Processing of Maize

The maize kernel is transformed into valuable foods and industrial products by two processes:

1. Dry milling
2. Wet milling

Dry Milling

Maize kernel is large, hard, flat and contains a large germ than other cereals (~12 per cent of the kernel). The germ is high in fat (34 per cent) and must be removed if the product is to be stored without becoming rancid. In dry milling, the aim is to recover the maximum amount of grits with the minimum amount of flour, with the least possible contamination of germ. Thus, the miller wants to remove the hull *i.e.* pericarp, seed coat and aleurone layers and germ without reducing the endosperm to small particle size. The most effective way to accomplish this is with a degerminator, a specialized attrition mill.

The grains are cleaned and conditioned by the addition of cold or hot water or steam (~ 21 per cent moisture), which results in loosening and toughening of the germ and bran. The endosperm is moistened to an ideal moisture content such that the yield of grits is maximum. The conditioned grain is passed through a degerminator which is composed of two cone-shaped surfaces, one rotating inside the other (stationary). They rub the corn to remove the hull and break the germ free. The stock after degermination is dried to 15-15.5 per cent moisture content and then sifted, to produce a number of fractions. Bran is removed by aspiration and then to plansifters. The fines go to the next break rolls and the coarse particles to purifiers and then to the germ rolls. The germ rolls flatten the germ so that it is easily removed by sifting.

Entoleters are also used for dehulling and degerming of corn. The entoleter is an impact machine rather than an attrition mill. The corn is fed through a centre opening in the entoleter and falls on a rapidly rotating disc containing pins on the surface. It is forcefully thrown against the wall and degermed by the impact. After the removal of hull and grerm, the endosperm is reduced to grits of the desired size by roller milling. The products in dry milling are:

1. Grits (40 per cent)
2. Coarse meal (20 per cent)
3. Fine meal (10 per cent)
4. Corn flour (5 per cent)
5. Germ (14 per cent)
6. Hominy feed (11 per cent)

Wet Milling

The largest volume of maize in developed countries such as the United States is processed by wet milling to yield starch and other valuable by-products such as liquid and solid glucose, corn syrup, maize gluten meal and feed.

Fig. 7.1 shows the outline of the wet milling process for maize. The steps to be followed are:

Steeping

After cleaning similar to that used in dry milling, the corn is steeped. Maize is first transferred into steep tanks. The steep water is a dilute solution (0.1-0.2 per cent) of sulfur dioxide designed to

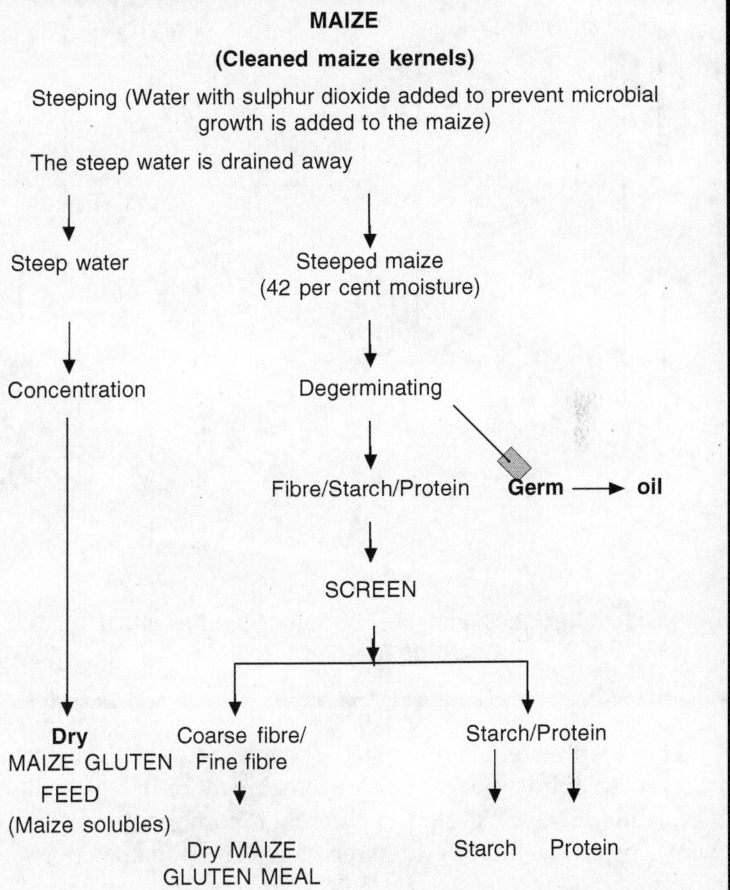

Fig. 7.1: The Wet-Milling Process for Maize

prevent excessive microbial growth. The bisulphite ions react with disulphide bonds in the matrix proteins of the corn, making them more hydrophillic and soluble (Fig. 7.2). Steeping is usually done for 30 to 48 hours at 48-52°C. As a result of steeping, the grain softens and swells to almost twice its size, taking upto 42 per cent moisture. The strong bond between the starch and protein in the endosperm is weakened, making it easier to isolate starch later on in the process.

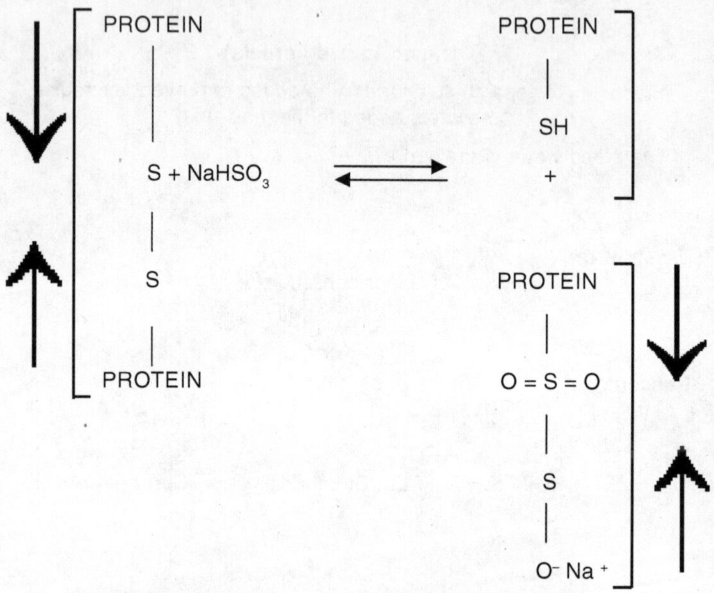

Fig. 7.2: Reaction of Sodium Bisulfite with a Disulfide Bond of a Protein

The steep water is not wasted. It contains significant amounts of dissolved solids, nearly half of which can be protein, which is called 'gluten'. Maize 'gluten' is different in composition from that of wheat gluten. The maize gluten recovered from steep water is used for animal feed (gluten feed). This can be concentrated by reverse osmosis membrane filtration to about 55 per cent solids and used as part of the media for growth of yeast and other microorganisms for purposes such as antibiotic production. Steep water is also used as a fur cleaner.

Milling

The softened steeped maize is ground coarsely in water by an attrition or degerminating mill to break open the kernel and to separate the germ away from the material in the kernel without breaking it into pieces. Two passes through the mill may be needed to free the germ, after which it is separated from the remainder of the kernel with a liquid cyclone separator, or hydroclone (Fig. 7.3).

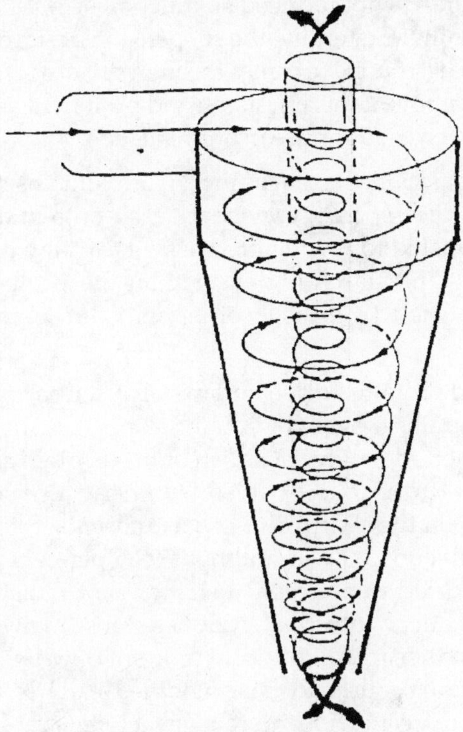

Fig. 7.3: Use of Hydroclone to Separate Material of Different Densities

Screening, Centrifugation and Washing

Germ is separated from the kernel using a liquid cyclone separator or hydroclone. The separators centrifuge the low density, germs out of the rest of the slurry. Starch suspension can be added to the slurry to make the specific gravity between 1.06 and 1.08, which is ideal for causing the germ to float and the starch plus cell debris to sink. The germs are screened and washed to remove the adhering starch and dried. It is then used to extract oil by hydraulic pressing or by using a solvent.

After the degerminated material obtained after sieving is ground in stone or steel burr mills or with an impact type of attrition mill.

The aim is to separate the starch, protein and fibre from each other. The hull fibre or bran is not reduced so much in size, hence can be removed by screening. Generally, the suspension of starch, protein and fibre is screened a number of times through various sized screens and is washed to remove adhering starch and protein from the fibre. The collected fibre is dried for use in animal feeds.

After fibre separation, the remaining stream contains the protein and starch in water. The specific gravity of starch-protein suspension (mill starch) is adjusted to 1.04 before passing through centrifugal starch separators. The starch is denser than the protein, hence, they can be separated from each other with large continuous centrifugation.

The recovered protein is dried and mainly used as animal feed. The starch still contains too much protein (~1 per cent) at this point and must be washed to remove as much of this protein as possible and centrifuging a further 8 to 14 times. Starch can also be purified with hydroclones on the same principle as those used to separate germ. Starch obtained from wet milling is 99.5 per cent pure. The washed starch is dried to between 10-15 per cent moisture using flash dryers and collect with dust cyclones. Most maize starch is converted into corn syrup, a significant amount of which is sold as unmodified cornstarch or used to make modified starches. The starch is also used to produce alcohol and food sweeteners by either acid or enzymatic hydrolysis.

Maize Products

There are more than 3500 different uses for maize products. Depending upon the maize variety, kernels are eaten whole, popped or used to make cornmeal, grits, corn flakes–breakfast foods and hominy (a coarsely ground maize meal boiled in milk or water). The grain is fermented to give *ogi* in Nigeria and other countries in Africa and is decorticated, degermed and precooked to be made into *arepas* in Columbia and Venezuela.

Maize flour dough does not have the elasticity essential for the leavened breads, but is ideal for flat breads such as tortillas. In Egypt, a maize flat bread, *aish merahra*, is widely produced. Maize flour is used to make a soft dough spiced with 5 per cent ground fenugreek seeds, which is believed to increase the protein content, improve digestibility and extend the storage life of the bread. The dough is fermented all night with a sourdough starter. In the morning, the dough is shaped into small, soft, round loaves which are left for 30 min to 'prove'. Before baking, the loaves are made into wide, flat discs. *Aish merahra* keeps fresh for seven to ten days if it is stored in airtight containers.

In Mexico, *tortillas* are made from lime-treated maize. Lime treatment involves addition of one part of whole maize to two parts of approximately 1 per cent lime solution. The mixture is heated to 80°C for 20 to 45 minutes and then allowed to stand overnight. The following day the cooking liquor is decanted and the maize is washed two or three times with water to remove the seed coats, the tip caps, excess lime and any impurities in the grain. The maize is converted into dough by grinding it a number of times with a flat stone until the coarse particles are fine enough and used for preparation of *tortillas*. Tortilla flour is a fine, dry, white or yellowish powder with the characteristic odour of maize dough. This flour when mixed with water gives a suitable dough for preparation of *tortillas* and other foods.

Some of the maize drinks are *colados*, *pinol* and *macho*, basically suspensions of cooked maize flour. Maize is also used as a substrate for fermented beverages called *Chicha*. As much as 12 per cent of world maize crop is fermented and the alcohol is mainly used as a fuel, but a significant amount is drunk as beer or whisky type drinks such as bourbon.

Hominy grits are ideal for making corn flakes. Cornstarch is used as a convenient food thickener or textile stiffener.

Corn germ is used for making corn oil. The germs are first steamed and then passed through expeller that forces out 95 per cent of the extractable oil and leaves the feed cake. The remaining 5 per cent can be removed with solvents such as hexane. The oil is filtered, bleached and refined. Maize oil, rich in essential fatty acids is used as a salad oil. It has a high smoke point, hence suitable for use as cooking oil.

Chapter 8

Processing of Sorghum

Flour made by grinding whole grain is occasionally used, particularly with the smaller millets, but in most places where sorghum and millets are consumed, the grain is partially separated into its constituents before food is prepared from it.

The first objective of processing is usually to remove some of the hull or bran–the fibrous outer layer of the grain which is done either by wet milling or dry milling. Dry milling is used to obtain products low in fibre, fat and ash, and wet milling to make starch and its derivatives. The steps involved in processing are:

1. Cleaning and dehulling through hand pounding
2. Decortication or attrition milling
3. Grinding and pulverizing

Cleaning and Dehulling through Hand Pounding

After cleaning, the grain is moistened with about 10 per cent water or is soaked overnight. Traditionally, the wet grain is pounded in a mortar with one, two or even three pestle throwers. With soft grains, the endosperm breaks into small particles and the pericarp can be separated by winnowing and screening.

When suitably prepared grain is pounded, the bran fraction contains most of the pericarp along with some germ and endosperm. This fraction is used as cattle feed. The other fraction, containing most of the endosperm and much of the germ along with some pericarp, is retained for human consumption.

Pounding moist or dry grain by hand is very laborious, time consuming and inefficient. A woman working hard with a pestle and mortar can at best only decorticate 1.5 kg to 2 kg of flour in an hour. Pounding gives a non-uniform product that has poor keeping qualities.

Decortication or Attrition Milling

In areas where sorghum and other millets are consumed as food mainly in India and Africa, they are often milled by decortication process because of two reasons. First, the grains are nearly round and do not have a crease. Second, the decortication process is similar to hand pounding which is traditional processing of grains. An important advance in the past 20 years has been the introduction of the PRL dehuller, which successfully removes the hulls from millet, sorghum and maize (Fig. 8.1). These machines are of intermediate scale, processing around 50 to 100 kg/hr. The hulls or bran, plus the germ make up approximately 10 per cent to 15 per cent by weight of the grains. The dehuller consists of a metal shaft on which a number of grinding stones or abrasive disks are evenly spaced about 2 cm apart. This rotor is enclosed by a semicircular sheet-metal barrel that is filled with grain. The abrasive disks, spinning at 1500-2000 rpm, rub against the freely moving mass of grain and abrade away the outer layers. The product is separated by mechanical winnowing into the hulls and endosperm. This machine is available in several designs, but the basic principles are the same.

Grinding and Pulverizing

Dehulled sorghum is milled to meal or flour using a hammer mill or burr mill. Whole sorghum is also milled in this way as in sorghum malt.

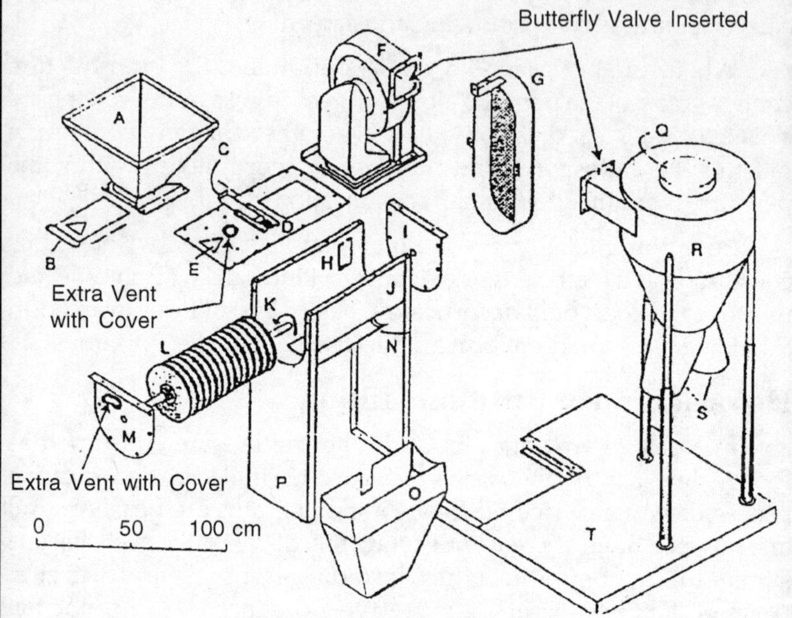

Fig. 8.1: The PRL Dehuller

Dry Milling

The clean and moistened grain (20 per cent) is milled by the conventional roller mills, to separate the endosperm, germ and bran from each other. Although maize and wheat milling systems have been used on sorghum but they are expensive. A small roller mill (500-1000 kg/hr) developed in South Africa for milling maize to meal has been found quite successful for sorghum and pearl millet but is more expensive to operate than the combination of PRL dehuller with a hammer mill.

The products of dry milling are:

1. Grit (76.7 per cent)
2. Bran (1.2 per cent)
3. Germ (11 per cent)
4. Fibre (10 per cent)

Bran and germ are further processed as in the case of maize, for the preparation of oils and feeds.

Wet Milling

Sorghum can be wet milled by the same method as used for maize wet milling. However, wet milling of sorghum is more difficult than that of maize because:

1. Sorghum is a small sized spherical grain.
2. It has a small germ.
3. Grain has dark-layered outer layers as pericarp contains polyphenolic pigments. These pigments leach out and give the starch an off colour during wet grinding.
4. Bran of sorghum breaks into small pieces that interfere with the separation of protein and starch.

Processing Malted Grains

Malting involves germinating grain and allowing it to sprout. The grain is soaked for 16 to 24 hours which allows it to absorb sufficient moisture for germination and for sprouts to appear. However, germinated sorghum rootlets and sprouts contain very large amounts of dhurrin, a cyanogenic glucoside, which on hydrolysis produces a potent toxic known as prussic acid, hydrocyanic acid (HCN) and cyanide. The fresh shoots and rootlets of germinated sorghum and their extracts must never be consumed, either by people or by animals. Removal of shoots and roots and subsequent processing reduce the HCN content by more than 90 per cent.

In the germination process, the grain produces α-amylase, an enzyme that converts insoluble starch to soluble sugars. This has the effect of thinning paste made by heating a slurry of starch in water, in turn allowing a higher caloric density in paste of a given viscosity, since as much as three times more flour can be used when the grain has been germinated. Thus using germinated grain can make food more suitable for certain categories of young children. Flour from malted grain is widely used in the production of weaning and supplementary food for children. When such foods are made from sorghum, great care must be taken to ensure that the levels of cyanide is adequately low, as children are particularly vulnerable to cyanide.

Malted sorghum is traditionally used in several countries in Africa. *Hullu-murr* is an important traditional food prepared from malted sorghum in Sudan. Alcoholic beverages and dumplings are prepared in Kenya from germinated sorghum and millet.

Processed Sorghum Based Products

India is the world's second largest producer of sorghum. At present most of the sorghum produced in India is consumed as a human food in the form of *roti* or *chapati* (unleavened flat bread). The various uses of sorghum in India are given in Table 8.1.

Table 8.1: Forms of Utilization of Sorghum in India

Food	*Product type*	*Form of grain used*
Roti	Unleavened flat bread	Flour
Sangati	Stiff porridge	Mixture of coarse particles and flour
Annam	Rice-like	Dehulled grain
Kudumulu	Steamed	Flour
Dosa	Pancake	Flour
Ambali	Thin porridge	Flour
Boorelu	Deep fried	Flour
Pelapindi	Popped whole grain and flour	Mixture of coarse particles and flour
Karappoosa	Deep fried	Flour
Thapala chakkalu	Shallow fried	Flour

Tortillas prepared in Mexico and Central America, are similar to *roti* except that the sorghum grain is lime-cooked and wet milled. Although corn is the preferred grain for making tortillas, sorghum is also widely used. Sometimes, tortillas are made by mixing corn and sorghum.

Injera (Ethiopia) and *Kisra* (the Sudan) are the major fermented breads made from sorghum flour. Use of sorghum and other millet based weaning foods prepared using extrusion and malting techniques have been found successful. Grits made from sorghum are cooked like rice in many countries. Sorghum grain can also be flaked. Decorticated grits are moistened with water and steamed or cooked to gelatinize some of the starch, dried to a moisture content of about

17 per cent and then either pounded in a special mortar or rolled between flaking rolls to produce a flat product. The flakes are further dried and can be stored for several months. In India, *poha* and *avilakki* are flaked foods based on sorghum and millet.

Porridge is prepared from the whole or decorticated sorghum grains. Porridges are either thick or thin in consistency. They are the major foods in several African countries. Fermented porridge is made in several regions in Africa. In eastern Africa, a suspension of maize, millet, sorghum or cassava flour in water is fermented before or after cooking to make a thin porridge. In the Sudan, a thin fermented porridge called *nasha* is prepared with sorghum. The *Chibuku* beer consumed in Southern Africa is basically a thin fermented porridge, usually made from sorghum (Fig. 8.2)

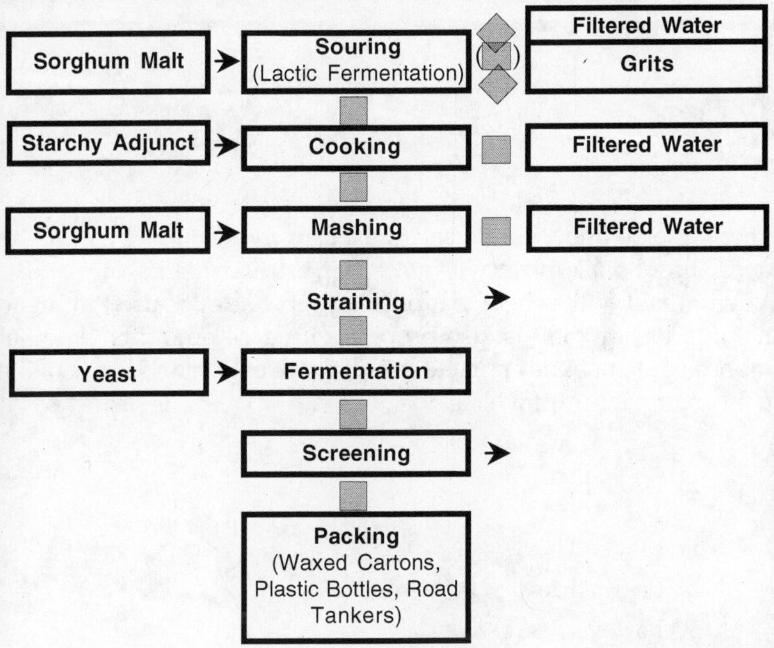

Fig. 8.2: The brewing of African Opaque Beer (*Chibuku*)

Chapter 9
Processing of Barley

Barley is the world's fourth most important cereal crop, after wheat, maize and rice. Barley is used in India mainly as human food. Barley flour is mixed with wheat or gram flour for making *chapatis*. When mixed with wheat, oat or rye flour, barley is used in bread making. Barley malt is also prepared in large amounts. Another important use of barley is in the manufacture of beer and for distilling in the manufacture of whisky.

Milling

Barley is milled to make:

1. Blocked barley
2. Pearl barley
3. Barley grits (groats)
4. Barley flakes
5. Barley flour

Blocked and Pearl Barley

After cleaning, the barley is conditioned by moistening or drying. The conditioned barley is subjected to blocking or shelling and pearling (rounding). The hull of barley is strongly attached to the pericarp. Therefore, it is difficult to dehull barley by the techniques used for rice or oats. Both blocking and pearling are abrasive processes differing in degrees of the removal of the superficial layers of the grain. Part of the husk is removed during blocking whereas remainder of the husk and endosperm gets removed by pearling. Aspiration is done to separate the abrasive portions.

Two types of machines are used for blocking and pearling:

1. First type consists of a cylindrical millstone which revolves at about 450 rpm.
2. Second type is a pearling machine consisting of rapidly revolving 6 to 8 abrasive discs coated with carborundum or emery. The hull and aleurone layer of barley are removed by rubbing against millstone or emery disc. The dehusked barley is pearled. After the third pearling, bran is almost completely separated along with a part of the aleurone layer. At this stage, the product may be graded and sold as pot or blocked barley. After the grain is subjected to 5 to 6 pearlings, the resulting pearl barley is small, round and white. Pearled barley is a common ingredient in soups.

Barley Grits

The blocked grain is cut into portions known as grits which are graded by size, rounded in a pearling machine and polished.

Barley Flour

The blocked or pearled grain is reduced to flour in roller mills. Whole barley can also be milled into flour. Flour is also a by-product of cutting, pearling and polishing processes. Barley flour is used in baby foods, breakfast cereals and for making leavened and unleavened breads.

Barley Flakes

Barley flakes are made from pearl barley by steam conditioning and hot rolling on smooth large diameter roller. The products are used in soups or in breakfast cereals.

Malting

Malting, a controlled germination process consists of the following stages:

1. Grain selection
2. Preparation and storage
3. Steeping
4. Germination
5. Kilning
6. Dressing

Grain Selection

1. The grain selected should be of an acceptable variety or mixture of varieties. It should not contain infested grains, insect damaged grain, weed seeds or the grains of other cereals, dirt or any other unacceptable levels of any fungicides, herbicides, insecticides or any other plant growth regulators.
2. The grain should appear bright and not stained (withered or discoloured) because of microbes.
3. The grain should have an even appearance and not be a mixture of different grades.
4. It should have no off-flavour when chewed.
5. When cut, the exposed grain endosperm should appear mealy and not steely (vitreous).
6. It should have a particular nitrogen content suitable for the malt being made. For many pale ale and large malts, total nitrogen contents of 1.5 per cent or 9.4 per cent protein are preferred whereas for highly enzymic malts, total nitrogen values might be 2.2 per cent or 13.8 per cent protein.

Preparation and Storage

For ventilated storage, the grain should contain less than 15 per cent moisture, 12 per cent moisture or less for cool storage at 15°C or less for upto about 6 months and preferably to 10 per cent moisture or less for periods of warm storage (upto 40°C) and for extended periods of cool storage (more than 6 months). During storage, the grain can attain full germinative powder. During storage, all kind of contamination, infestation and deterioration should be avoided. Heating should not occur.

The germinability of dormant grain improves and its water sensitivity declines during initial stages of storage immediately after harvest. This post harvest maturation or ripening, may be accelerated by a period of warm storage (1 to 3 weeks, 30-40°C). This allows secondary ripening processes to occur.

Steeping

A weighed amount of cleaned and selected stored barley is steeped in water. The grain may be washed by a countercurrent of water before it is loaded into the steeps, which are already partly filled with water. The time required for steeping depends on the temperature and extent of aeration of the steep water. Usually the temperature of steep water is controlled at around 16°C and steeping is done for 50-70 hours. Compressed air is frequently blown into the base of the steep during or soon after loading grain into the water to help mix the grain with water and clean the grain.

At intervals, usually twice in a 2-to-3-day steeping period, the water is drained from the grain and during the several-hour air rest, when the grain is not covered with water, air is sucked down through the grain. This process removes carbon dioxide, supplies oxygen, cools the grain and ensures that it can respire. This accelerates the rate and uniformity of subsequent germination. After each air rest, the grain is covered with fresh water and is periodically aerated.

During steeping, the water dissolves material from the grain, becomes yellow and frothy and develops a characteristic smell. Steeping is continued until the grain has reached a selected moisture content *i.e.* approximately 45 per cent fresh weight.

Germination

The steep is then drained off and grain is transferred into a separate germination vessel where it remains for 4 to 6 days. Grain can also be spread on floor for 7 to 8 days for germination. The grain bed is leveled when the steeped grain is put into the germination vessel. The bed depth before germination may be 1.4 to 1.5 m. The depth of grain bed increases upon germination. By the end of

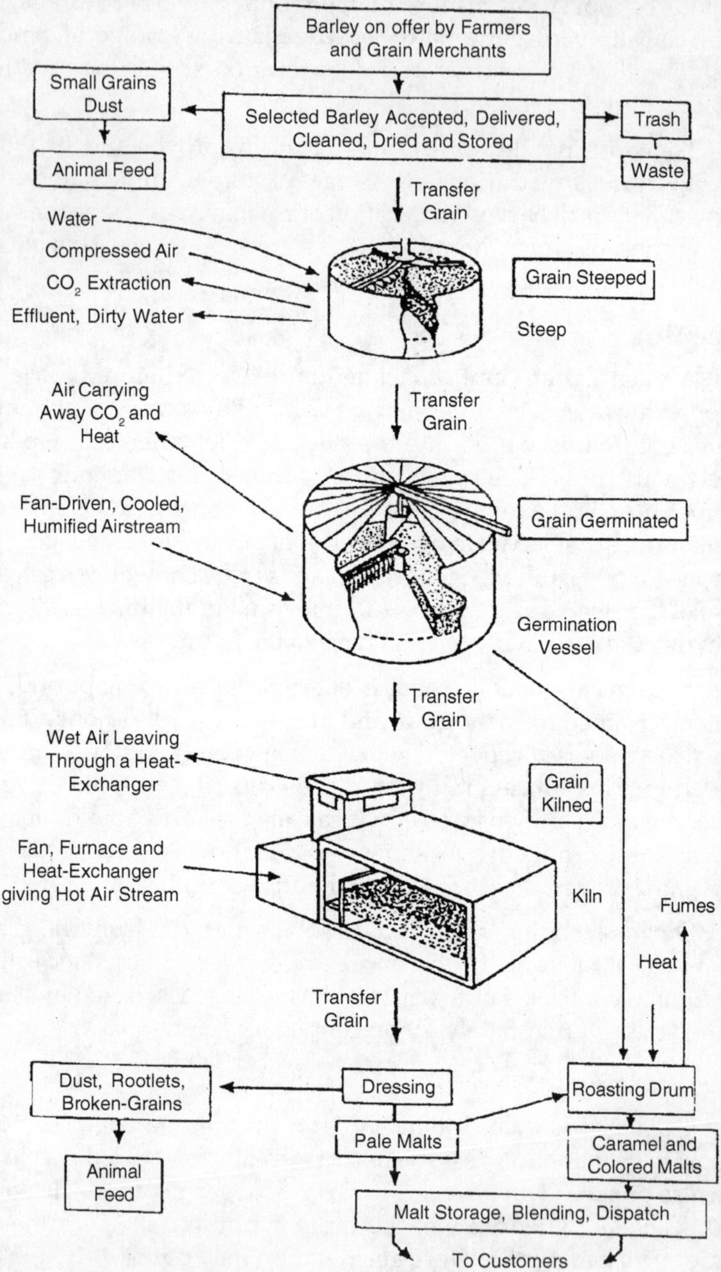

Fig. 9.1: Outline of Malting Process

germination period, about 18 per cent of the starch is degraded and grain will be richer in soluble sugars and amino acids due to activation of proteolytic and amylolytic enzymes. There will be a loss of about 10 per cent dry matter relative to the original barley because of soluble material lost in steeped water (0.5-1.5 per cent), lost as carbon dioxide and water due to respiration (5-6 per cent) and materials lost as rootlets (3-4.5 per cent).

Kilning

The grain malt is transferred from a germination unit to a kiln to arrest the enzymatic activity. The grain malt is partly cooked too.

Kilning is an expensive process because it uses much fuel to generate the heat used to evaporate water from the grain. The hot air is generally fan driven in kilns. The final moisture content of the malt is in the range of 2 per cent to 5 per cent (fresh weight).

Dressing

After kilning, malt is cooled and dressed *i.e.* the rootlets are broken up and they and dust are separated from the grains. Rootlets and dust are used in animal feed. The dried and dressed product is malt.

Uses of Barley Malt

The malts are mainly used in manufacture of beers and whiskies. Some are used for making vinegar, extracts or flours that are used in drinks, foodstuffs, *e.g.* breakfast cereals, infant foods, bakery products, malted milk concentrates and sweets.

Chapter 10

Processing of Oats

The oat grain is harvested with its hull on. It is a covered cereal and its hull constitutes 25 per cent of the total weight. After the removal of hull, oat is known as groat. The hull is tough and fibrous and its function is to protect the groat. It is of little nutritional significance. The groat is made up of three major tissues:

1. Outer bran layers
2. Starchy endosperm rich in protein, oil and several enzymes
3. Embryo or germ

Milling

During milling, the main objective is to remove the hull from the groat and to obtain high yield of clean groats. The steps involved in oat milling are (Fig. 10.1).

Cleaning

The oat grain samples are cleaned of the extraneous matter *i.e.* loose hulls, weed seeds, straw, dust, thin and light grains and extraneous metal etc. This is achieved in a multistage cleaning process that uses magnetic separators, sieves, aspirators and indented cylinders.

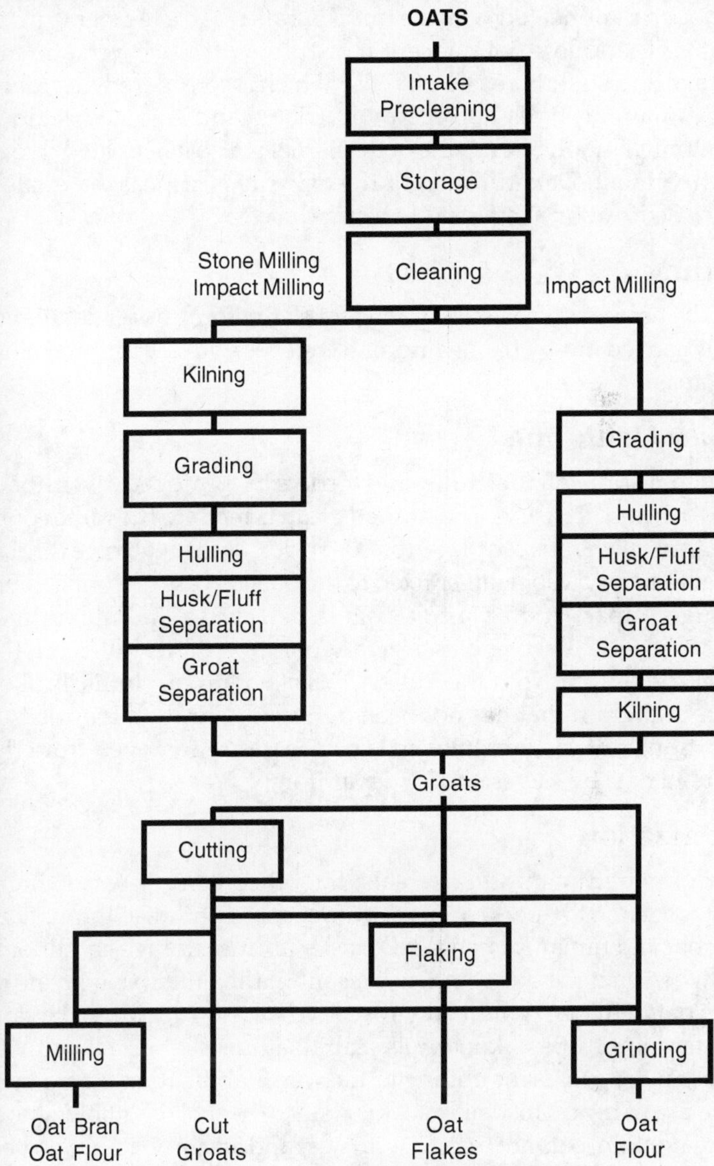

Fig. 10.1: A Flow Diagram Showing Possible Mill Streams for the Production of Oat Mill Products

After cleaning, the oats are heat treated or dried for about 1 hr in large open pans heated with steam. The oats reach a temperature of about 93°C and lose 3-4 per cent moisture. With such a treatment, oats take on a slightly roasted flavour which is considered desirable. Besides flavour, hulls become more friable and easier to remove after drying. Lipolytic enzyme of the kernel is also inactivated due to heat treatment. Denaturation of the enzyme is critical if a quality product with good shelf life is to be produced.

Grading

The heat treated oats are graded for size before impact dehulling. This is carried out by using automated sieves with rectangular slots of increasing size.

Impact Dehulling

Separation of the hulls and groats is achieved by impact (Fig. 10.2) and abrasion. The graded grain is fed into the huller onto the rotor, which rotates at 1500 to 2000 rpm. Centrifugal force throws the oats against a rubber liner fixed to the outside case of the machine. Through impact and abrasion, hull is detached. The rubber liner reduces the breakage and assists in separation of the hull from the groat. The output from the huller consists of groats, hulls, broken groats and grain that has not been dehulled. Through scouring or aspiration, hull can be removed. The groats are removed from the unhulled oats by sieves or disk separators.

Stabilization

Compared with other cereals, the oil content of oats is high. Groats contain 5 to 9 per cent oil which is evenly distributed throughout the groat and remains unchanged under normal storage conditions. The lipase enzyme, however, is present in the outer bran layers of the groat. This enzyme can cause hydrolytic rancidity. Hence, inactivation of lipase known as stabilization is essential prior to processing of groats for milling or flaking. Stabilization is achieved by the use of heat. Most mills now use steam to achieve stabilization. In radiator kiln, oats are treated with heat and steam. Oats are heated to more than 100°C for 1.5 to 2 hours in the kiln. The moisture content is increased from 13.5 per cent to more than 17 per cent. Then oats are cooled to 20°C and moisture content is reduced to 10 per cent. The advantages of this process are:

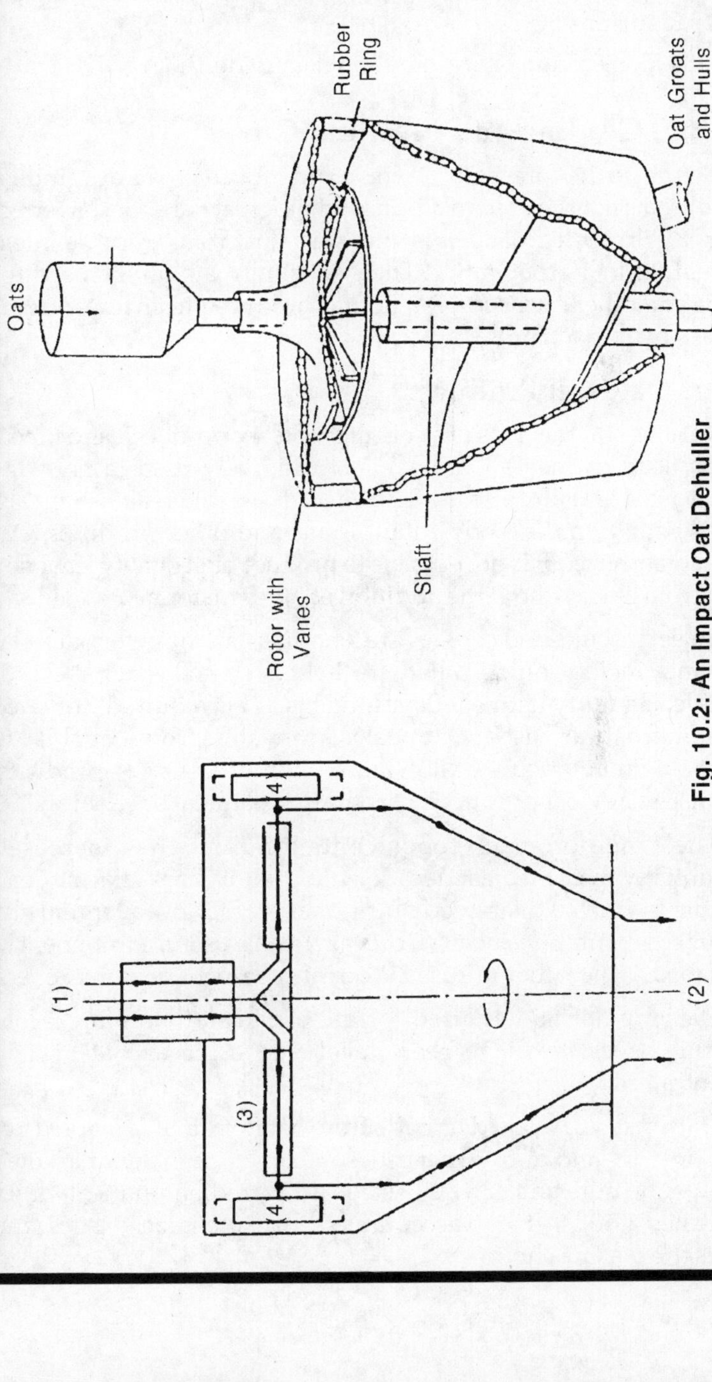

Fig. 10.2: An Impact Oat Dehuller

(1) Grain inlet, (2) Outlet, (3) Rotor, (4) Impact ring.

1. Lipase is completely inactivated.
2. This process also destroys bacteria and fungi on the surface.
3. Typical nutty oat aroma and flavour develop.

Cutting, Grading and Cleaning Groats

Before further processing, whole and broken groats are graded. Whole groats may be used to produce whole groat flakes or converted, along with broken groat pieces, into steel-cut groats using stainless steel knives in a groat cutter. The steel cut groats can be used for flaking and other purposes. Oat flour is produced from fines, groats or flakes by impact mills.

Use of Oat Mill Products

Various size fractions of steel-cut groats are produced as oatmeal (*e.g.* pinhead oatmeal). Oatmeal is traditionally used in porridge and oatcakes. Oats are also used in the ready-to-eat breakfast cereals, bakery goods, snack foods, infant foods and other products. Oat lacks gluten, hence, it is not possible to produce high quality leavened bread from oats without the addition of other materials.

Sweet biscuits and cookies are a popular medium for oats. Oat forms may include quick, rolled, steel-cut or crushed oat flakes. For example, if a nutty oatmeal flavoured biscuit is required, softened steel-cut groats are used. Oatmeal is a versatile product in biscuit and cookie manufacture, allowing a wide diversity of products. Muffins are a sweet product incorporating oatmeal or oat bran.

The range of snack foods containing oats has increased substantially over the past decade with granola bars taking a lead position. In view of their good nutritional profile, low allergenicity, flavour compatibility, and cost, oats are used a useful component of infant foods, where they are used in cereal-type foods or as thickeners.

Oats are not widely used for the production brewing. Non-alcoholic beverages have been developed using an oat protein concentrate.

Oatrim is a dry powder made from oat flour that is made up of malto dextrins and upto 10 per cent soluble β-glucan. It is marketed as a fat substitute and can be used as an ingredient in meat, dairy and baked goods. It has acceptable sensory characteristics and lowers the plasma cholesterol.

Chapter 11

Quality Evaluation and Functional Properties Used in Baking

The term quality is defined as fitness for purpose or as fulfilling the requirements for a particular process. Therefore, there can be no absolute definition of quality, because it varies according to the requirements of the process and the ultimate end use of the product. For example, in selecting wheat the miller needs to know how well a particular sample wheat will perform in the mill in terms of the final amount of flour obtained from the wheat, the ease of separation of bran from endosperm, its breakability, and the flow properties of the flour. Bakers will have different requirements from the miller, particular whether the flour will produce good bread and give no problems in processing in the bakery. Specific raw material quality is required to meet the needs of these processes. This enables millers to maximize throughout yield and to prevent any interruptions in production caused by unexpected variations in the wheat quality.

A quality test tries to predict the performance of the wheat in later processing during milling and baking. An experienced miller can predict the quality of a wheat sample by its smell and appearance and by biting and chewing a few grains of wheat. The act of biting and chewing encompasses the whole process of milling and mixing the flour with water to produce dough. The aim of quality testing is to try to reproduce on a formal quantitative basis what the miller does subjectively. General European Union quality standards for various cereal grains are given in Table 11.1.

Table 11.1: General Minimum EU Quality Standards for Various Cereals

Parameters	*Bread-making Wheat*	*Durum Wheat*	*Malting Barley*	*Maize*	*Rye*	*Sorghum*
Maximum moisture (%)	14.5	14.5	14.5	14.5	14.5	14.5
Specific weight (kg/hL)	72 (min.) 75(max.)	78	62	72-78	68	—
Maximum total screenings* (%)	12	5	12	12	12	12
Broken grains	5	6	5	10	5	5
Grain impurities from	12	5	12	5	5	5
sprouted grains (%)	6	4	6	6	—	—
shrieveled grains (%)	7	5	12	—	—	—
infested grains (%)	0.5	—	—	—	—	—
Ergot	0.05	0.05	—	—	0.05	—
foreign seeds	0.1	0.1	0.1	0.1	0.1	0.1
Heat damaged	0.5	0.5	3	3	3	3
Hagberg index	220 (min.) 250 (max.)	220	—	—	—	—
Protein (N × 5.7)	11-12	11.5	—	—	—	—
Alveograph index	P/L <0.6W>170	—	—	—	—	—
Zeleny Index (min)	20	—	—	—	—	—
Gluten content						

Note: Screenings = any material that is not 100 per cent fault free cereal

Source: Dendy, D.A.V. and Dobraszezyk, 2001.

In addition, for wheat traded on the international market the specific quality requirements include strict restrictions on insect and fungal contaminants and insecticide residues.

Sampling

For quality testing, the first step is to obtain the cereal sample which is very important as well as crucial as the outcome of any quality test depends on how representative of the whole batch that sample is. Much relies on the accuracy of sampling and testing procedures, which highlights the need for objective, internationally accepted standard methods.

In modern mills, large quantities of wheat can be delivered in one batch, and the batch may often be heterogeneous because of segregation during transport or contamination with non-wheat, diseased or substandard wheat material. Small sub-samples of wheat are generally taken from different points in a batch of wheat using sampling probes (Fig. 11.1) to achieve a representative sample from the incoming wheat, and these are often mixed back together to obtain an average value for the whole sample. This will give a mean value but no information on the variation within the bulk, which can only be achieved by testing several individual samples and performing simple statistical analysis to estimate the range of variation. Alternatively, a large number of single grains can be tested with modern rapid single grain analysis.

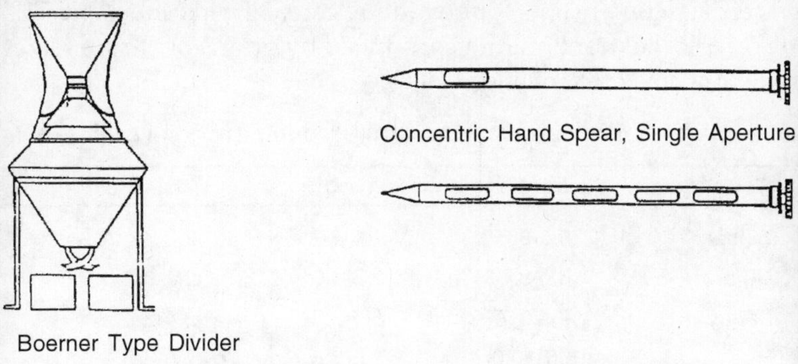

Fig. 11.1: Instruments Used for Sampling of Cereals

Appearance

Visual appearance can provide a lot of information about the general soundness and quality of any particular batch of cereal grain to the experienced eye. Visual inspection can reveal sample purity, contamination or infestation. The size, shape, colour and plumpness of the grains have long been used to classify and grade cereal grains according to their potential processing quality. Traditionally, plump grains are known to give better extraction, and dark glassy looking vitreous grains are associated with higher protein content and wheat hardness.

Size and Shape

Size and shape of grains are associated with the extraction rate (the total proportion of white flour extracted from a given weight of wheat). The surface area of a given grain is roughly inversely proportional to the average diameter of the grain. The larger the grain, the greater the ratio of volume to surface area. This is because of the well known cube-square relationship between volume and surface area of a body. As an object increases in size, the volume increases as the cube of its length or radius, whereas the surface area increases only a the square of its radius.

Wheat grains vary in size and shape and it is, therefore, expected that larger, plump grains will have a lower proportion of surface area (bran) to volume (endosperm) than small thin grains. This should then have an impact on the maximum grains. Table 11.2 gives typical dimensions found among cereal grains and Table 11.3 shows typical extraction rates produced by grains of various sizes throughout break roll milling.

Table 11.2: Typical dimension (mm) found in cereal grains

Cereal type	*Length*	*Width*	*Thickness*
Wheat	5.0-8.5	1.6-4.7	2.0-3.4
Durum	6.0-8.5	2.8-4.0	2.4-3.2
Barley	7.5-9.7	3.5-3.8	2.4-2.9
Rye	5.0-10.0	1.5-3.5	1.5-3.0
Oats	9.5-11.0	2.5-3.1	1.8-2.3
Maize	8.5-10.6	7.5-10.0	4.3-6.5
Sorghum	4.7-5.6	4.0-4.6	2.0-2.6

Table 11.3: Percentage Extraction of White Flour obtained from Wheat Grains of Various Sizes through Break-roll

Break No.	*Large*	*Medium*	*Small*
I	37.14	24.80	20.57
II	49.25	44.38	42.11

Source: Svensson *et al.* (1997).

Most wheat grading systems rely on visual inspection and comparison of the morphology of grain samples. This is highly subjective procedure that requires considerable training and expertise to achieve consistent results. Now-a-days, Digital Image Analysis is being used to quantify both the size, shape and colour (*e.g.* Grain Check 310) of samples of wheat grain and to discriminate between different varieties.

Impurities: Screenings

Wheat is inspected thoroughly on arrival at the mill for impurities such as foreign bodies; non wheat grains; damaged shriveled, and diseased grains and other contaminants. Such impurities are generally known as screenings in the UK, dockage in the US and besatz in Continental Europe, although each term has a slightly different meaning because of the use of different methods to separate and measure the total proportion of impurities. Admixture is a term used to describe all material that is not whole grain. Screenings are determined by passing wheat through slotted or mesh screens, with the size of the slots depending on the end use of the wheat. Table 11.4 shows some of the European Union Standards specified for impurities in various grains. If the batch fails to meet the necessary quality requirements, the batch may be rejected or adjustments to the price paid can be negotiated.

Smell

It is important in initial assessment of grain quality as it can indicate the presence of fungal or insect contaminants. The limitation is that this test is highly subjective and variable. New methods are being developed that attempt to quantify smells and odours by the use of thin-film conducting polymers and metal oxide sensors, as in the 'electronic nose'.

Table 11.4: Quality Standards for Allowed Levels of Impurities in Various Grains

Quality Standard	*% Impurities Allowed*	*Method Used*
Wheat milling (NABIM)	2% screenings + 2% admixture	Slotted screen: 2 + 3.5 mm
Wheat and barley (export)	2% admixture	Slotted screen: 2.0 wheat, 2.2 barley
Malting barley	2% screenings	Slotted screen: 2.25 mm
Food grain	2% maximum	Slotted screen: 2.0 wheat, 2.0 barley
Intervention grain	12% maximum	Slotted screen: 2.0 wheat, 2.2 barley

Vitreousity

Vitreousity is a description of grain appearance. Vitreous grains have a dark, translucent, glassy appearance as opposed to mealy grains, which have a light, opaque appearance. Various methods are used to examine vitreousity that attempt to reduce subjectivity. The Pohl Farinator is used to cut 50 grains simultaneously to give cross sections that can be examined in reflected light. The other way is that whole grains or sections can be illuminated by transmitted light through a glass plate. The other way is that whole grains or sections can be illuminated by transmitted light through a glass plate. The opaque appearance of mealy grains is caused by porous nature of the endosperm, scattering reflected and transmitted light to give a more opaque, white colour. In vitreous grains, the absence of air pores gives a more translucent glassy appearance. Generally, vitreousity has frequently been associated with increased density, hardness and higher protein content, giving better milling quality. Density, hardness and vitreousity are all interrelated with large differences in the fracture energy and indentation hardness observed between vitreous and mealy grains but little difference in the hectolitre weight (Table 11.5).

Specific Weight

It is also known as test weight or hectolitre weight (kg per hectolitre). It is the most widely used indicator of wheat quality in commercial trading. It is measured by the weight of grains required to fill a container of known volume under controlled conditions.

Table 11.5: Typical Values for Endosperm Density, Hardness, Fracture Properties and Specific Weight for Vitreous and Mealy Wheat Grains

Type of Endosperm	*Mean Density (g/cm³)*	*Thousand Grain Weight*	*Hectolitre Weight*	*Fracture Energy (kj/m²)*	*Indentation Hardness (Vickers)*
Vitreous	1.43-1.45	30.2	80.2	6-7	16
Mealy	1.35-1.41	46.4	75.4	1-2	11

Specific weight is associated with extraction–the amount of flour produced per unit weight of wheat. It may not always be a reliable indicator because of its susceptibility to extraneous factors such as grain packing density, grain shape and size, grain surface condition, impurities, moisture and disease and therefore, cannot be considered a reliable indicator of milling quality or extraction.

Thousand Grain Weight

Thousand grain weight or thousand kernel weight is usually expressed as the weight of a thousand grains of wheat in grams. It is normally determined automatically by electronically counting and weighing 1000 grains of cleaned wheat (Fig. 11.2). It is used to predict how much flour will be extracted from a given weight of wheat. It is probably more highly correlated with milling extraction, because it is directly related to grain size, which is known to be related to extraction.

Density

The density of wheat is defined as the density of the endosperm, rather than the apparent density or specific weight of bulk wheat samples. The density of endosperm as measured by most methods will normally contain the combined contribution of air pores (2-13 per cent) and the solid endosperm material. The density of wheat is largely influenced by the porosity and the packing of the endosperm components within the grain and, therefore, will be closely associated with physical hardness, vitreousity and milling performance of wheat. Table 11.6 shows typical density ranges found in common cereals.

Fig. 11.2: Electronic Grain Counter Used to Determine Thousand Grain Weight

Table 11.6: Typical Density Ranges of Common Cereals

Cereal	*Density (g/cm³)*
Wheat	1.280-1.478
Hard	1.360-1.478
Soft	1.280-1.430
Durum	1.450-1.480
Oats	1.10-1.20
Barley	1.28 (mean)
Rye	1.34 (mean)
Rice	1.35-1.39
Sorghum	1.23-1.33
Maize	1.25 (mean)

Mealy grains have lower density than vitreous grain. Lower density is due to the presence of air pores within the endosperm. Degree of compactness of the protein of the protein matrix which is influenced both by genetic and environmental factors can be responsible for observed differences in density and hardness between soft and hard wheats.

There are various methods to determine density of individual cereal grains:

1. Displacement of air or liquids by pyknometer. This method is suitable when a number of grains is being measured but is not suitable for measuring individual grains.
2. Floatation in a liquid whose density is adjusted by titration to equal that of wheat grain. This method is time consuming because each grain requires a separate titration and measurement of the liquid density.
3. Floatation is a variable density gradient. This is used to measure the density of single pieces of endosperm.

Hardness

Hardness is the most important factor in assessing the quality of wheat. It is a characteristic which is often used in the milling industry to classify wheat varieties according to the desirability of their milling and breadmaking properties. Some workers define wheat hardness (endosperm texture) as a mechanical property of the individual wheat grain or the resistance to deformation or crushing whereas others define hardness in terms of varietal or genetic differences, with certain wheat varieties classified as hard and others as soft. Methods like–energy or time taken to produce a given volume of flour under standardized grinding conditions *e.g.* the Stenvert test and pearling index are used to measure wheat hardness. Perten Single-Kernel Characterization System (SKCS 4100) in the instrument which is used to measure grain hardness directly. A hard wheat is one that can be milled to produce flour with the high levels of starch damage desirable for bread production, and that grinds to give relatively angular particles that flow easily and are easy to handle. Soft wheats mill to give flours with relatively small irregular-shaped particles that do not flow easily and tend to block sieves in the mill. These are used for cake and cookie production because of their fine particle size and low starch damage.

Moisture

It is regarded as one of the most important quality characteristic of grains because it directly affects the specific weight and value and its effect on the microbiological stability of cereal grain during storage.

Millers do not want to pay for the water. Moisture content depends on the climatic conditions during harvesting. Normally wheat is dried on the farm directly after harvesting. Optimum storage moisture for wheat is less than 12.5 per cent whereas optimum milling moisture is between 14 and 17 per cent, necessitating the addition of water (conditioning) to the wheat before milling. Different methods for moisture determination are:

1. Evaporation of moisture at atmospheric pressure in ovens at various temperatures (100-130°C).
2. Evaporation of moisture from ground grain at 50°C under vacuum in the presence of P_2O_5 (Karl Fischer method).
3. Rapid moisture method: NIR reflectance is the principal rapid method used for moisture and protein determination (Fig. 11.3).

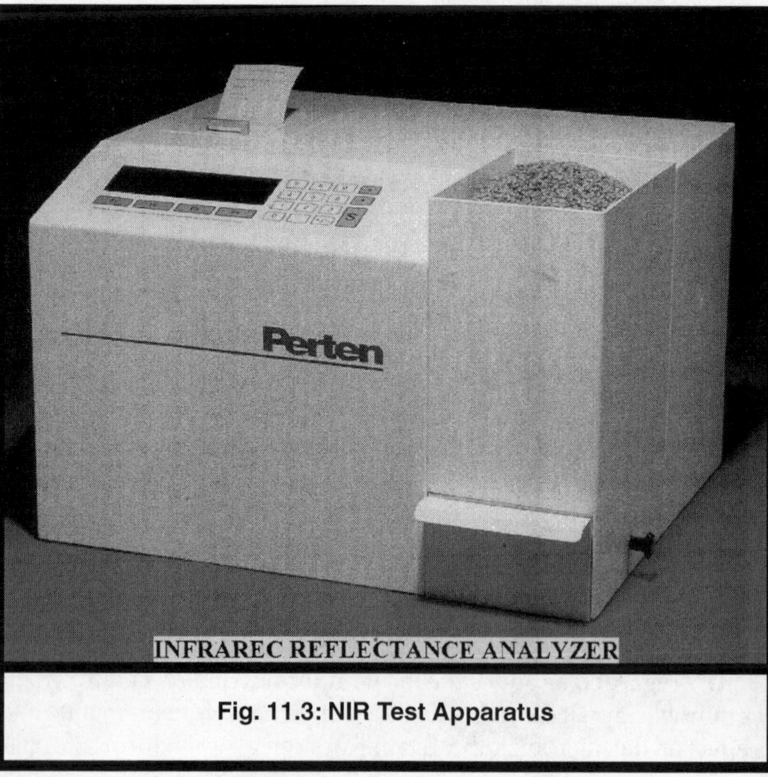

Fig. 11.3: NIR Test Apparatus

Protein

Wheat flour can contain between 6 per cent and 20 per cent protein, most of which is in the form of gluten. Both the quality and quantity of gluten protein are key indicators of wheat quality, especially in relation to breadmaking. Gluten is responsible for the gas-retention properties of bread doughs during baking. Loaf volume which is generally used as an indicator of baking quality, increases with an increase in the protein content of the flour. It is not possible to prepare bread from wheat flour containing protein below 8 per cent and normally flour with atleast 11 per cent protein is preferred for breadmaking.

Two main fractions of gluten are gliadin and glutenin. These fractions can be separated by gel electrophoresis which represent particular subunits within the glutenin fraction and can also be used to identify wheat varieties. Certain subunits have been associated with good breadmaking quality: subunits 5 and 10, 1, 17, and 18 are known to confer good baking performance, whereas subunits 2, 6, 8 and 12 are associated with poor breadmaking quality. As these subunits are inheritable traits, it is possible to selectively breed wheats that contain the good protein fractions.

Normally for protein determination, microkjeldahl method is used. By this method, nitrogen content is determined first which is multiplied by a factor to estimate protein content. Recently, rapid methods for determining wheat protein content have been developed using NIR reflectance.

The Pelshenke test is used in many countries predicting the breadmaking quality of gluten. A dough ball is made up from the whole wheat meal with a yeast suspension, and these are immersed in water at a constant temperature. The dough balls fall apart after a given time, and the elapsed time between immersion and the start of disintegration is called the Pelshenke test number.

Another rapid test used as a gluten quality test at wheat intake is the gluten washing method. Wheat is coarsely ground, sieved and made into a dough by mixing with water. The starch is then washed out by passing through water through the dough in a machine such as Glutomatic (Fig. 11.4). The insoluble gluten remains, and the starch is carried away in suspension. The gluten produced is tested for quality by measuring its extensibility and strength either by hand

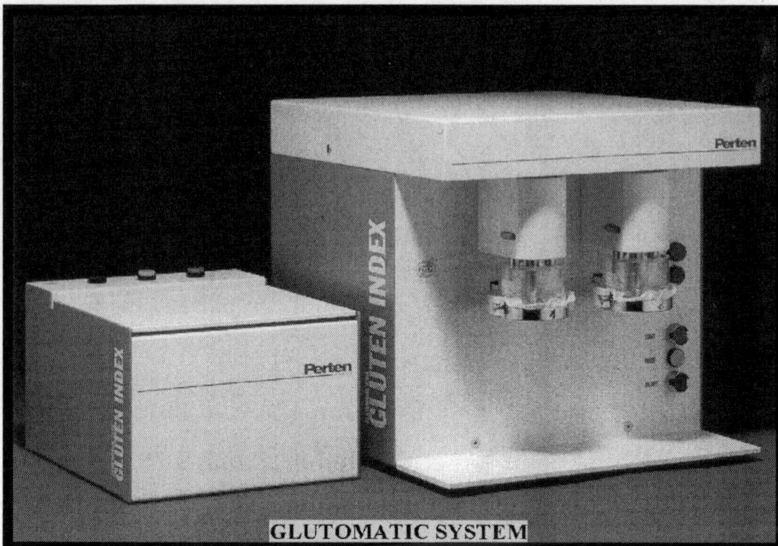

Fig. 11.4: The Glutomatic System

or in an Extensometer. Good extensibility and strength generally indicate that the protein is of good quality and suitable for breadmaking.

Alpha-amylase Activity and Hagberg Falling Number

Alpha-amylase is an inherent enzyme of the wheat which breaks down the wheat starch into simple sugars during germination. It is used as one of the key indicators of wheat baking quality. The flour having high level of α-amylase activity requires less amount of water for mixing, softens the dough, weakens the bread structure and produces a soft, sticky crumb (Fig. 11.5).

α-amylase activity is measured using the Hagberg falling number test (Fig. 11.6). A sample of ground wheat is suspended in water using a standard glass tube. The tube is placed in the Falling Number apparatus, where the suspension is heated in a waterbath at 100°C and stirred for 60 seconds. The α-amylase breaks down the starch in the suspension, causing a reduction in the viscosity which is measured using the time taken for a plunger to fall through the suspension. The time in seconds is taken as the Hagberg Falling

Fig. 11.5: Normal Loaf on Left, Bread Baked with Low Hagberg Falling Number on Right

Fig. 11.6: Hagberg Falling Number Test

Number. The greater the number, the higher the viscosity and the lower the α-amylase activity. Falling number values of greater than 250 seconds are generally acceptable for breadmaking.

DNA Fingerprinting

Recently, some genetic techniques such as polymerase chain reaction (PCR), commonly known as DNA fingerprinting are used to assess the wheat quality characteristics. PCR methods are the rapid ones for identification of cereal varieties and adulteration.

Flour Quality Testing

Flour Colour

Whiteness of flour is regarded as a quality attribute because it can finally affect the colour of the final bread and can also indicate the amount of bran remaining in the flour after milling and the whiteness of the endosperm material. A number of factors *e.g.* variety, fungal contamination, conditioning and incorrect grinding and sieving conditions can lead to high flour colour. The standard test for flour colour is the Kent-Jones and Martin flour colour Grader. Using image analysis techniques, the bran content of white flour can be determined.

Ash

It is an indicator of the amount of mineral matter present in the flour and is commonly considered a quality index for flour. The ash content is measured by the combustion of flour at high temperatures *i.e.* 550°C. All the organic matter is oxidised to gases at this high temperature and only inorganic matter is left.

The flour having high bran content will contain more of ash content as bran has a higher mineral content than the endosperm. High ash content of flour is not considered good for baking performance because bran itself and some of its components have adverse effects on breadmaking quality.

Starch Damage

Some of the starch granules get damaged during the milling process. Using polarized light, damaged starch can be under microscopic examination. Damaged starch absorbs more water than the undamaged starch and also is more susceptible to attack by α-amylase. Damaged starch can give rise to problems similar to excessive levels of α-amylase, such as sticky crumb and weak bread structure. Hard wheats generally have more starch damage than soft wheats, leading to an increased water absorption.

Sedimentation Value

Sedimentation test is used to assess the gluten quality and bread making potential of the flour by observing the way in which a ground wheat or flour suspension coheres and settles in the presence of sodium dodecyl sulphate or SDS (Tables 11.7 & 11.8)). It takes up to 30 minutes for ground wheat and 50 minutes for white flour. Hard wheat flour having high content of glutenin proteins showed high sedimentation value as compared to soft wheat flour.

Rheological Tests

Rheological tests are used to predict baking performance and behaviour of the dough during processing before baking. These measure the following mechanical properties of dough with the help of farinogrpah, mixograph, extensograph, alveograph and amylograph.

(1) Viscosity, (2) Elasticity, (3) Consistency, (4) Extensibility

Table 11.7: Threshold Values of Important Quality Traits Needed for End Uses

Quality Character	*Bread*	*Biscuit*	*Chapati*	*Pasta*
Test weight (Kg/hl)	>78.0 (Available)	Preferably> 76.0	Not specified	>80.0 (Available)
Protein content (%)	>12.0 (Available on certain locations)	<10.0 (Available on very few locations)	10-12 (Available)	>12.5 (On certain locations)
Sedimentation value (ml)	>60 (Scarce)	<40 (Available)	40-50 (Available)	>40 (Scarce)
P/L ratio	~1.0 (Scarce)	<0.5 (Scarce)	Not specified	—
β-carotene (ppm)	Not required	Not required	Not required	>7.0 (Scarce)
Yellow Berry (%)	-do-	-do-	-do-	<10.0 (Available)

Parenthesis description denotes the quality status of Indian wheat.

Table 11.8: Influence of Some Physico-chemical and Rheological Properties on Loaf Volume of Bread

Properties	*Bread Quality Classes*			
	Very good	*Good*	*Average*	*Poor*
Loaf volume range (cc)	>550	>450-<550	>400-<450	<400
Loaf volume (cc)	573	495	434	391
Protein (per cent)	12.26	11.99	11.04	10.26
Sedimentation value (ml)	48	47	45	44
Hectolitre weight (kg/ha)	76.1	78.1	79.3	79.8
Pmax	63.27	82.05	84.34	97.11
L	57.98	53.51	47.80	39.36
P/L ratio	1.28	1.78	1.98	2.67
W	159.5	140.6	135.0	124.8
No. of samples	17	166	87	30

Farinograph

With the help of this instrument, force or torque during mixing of small quantities of dough is measured and is generally used as a physical dough-testing machine in cereal laboratories. Its main uses are:

1. to predict the amount of water to be added to flour to get a fixed consistency during mixing.
2. to measure the mixing characteristics of a flour.
3. to predict baking performance.

A fixed amount of flour (normally 10–500 g) is mixed with water until a required consistency (usually 500-600 BU in UK) is reached. Consistency is measured as torque recorded as Brabender Units (BU) on standard chart paper by means of a pen attached by a series of levers to a torque-recording device. The amount of water added to achieve a required consistency is known as the water absorption which can vary between 50 per cent for a cookie flour to almost 70 per cent for standard UK breadmaking flours at 600 BU consistency. Prior measuring of consistency and water absorption help to predict the processing behaviour. If too much water is added to flour, a dough with low consistency will be obtained. It is difficult to handle such a dough as it shall be sticky. If little water is added, the dough will be stiff and difficult to process.

The farinograph is also used to measure the mixing characteristics of a dough (Fig. 11.7). A poor breadmaking flour produces a trace that rises rapidly to maximum consistency and then decreases rapidly. A good breadmaking flour takes longer to reach its maximum consistency and is much more stable (Figs. 11.8 and 11.9). This is probably related to the stability of the gluten macromolecular proteins during mixing.

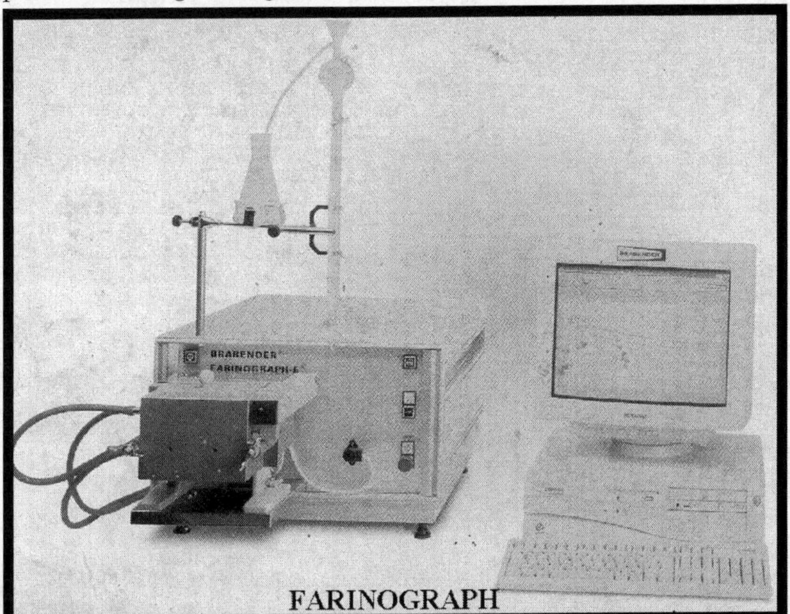

Fig. 11.7: Farinograph

Mixograph

It is a recording mixer which uses planetary rotating pins oriented vertically to mix the dough instead of blades (Fig. 11.10). Torque during mixing is recorded either by a pen or chart paper or electronically by a torque transducer or by recording electrical output from the motor driving the pins and mixing traces similar to those recorded by the farinograph are obtained. Small amount of sample

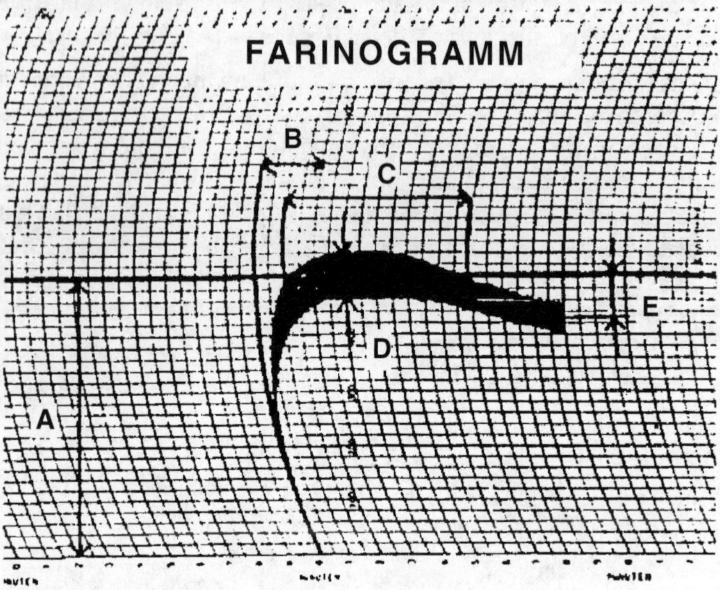

Fig. 11.8: Brabender Farinogram

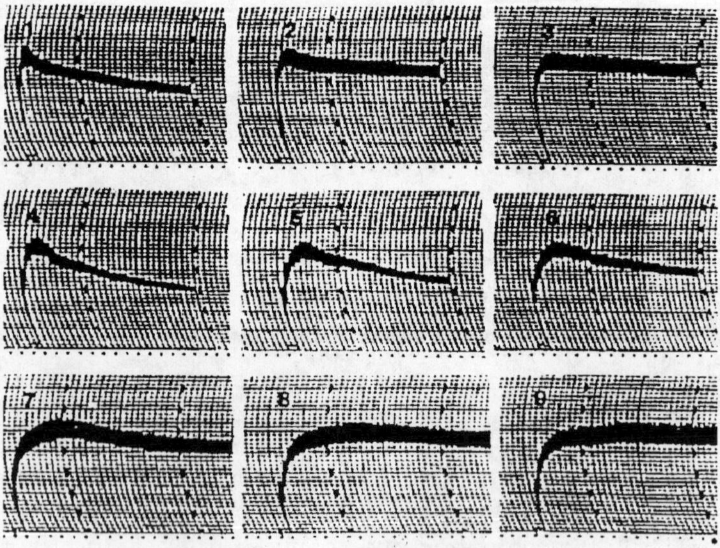

Fig. 11.9: Typical Farinograms
From top to bottom the flours become elastic, from left to right the flours are stronger.

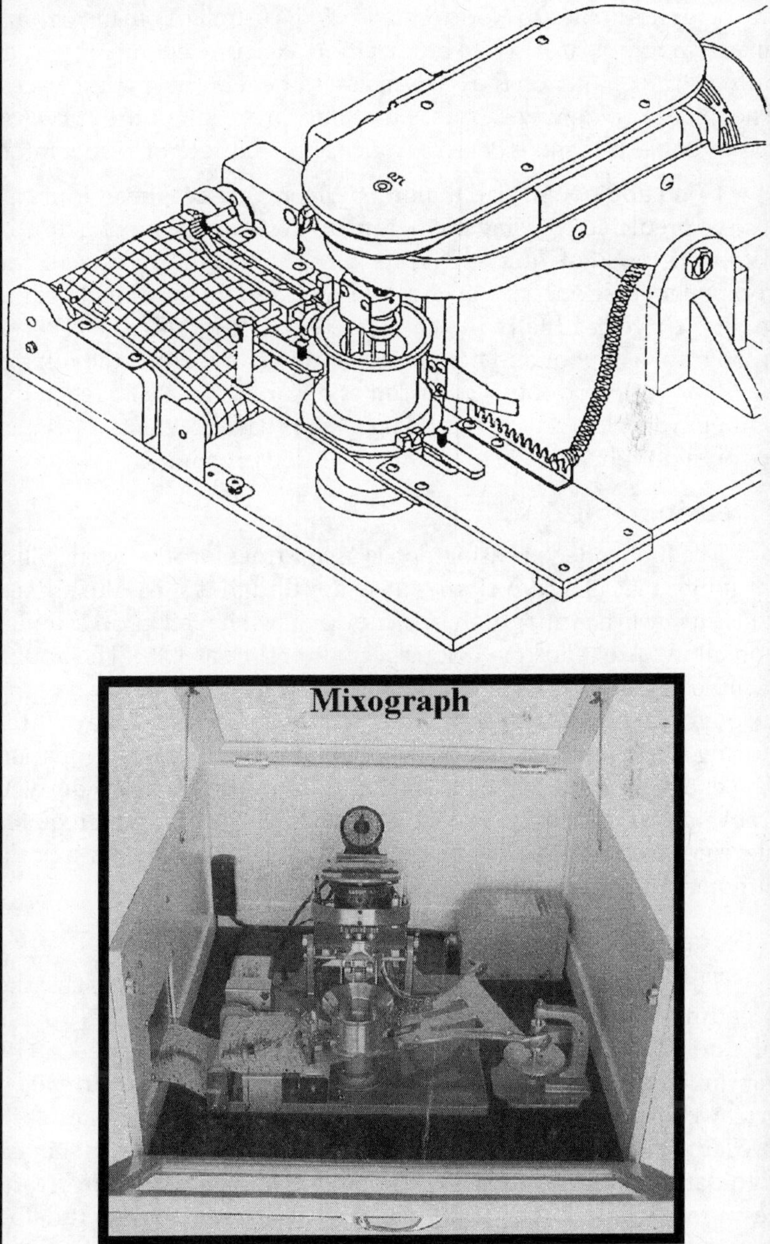

Fig. 11.10: The Mixograph

i.e. only 2 g of flour is used in new models of mixographs. The use of mixograph is limited to North America and Australia. Both mixograph and farinograph are used to predict the dough processing properties and baking quality on the basis of assessment of the mixing traces. The major problem with this is that interpretation of the curves is highly subjective and is based as much as on the 'feel' of the operator.

Good and poor bread making performance of wheat flour can also be predicted by using mixograph to measure the mixing time of different types of flours. Mixing time is the time when all the components of flour have been rehydrated and thus the height of the mixing curve gradually increases to peak dough (Fig. 11.11). The mixographs of poor and good wheat flour showed that the mixing peak for various doughs occurred at different times. To reach the optimum development, good and poor flours have different work input to mix a dough. It is due to quality of gluten proteins.

Extensiograph

The Brabender extensiograph is used to measure the extensibility of dough Fig. 11.12). A flour-salt-water dough is mixed to a fixed consistency in a farinogrpah, and the dough is shaped into a cylinder and allowed to relax for various periods of time at 30°C. The dough sample is clamped in a cradle and stretched by a hook passing through the centre of the sample at constant speed. A trace of force during stretching versus time is recorded by a pen on chart paper. The extensibility (E) and resistance to extension (Rm) are derived from the force-time trace (Fig. 11.13). Good breadmaking flour requires a greater resistance to extension than the poor breadmaking flour, although the extensibility of both flours is similar.

Alveograph

This instrument is widely used in France to assess the breadmaking potential of wheats. The alveograph inflates a bubble of dough from a flat circular sheet of dough clamped at its circumference. A dough is prepared with an integral mixer to a fixed water content and then extruded from the mixer after standard procedures. After a fixed rest period of 20 min, the dough is shaped into flat disks, and each disk is inflated at a constant inflation rate, resulting in an expanding bubble of dough. The bubble is inflated

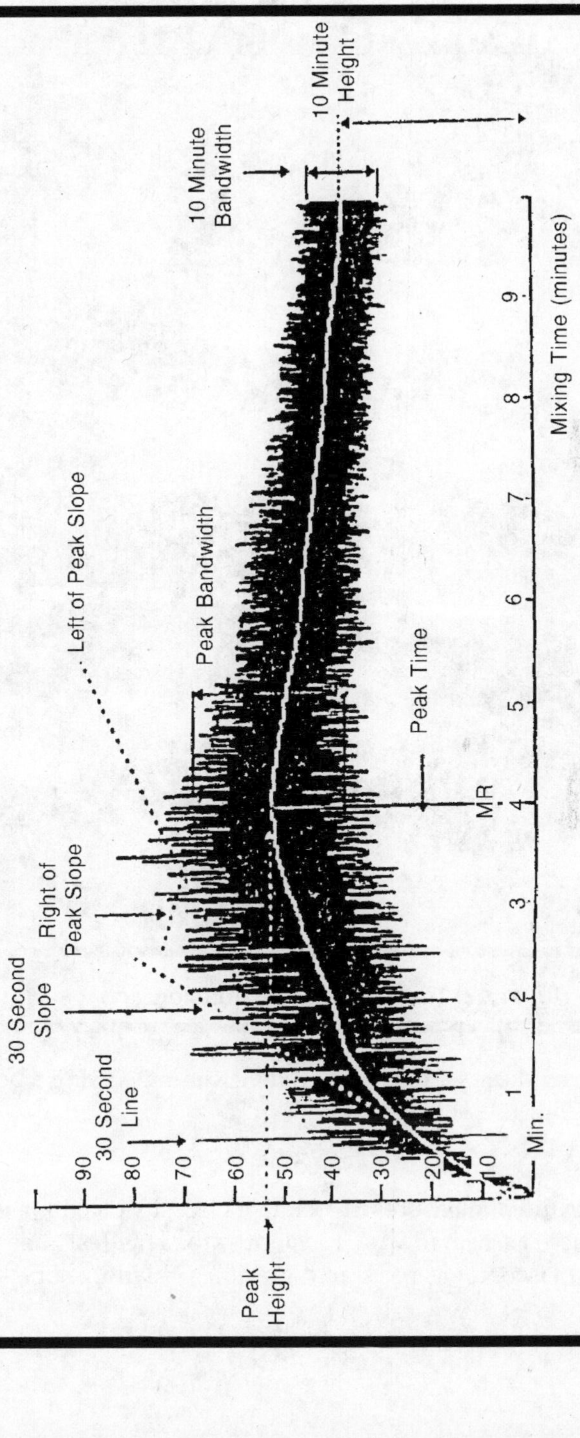

Fig. 11.11: Representative Trace from a Mixograph Showing Commonly Measured Parameters

Fig. 11.12: The Brabender Extensiograph

until rupture, and pressure is recorded versus-time using a pen on chart paper (Fig. 11.14).

Amylograph

This instrument measures the relative viscosity of a flour-water suspension as it is heated at a constant rate. This test measures the change in viscosity as the starch granules gelatinize and swell

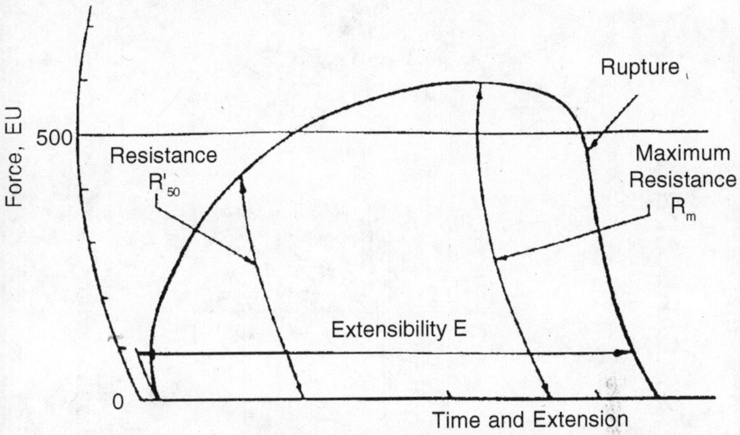

Fig. 11.13: Representative Trace from an Extensiograph Showing Commonly Measured Parameters

during heating. A suspension of flour and water is prepared according to standard procedures. The mixture is heated from 30°C to 92°C in a rotating bowl at a heating rate of 1.5°C/min. A paddle inside the bowl is attached to a force measuring device, which records relative viscosity as Brabender Amylograph Units (AU) against time or temperature. Good breadmaking performance is related to a gelatinization maximum between 300 and 700 AU. If the flour has very low levels of α-amylase activity (corresponding to a Falling Number Value <300), the breadmaking quality of the flour is adversely affected, and α-amylase is added to the flour as an improver. A recent alternative to amylograph is the Rapid Visco-Analyzer.

Test Baking

This is a measurement of the baking performance of a given flour. Any batch of wheat or flour delivered to a mill or bakery, has to be assessed for its breadmaking quality as no other tasts are accepted as valid by the baking industry. A small amount of flour (1-2 kg) is mixed and baked using a well-controlled and standard baking procedure. The loaves prepared are compared with so-called

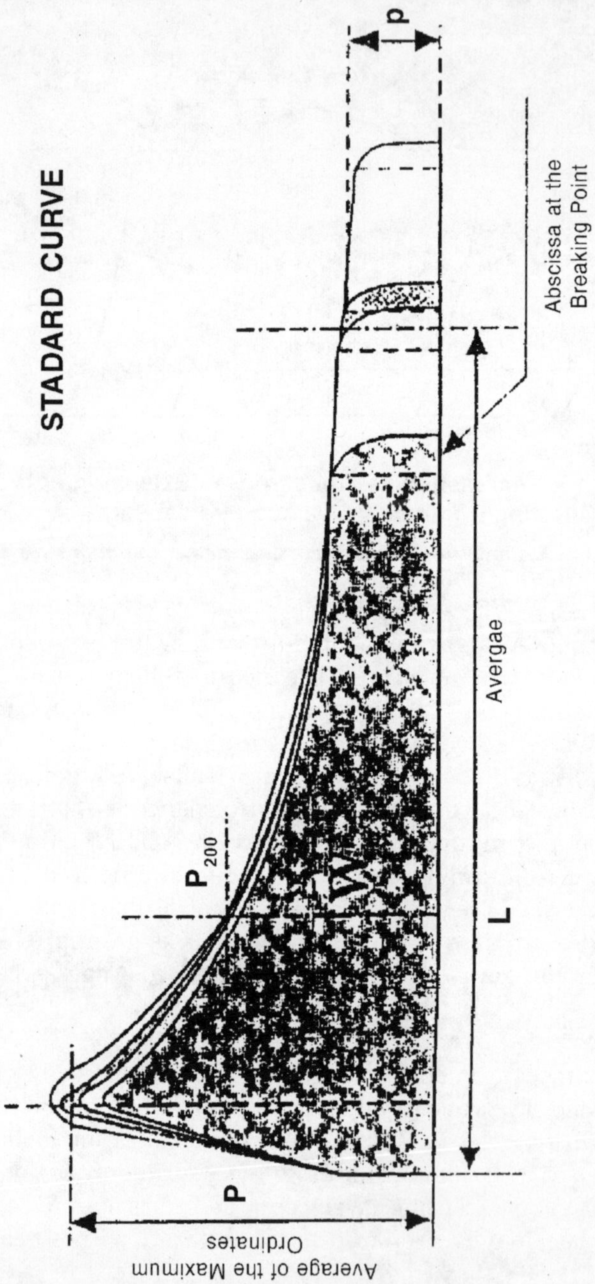

Fig. 11.14: Representative Trace from the Alveograph Showing Commonly Measured Parameters

standard control flours of known quality. The key performance indicators measured are loaf volume, measured by seed displacement, loaf height measured by a ruler; and a subjective visual assessment of colour and texture by a trained expert. Although test baking is still regarded as the 'golden standard' in the baking industry, it is slow, expensive and time consuming, labour intensive and requires high trained staff and specialized facilities and equipment. The milling and baking industries need rapid and small scale methods with the ability to differentiate between wheats of different quality so that they can assess raw material quality effectively and efficiently.

Chapter 12
Characterization and Importance of Wheat Gluten Protein in Baking

Functional properties are physico-chemical properties which give information on how a particular ingredient (*e.g.* protein, carbohydrates) will behave in a food system. The functional properties of plant foods are determined by the molecular composition and structure of the individual component and their interactions with one another. Characterization of functional properties which are generally referred and have found wider applications in formulation of baked products have been discussed in detail in chapter 11. Hence in this chapter, functional properties of wheat gluten and its importance in baking would only be discussed.

Gluten Proteins

Wheat flour proteins have long been known to be crucial in relation to bread making quality, both protein quantity and quality being important. The major wheat endosperm storage proteins, the gluten proteins, comprising two prolamin groups, gliadin and glutenin, have been studied extensively because they confer the viscoelastic on doughs considered essential for bread making quality. Qualitative differences in their composition and properties account for much of the variation in bread making quality between wheat cultivars. Glutenin, comprising polymers with subunits linked by disulphide bonds, is particularly, important.

Besides bread making quality, the flour milling performance of wheat is also of considerable technological importance. Much less is known about the factors that affect intercultivar variation in milling quality than those that affect bread making quality but starch damage level, which in turn affects water absorption and dough rheology is an important characteristic. A minor protein fraction associated with starch granule surface has been implicated recently as having a role in controlling grain endosperm texture (hardness), an important component of milling quality.

Importance of Gluten Proteins to Bread Making Quality

Wheat flour is known to be a complex mixture of starch (70-80 per cent), proteins (8-18 per cent), lipids (2 per cent), pentosans (2 per cent), enzyme and enzyme inhibitors and other minor components. A good bread quality flour encompasses an optimum blend of all these constituents. However, the technological importance of wheat flour is attributed mainly to its glutenin proteins (water-insoluble complex proteins). This is fact that upon fractionating wheat flour into gluten, starch, lipid and water-soluble; gluten alone possesses visco-elastic properties *i.e.* it exhibits rubber like characteristics. Also, if the gluten proteins are removed from the flour, then the property of forming a viscoelastic dough is lost. It is generally agreed, therefore, that the unique viscoelastic properties of gluten proteins are responsible for uniqueness of wheat flour. Inter-cultivar differences in bread making potential may also be linked to the differences in gluten viscoelasticity.

Characterization of Wheat Gluten Proteins

Proteins of wheat endosperm can be separated into non-gluten forming and gluten forming groups, when a wheat flour is wetted and mixed with water. The term gluten refers to a viscoelastic protein mass which is recovered after aqueous washing out of starch and water-soluble components from wheat flour. When dried it yields a cream-coloured free-flowing powder of high protein content (75-80 per cent) and bland taste. When rehydrated, it regains its original viscoelastic properties. The non-gluten protein class accounts approximately 10-20 per cent of the total flour proteins and their amounts are relatively constant from one flour to another.

Traditionally, gluten forming proteins, which represent 80-90 per cent of the total proteins of wheat flour, have been classified into two major groups, *viz.*, gliadin and glutenin based on their extractability and unextractability, respectively in 70 per cent alcohol. Gliadin contains very high contents of proline and glutamine. Glutenin fraction is extractable in dilute acid or dilute alkali. Some protein usually remains unextracted after alcohol and acid extraction, and is referred to as 'residue protein'. Gliadin occurs as monomeric proteins, and linked with intra chain disulphide bonds whereas glutenin comprises high molecular weight polymeric proteins whose component polypeptides are linked by inter and intra chain disulphide bonds.

Gluten proteins can be divided into three main categories, namely sulphur-poor prolamins, sulphur-rich prolamins and high molecular weight prolamins (Fig. 12.1).

Gliadins

Gliadins are usually classified into four main sub-categories, α-, β-, γ- and ω-gliadins. The molecular weight of α-type and γ-gliadins are between 30,000-45,000, whereas, ω-gliadins generally have molecular weight of 44,000-80,000. The γ-gliadins, in general, have somewhat higher molecular weight than α-type gliadins. Gliadin behaves mainly as a viscous liquid, when hydrated, and confers extensibility, allowing the dough to rise during fermentation.

Glutenins

The polypeptide components of glutenin are fractionated into low and high molecular weight subunits (also known as A subunits) by sodium dodecyl polyacrylamide gel electrophoresis (SDS-PAGE) under reduced conditions. High molecular weight subunits contain highest level of glycine residues among gluten proteins. Their

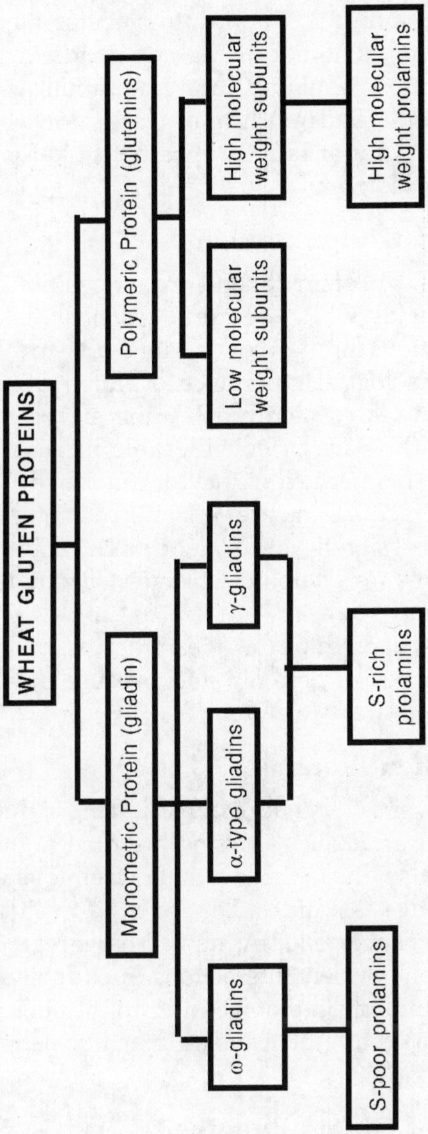

Fig. 12.1: Classification of Wheat Gluten Proteins

molecular weight measured by SDS-PAGE, range from 80,000-160,000. The high molecular subunits are further divided into X-type and Y-type. The X-type subunits are somewhat larger polypeptides than Y-type subunits. The low molecular weight subunits of glutenin, after reduction of disulphide bonds, can be divided into two main groups, B subunits and C subunits. It has long been thought that the gliadin/glutenin ratio, low/high molecular weight glutenin subunit ratios are responsible for the inter-activity variation in bread making quality.

Structural Properties of Gluten Proteins

The structural features of protein depend on composition and sequence of their amino acids which determine their ability to participate in chemical reactions through covalent and non-covalent interactions which have technological importance for gluten proteins. Disulphide bonds are the principal covalent bonds within and between gluten polypeptides and they are of considerable importance technologically. Non-covalent interactions include ionic, hydrogen as well as van der wads interactions and are generally much weaker than covalent bonds. The most significant covalent bonds, evident in the structure of gluten proteins are disulphide linkages. Gliadins have either intramolecular (as in α-type and γ-gliadins) or no (ω-gliadins) disulphide linkages, whereas these are both inter and intra-molecular in glutenin and because of these linkages glutenin provides elasticity to gluten.

Charge Density of Gluten Proteins

Gluten proteins have very low charge density. This is due to their low level of basic amino acids, such as lysine, histidine, arginine as well as tryptophan and also due to the fact that glutemic as well as aspartic acid occur mainly as amides. Due to this low charge density the gluten proteins are not repelled by mutual charge repulsion and associate strongly by non-covalent interactions. Such behaviour is important to baking technology in that it results in the ability of gluten proteins to form viscoelastic gluten and a gluten film network that is essential for gas retention.

Quality and Quantity of Gluten Proteins

During mixing of a wheat dough, gliadin and glutenins absorb a certain amount of water, thus, hydrated constituents are then transformed into a coherent protein mass, called gluten. Starch, added yeast and other dough components are embedded in this gluten skeleton. The bread making quality of a dough depends upon two factors; the quantity and quality of its gluten.

When the total protein content of wheat grain increases, the total amount of gluten protein also increases, but the amount of the non-gluten forming proteins (*i.e.* albumins and globulins) changes very little. For this reason, there is close positive relationship between the total protein content and gluten content of wheat flours. Thus, wheats of high protein contents usually have a higher proportion of gluten proteins compared with those having lower protein contents.

It has been recognized that mixing properties and bread making quality of wheat flours are governed by the quantity and quality of their proteins. It was indicated that the mixing characteristics of flours from wheat cultivars in the medium-strong range are significantly influenced by their gluten contents. On the other hand, the mixing properties of 'strong' or weak flours are relatively less affected by their gluten protein contents, but gluten protein quality primarily controls their behaviour during mixings. Weak gluten develop quickly whereas strong glutens need a longer time to mix to peak dough development *e.g.* gliadin fraction generally decreases mixing time, whereas glutenin fraction increases the mixing requirements of a wheat flour.

Gliadin/Glutenin Ratio

Differences in gliadin to glutenin ratio among wheat cultivars have long been considered an important source of inter cultivar variation in physical properties and bread making quality. The technological significance of gliadin and glutenin in bread making has been attributed to their contribution to dough extensibility and elasticity, respectively. Doughs that are too elastic and inextensible or vice-versa give poorer bread making performance than do doughs that have an appropriate balance of extensibility and elasticity. Therefore, it has been considered that an appropriate balance of these fractions must be responsible for the bread making potential of wheat flours.

High Molecular and Low Molecular Weight Subunits of Glutenin in Rheology and Bread Making Performance

The type and composition of HMW glutenin subunits have also been considered important for determining the mixing characteristics and bread making performance. Upto 20 different high molecular weight subunits have been identified in different bread wheats. Each bread wheat cultivar contains 3-5 high molecular subunits, which together account for about 1 per cent of the dry weight of the moisture endosperm of a wheat grain. This indicates that, although high molecular subunits are quantitatively minor, but they are functionally important polypeptides gluten proteins.

It is also noted that the good bread wheats contain superior high molecular weight subunits such as subunits 5+10, 1, 2*, 17+18 and 7+8 and the poor bread making wheat cultivars generally have inferior high molecular weight subunits such as 2+12, 6+8, 3+12 and 20. It is generally considered that subunits 5+10, 17+18, 1 and 2* are related to longer mixing times, dough strength and superior bread making quality, whereas subunits 6+8, 2+12, 3+12 and 20 are related to shorter mixing times and dough weakness. However, it is indicated that an appropriate balance of high and low molecular weight glutenin subunits must be responsible for the good bread making potential of wheat flour.

Chapter 13
Role of Bakery Ingredients

There are fundamental and basic considerations in the production of breads and other bakery products such as ingredients or raw materials and machinery. The baker should have an understanding of the normal use of ingredients in baking. Function of baking is to present cereal flours in an attracting, palatable and digestible form.

Functional Classification of Ingredients

Structure builders: Flour, eggs and milk

Tenderizers: Fat, sugar and baking powder

Moisteners: Milk, eggs

These can be classified depending upon their functions in bakery:

Structure Builders

Provide the structure and texture to the cake *e.g.* flour, eggs, milk.

Tenderizers

Provide softness and shortness in the product *e.g.* fat, sugar, baking powder.

Moisteners

Provide moisture and keeping quality *e.g.* Milk, water, eggs, syrup.

Driers

Absorb and retain moisture and provide the body of the product *e.g.* Milk solids and starches.

Flavours

Provide natural flavour *e.g.* Cocoa, chocolate, butter, eggs, and other natural flavour bearing ingredients.

The different ingredients used in baking are:

1. Flour
2. Sugar
3. Shortenings
4. Leavening agents
5. Eggs
6. Water
7. Salt
8. Milk and milk derivatives
9. Minor ingredients

Flour

Wheat flour is the basic structural component of most batter and dough products. It is able to perform this textural function because of gluten content, which allows expansion of air cells and provide rigidity after baking. Flour is obtained through the milling process in which bran and germ part of wheat grains are removed as far as possible.

Wheat flour is unique among the cereal flours, when mixed with water in correct proportions, the protein will form an elastic dough which is capable of holding gas and which will set to a spongy structure when heated in oven. Commercially flour is obtained from two types of wheat:

1. Hard wheat
2. Soft wheat

Hard Wheat

Hard wheat is mostly desirable in bread production. They mill well and yield good quantities of flour that is high in good quality protein from which strong elastic dough can be made. Hard wheat dough has high water absorptive capacity, excellent gas-holding properties and will yield bread with good volume, grain and texture.

Soft Wheat

Soft wheat is low in protein and yields flour having low water absorption capacity and poor tolerance to mixing and fermentation. They are undesirable for bread production but are highly desirable in production of cakes, pastries and cookies.

Flour builds the structure of the cake and holds other ingredients together in an evenly distributed condition in the cake. Cakes made from too strong flour will peak in the center and will be tough and dry. Cakes made from too weak flour may flatten or even sink in the center.

It is the wish of every baker to use flour having the following characteristic for the production of quality bread:

Colour

The flour should have a trace of creamish colour, otherwise, the bread will have a dead white crumb.

Strength

Strength is often said that the flour is strong or the flour is weak. Such statements refer to strength of flour which is capable of producing a bold, large volume, well risen loaf.

Tolerance

The ability of flour to withstand the fermentation process and to produce a satisfactory loaf over a period of time, in excess of what normally is required to bring about the correct degree of ripeness for that practical process, means, tolerance.

Water Absorption

This refers to the ability of flour to take on and hold the maximum amount of moisture without additional mixing for full development of dough. Absorption varies from 54-65 per cent based upon the weight of flour and way the flour is to be used. If the dough is not given the required mixing time because of limited mixing capacity, or for other reasons, the baked product will lack volume and have a dry crumb and inferior eating and keeping quality.

Uniformity

This is also an important aspect which should not be overlooked. Bakery should get uniform flour to obtain good quality end product.

pH

Flour with pH value below 5.0 are generally too acid and give poor result in bread baking; the range for satisfactory flours is usually between pH 5.5 and 6.5.

Composition

Major components of flour are starch (70 per cent), protein (11.5 per cent), water (14 per cent) and minor components are ash (4 per cent), sugar (1 per cent) and fat (1 per cent.). Gluten protein [glutenin and gliadin] is insoluble in water or dilute salts solution. These proteins are responsible for elastic properties of flour dough. Glutenin portion provides strength and firmness to gluten and gliadin adheres to glutenin and holds it together. Carbohydrate is present in the form of starch with small amount of dextrin and sugars, cellulose and gums.

Sugar

It imparts sweet taste. It has tenderizing action on flour proteins and it makes the cake tender. Being hydroscopic, sugar helps to retain moisture in cakes, which improve its shelf life. The golden brown crust and colour of cakes is due to caramelization of sugar. Sugar has lubrication effect on gluten strands and helps in acquiring volume in cakes. Sugar is essential for fermentation activity of yeast to produce CO_2 gas which raises the dough and imparts proper volume to the bread. It enhances flavour and helps in moisture retention due to its hygroscopicity.

Bread flavour depends on the type and quality of ingredients, fermentation and processing of dough and sugar has most pronounced effect on flavour (except salt). Sucrose is superior to the other sweetners in its contribution to flavour. It influences bread flavour by making possible, more rapid baking.

Sugar does not act as softening agent but by developing crust colour quickly it makes possible a reduction in baking time and retention of more moisture in the bread. It also contributes little to anti-firming properties. Browning of crust is due to part of caramelization, as well as to sugar-amine reaction (Mallard reaction). It also act as tenderizing agent.

Amount of sugar used in bread or rolls is entirely within the discretion of the baker and depends on type of bread. Sugar influences the bread yield by adjusting the baking time and temperature to produce loaves of high original moisture. Sugar has little effect on absorption of the dough but additional mixing is required if percentage of sugar is increased. Sugar also increases the time required to get maximum dough development. Crust colour reflects the type and amount of sugar used. As sugar percentage is increased, the crust becomes darker *i.e.* sucrose results in more reddish brown crust. High concentration of sugar interferes with gluten formation.

Uses of Sugar

It serves the following purposes:

1. Gives the necessary sweetness in cakes,
2. Serves as a form of food for the yeast in fermentation,
3. Is used in the preparation of a variety of icings for baked products,
4. Assists in the creaming and whipping process of mixing,
5. Provides good grain texture in the product,
6. Aids in the retention of moisture and prolongs freshness,
7. Promotes a good crust colour
8. Adds nutritional values to the product.
9. It increases gas production.

Different Types of Sugars

1. Fermentable sugars which are naturally present in flour *e.g.* glucose, fructose, sucrose, maltose
2. Non-fermentable sugars which are oligosaccharides.

Commercial Available Sugars

Medium Granulated Sugar

It is coarse crystal sugar. Used for sanding cookies, pies and other bakery products in which very coarse grain is desired. Used for decorative purposes also.

Sanding Sugar

Most frequently used for sparkling or sanding purposes for cookies, pies, bread etc. It has property of reflecting light and give sparkling appearance to the product on which it is used. It is the lightest colour sugar.

Extra Fine Granulated Sugar

Most frequently used product in baking industry. It dissolves readily in water or in other liquefying agents of bakery.

Icing Sugar

As name implies, it is used for high quality icing production. It promotes higher gloss, rapid crusting.

Brown or Soft Sugar

Brown sugar is offered in a wide range of colours from light yellow to dark brown. They are used for flour development to baked products. It is used in dark breads, many cookies and in devils food, spice and other dark cakes.

Shortenings

Fat lubricates the structure of a baked product. These are essential ingredients of most types of bakery products which shorten pastry, cake *i.e.* any fat fit for such use *e.g.* lard, butter and some vegetable oils. It has tenderizing effect on flour proteins and makes the product tender. It is fat part of the mixture which holds large number of air cells incorporated during creaming. Fat used in cake making should be smooth as it can incorporate and holds air cells as granular fats do not fulfill this function. Therefore use of granular fat should be avoided. Vegetable oil is also used for shortening *e.g.* coconut oil, corn oil, cottonseed oil, peanut oil and soybean oil.

Uses of Shortenings

These

1. Impart shortness, richness and tenderness to the product,
2. Improve the eating qualities of the product
3. Provide aeration
4. Contribute to flavour, particularly special fats such as butter,
5. Promote a desirable grain and texture,
6. Develop flakiness in product
7. Lubricate the gluten for development of yeast-raised dough,
8. Act as emulsifiers for holding of liquids.

Shortenings should be stored at a temperature of 70-80°F. At low temperature it becomes hard and brittle and difficult to work and at high temperature they become excessively soft and show impaired creaming quality. Shortening should not be stored near odourous material because fats are more prone to absorb many foreign odours which are undesirable in shortening. Emulsifier is widely used ingredient in shortening for cakes, icings and bread.

Properties of Shortening

It should have

1. Bland flavour
2. White appearance
3. Good plasticity
4. Flavour and oxidative stability.

Butter

It is considered to be the best of all baking shortenings from a flavour standpoint. It imparts desirable flavour to the finished baked products. It is widely used for specialty breads, sweet goods, cookies and pastries. It has good shortening value. Cake made with butter is generally lower in volume and has coarser grain. But it deteriorates easily by bacterial or mold action. Salt added would act as preservative but not sufficient to avoid deterioration because salt added in separated butter may not be evenly distributed, leaving some water droplets which results in bacterial infection deterioration. Oxidative deterioration results in tallowy flavour.

Lard

Fat rendered from fresh, clean, sound, fatty tissues from hogs in good health at the time of slaughter. Lard has distinctive natural flavour and odour, which is considered desirable in certain baked products primarily bread, crackers and pie crusts. It is most widely used shortenings for bread, pies, soda crackers and find extensive use in pan greasing and in cookie dough.

Leavening Agents

Leavening agents contribute significantly to the textural properties of baked products by expanding the batter or dough, sometimes during mixing and always during baking. Any process by which dough or batter is filled with holes, which are retained upon baking, is a leavening process. Any material which brings this process is called leavening agent.

Generally two types of leavening agents are used:

1. **Biological Agents**: Yeast.
2. **Chemical Agents**: Baking powder, baking soda, ammonium carbonate, etc.

Yeast

Function of yeast in bread making is to lighten the dough and impart to it a characteristic aroma and flavour. Generally four kinds of yeast are available to the bakers- living yeast for leavening, dead dried yeast for nutritional and flavour enhancement, bakers' yeast for white bread and food yeast for rye bread.

Baker yeast is an oval shaped, one celled, and colourless, microscopic plant called *Saccharomyces cerevisiae*. Yeast is universally distributed, generally growing harmlessly on various plant parts wherever sugar is available. One important process it causes in baking is fermentation.

Characters of Yeast

1. Yeast exists and is active in air as well as in absence of air.
2. In presence of air it grows rapidly and forms little alcohol.
3. In absence of air it grows slowly but alcohol formation increases.

In addition to glucose, baker yeast ferments hexose, fructose and mannose, disaccharides sucrose, maltose, the trisaccharides-raffinose and tetrasacharides stachyose. Lactose (milk sugar) is not attacked by baker yeast. Nitrogen compounds are required in abundance to build protein and nucleic acids. Inorganic ammonium salts, urea and amino acids are metabolized readily. Nitrogenous compounds are present in dough in plenty but ammonium chloride is added to stimulate fermentation. Most favourable temperature for baker yeast growth and fermentation is in the range of 84°F-90°F depending on strain used. Temperature above 95°F decreases yeast activity. Yeast grows and ferment best in acidic environment, tolerating acidities as low as pH 2.

Role of yeast in bread making is to lighten or raise the dough, thereby improving its ultimate palatability, simultaneous production and concentration of alcohol, aldehydes, ketones and acids contributing to aroma and flavour. The principal disadvantage is that it is difficult to control and in some items, fermentation flavour can be undesirable. It is also more expensive than chemical agents.

Baking Soda

It is chemically known as sodium bicarbonate. It will liberate CO_2 gas, a leavening gas, when heated. It also liberates the same gas when mixed with an acid, either hot or cold. When baking soda is heated, the products formed are:

$$2NaHCO_3 \xrightarrow{\text{heat}} CO_2 + H_2O + Na_2CO_3$$

If soda is alone used as a leavening agent a residue of washing soda will remain in the cake. This residue when present in excess, gives the dark colour and taste. The reason is that the washing soda so formed will act upon the shortening which is in the cake batter forming soap. This causes an unpleasant taste brown colour and alkaline odour. Therefore, bicarbonate is not used alone and when used, a suitable quantity of acid is added so that neutral residue is formed.

Baking Powder

Quantity of baking powder should be carefully regulated in the formula in order to achieve good results. If a formula calls for use of more moisture the setting of structure of end product will be delayed. Baking powder will start evolving CO_2 gas as soon as the product is placed in oven, but the batter being too soft, the gas will not be held by gluten framework and will escape before the structure is set resulting in loss of volume. The quantity of baking powder should be increased in the formula and baking should be done at higher temperature in order to have faster set.

Baking powder is combination of sodium bicarbonate and an acid salt when moistured and heating will evolve gas which leaven the product giving it volume and making light and easy to digest. Baking powder must yield not less than 12 per cent available carbon-dioxide and concept of neutralization value was developed.

Neutralization value = gm of $NaHCO_3$ × 100/100gm of acidic salt

Baking powder is of three different kinds:

Fast Acting

This type of baking powder releases most of its CO_2 gas during bench operation and very little gas is released during baking *i.e.* mixing operation.

Slow Acting

Such baking powders do not release much of gas during bench operation and all the gas is released when it comes in contact with heat.

Double Acting

This type of baking powder is most widely used by bakers. This baking powder releases part of gas during bench operation, increasing fluidity of cake batter. This action makes the weighing operation easy enabling the baker to apportion the batter in moulds correctly. The remaining of CO_2 gas is released in the oven, which gives volume to the end product.

Baking powder also contains an inert filler which is common corn starch. A baking powder should release its gas in the batter to saturate it with CO_2 gas and liberate the gas uniformly during baking to hold the raised batter until set. This tends to give a uniform crumb and prevent shrinkage and cakes from falling. The starch serves two purposes;

1. It act as a buffer between soda and the acid and prevents reaction when exposed to air by absorbing moisture.
2. It also helps the powder to release standard amount of CO_2.

Sometimes powdered and dried egg albumen is added to baking powder. It dissolves in cold water and increases the viscosity of the dough which helps to hold gas bubbles in the dough, this increase the effectiveness of the baking powder. Baking Powder releases 12-14 per cent available CO_2.

The baking powders are named after the acid ingredient used in the powder *i.e.* tartrate powder, phosphate powder etc. The time and rate of gas evolution from baking powder can be regulated by the selection of different baking acids that react faster or slower with sodium bicarbonate. Commonly used leavening acids components are:

Tartrates (Mono Potassium Salt of Tartaric Acid)

Tartrates are commonly used as the acid component of baking powder in the form of tartratic acid or potassium hydrogen tartrate. It reacts readily at room temperature and is relatively expensive.

Phosphates

A number of sodium acid pyrophosphate powders are available. They vary in their reaction rates, depending upon how they are made.

Monocalcium Phosphate

Cream of tarter being relatively expensive has been largely replaced by phosphate, reacts readily at room temperature and is widely used as the fast acting component in double acting baking powders. Phosphate powders react somewhat slower than tartrates at room temperature but still lose a high percentage of their gas before baking.

Sulphates

To overcome the above defect, slow acting powders are used. Such powders give very little gas at room temperature but release all the available gas only at the temperature of the oven.

Ammonium Carbonate or Bicarbonate

When ammonium carbonate or bicarbonate are heated , CO_2 and NH_3 are roduced. No solid is left behind in this reaction. However, the ammonia imparts a detectable odour unless it is completely removed. It is used as leavening agent in baking biscuits and crackers as they have large surface to mass ration and ammonia escapes when baked at high temperature. Ammonium bicarbonate can be used in products that are to be baked at low moisture.

Either ammonium carbonate or bicarbonate is used to a small extent as a leavening agent. Its use is primarily limited to a certain types of cookies.

Eggs

Most important function of eggs is to provide structure to the cake. It provides moisture to the cake. It improves the taste and nutritive value of cake. Eggs used in excess amount will give abnormal volume to the cake. Crust will be dark, thick and peeld off as a flake. Texture will be dry and rough due to evaporation of moisture.

Proteins of eggs are of particular importance. Coagulation of protein during baking contributes to the structure of finished product and reduces tenderness.

Function of eggs:

1. Binding action
2. Leavening action
3. Emulsifying action
4. Flavor
5. Colour
6. Nutritive value

Egg White

It is used in candy and baking industry because of its ability to form foams which are stable enough to support large quantities of flour or sugar. These foams must be capable of holding the other ingredients until heat coagulation can occur in the oven and a stable protein matrix develops. Egg white has characteristic property of good foam formation. Globulins are primarily responsible for lowering surface tension and increase viscosity where air gets incorporated. As foam develops bubbles become smaller, surface is greatly enlarged and ovomucin (protein) undergoes surface denaturation to form a solid film, which contributes to the stability of the unheated foam and volume of foam increases. Ovalbumin, which is readily heat coagulable, set up in heat and supports many times its weight of sugar and flour. Albumin having pH 6.5-9.5 has greatest foaming power. The pH of egg white is 7.6.

Egg Yolk

Yolk is not commonly employed as a foaming agent with the exception of a yellow sponge type baked product. It does have characteristic foaming ability. Type of foam is quite different than egg white which is oil-water-air emulsion. It is mostly used in manufacture of mayonnaise and salad dressings. pH of egg yolk is 6.0

Following actions should be kept in mind while using egg as ingredients:

1. Weight of sugar should exceed the weight of flour.
2. Weight of total liquid should equal or slightly exceed the weight of sugar.
3. In pound or layer cake, the weight of egg solids should approximate $1/4^{th}$ of the weight of shortening.
4. In white cake the weight of egg white solids should exceed $1/10^{th}$ of the weight of shortening.

Water

In its pure form, water is a tasteless, odorless and colorless liquid. It is an essential dough ingredient which helps to form gluten, starch-swelling process and to bring dough ingredients into intimate contact with each other so that the complex reaction of bread making can take place. Amount of water added depends on the optimum dough characteristic for proper and easy handling as well as for the best quality bread obtainable. In general water of medium hardness (about 50-100ppm) with a neutral or slightly acidic pH is preferred for baking. Too soft water can result in sticky dough because of absence of gluten tightening minerals. Too hard water may retard fermentation to a certain extent by toughening the gluten. So medium hard water is the best for use in bread production.

Some of the mineral component of water, which does not have any effect on fermentation, is copper salts, iron salts, aluminum salts, tannic acids, silicates and phosphates. Probable effects of following salts are found *i.e.* calcium oxide, calcium carbonate, calcium sulphate, magnesium chloride, magnesium oxide and sodium carbonate. If the problem in bakery is suspected to be due to water supply, several common tests can be performed which include alkalinity, pH and hardness.

Functions of Water in Baking

Water has several functions in bread making. It makes possible the formation of gluten. Gluten as such does not exist in flour. Only when flour proteins are hydrated, gluten is formed. Water controls the consistency of dough. Water assists in the control of dough temperatures and warming or cooling of dough can be regulated through water. It dissolves salts, suspends and distributes non-flour ingredients uniformly. Water wets and swells starch and renders it digestible. Water also makes possible enzyme activity. Water keeps bread palatable longer if sufficient water is allowed to remain in the finished loaf. It dissolves salts, sugar and suspends other material in dough. It helps the enzymes to carry out their activity and wets and swells the starch to make it digestible.

Salt

Common salt is used for bringing out the flavour of other ingredients, which are used in cakes, and to impart taste to the bread and to other products. Instead of reducing sugar in the cake it can be used as an adjustment of sweetness if the cake is too sweet. Salt also lowers caramelization temperature of cake batters and aids in obtaining crust colour.

In bread, it is used for taste and helps to improve flavour and characteristic of bread. Without salts, dough is wetty. It, therefore, improves grain and texture of loaf by strengthening the dough, thus indirectly helping colour, grain and texture. Salt helps to control the yeast activity, therefore controls fermentation. It also prevents the formation and growth of undesirable bacteria in yeast-raised dough.

Amount of salt to be used depends on several factors but mainly upon the type of flour. Weak flour will take more salt, because salt gives strengthening effect to proteins. The mineral content of water will also affect the amount of salt. When using hard water the amount of salt will need to be reduced. Under normal conditions the amount of salt to use will range between 2—2.25 per cent. Salt is added to develop flavour. It also toughens the gluten and gives less sticky dough. Salt slows down the rate of fermentation. Generally all levels of salt suppress yeast activity.

Functions of Salt

1. It increases gluten stability,
2. Controls fermentation,
3. Develops flavour,
4. Retains water.
5. Contributes to the crust and crumb formation.

Common salt should have the following characteristics for use in the bakery:

1. It should be completely soluble in water.
2. It should give a clear solution. Cloudy solution will indicate presence of certain impurities.
3. It should be free from lumps.
4. It should be pure.
5. It should be free from a bitter or biting taste.

Milk and Milk Derivatives

Milk solids perform the function of structure formation in the cakes. Milk enriches the cake nutritionally and it also provides moisture in cake. Milk is the basic mean of supplying liquid to the dough. It contributes to the crust browning because of its proteins and sugar content and to softening of crumb texture because of its fat content.

Proper incorporation of milk in dough will result in increased loaf volume. The grain texture of finished bread is also improved by using non-fat dry milk. High moisture content of milk bread permits it to remain soft for longer periods than bread made without milk. Milk solids have a binding effect on flour protein, creating a toughening effect. Milk contains lactose which regulates crust colour.

Liberal use of milk in bakery products brings about nutritional improvements *i.e.* increases mineral content; improves protein quality and supplements carbohydrates to the bread. Wheat is deficient in essential amino acids (lysine, tryptophan and methionine) which can be increased by adding 6 per cent level milk solids *i.e.* lysine increases to 46 per cent, tryptophan 10 per cent and methionine 23 per cent. Greatest advantage of milk solids in bread is to improve sensory quality.

Milk solids also contribute in cakes:

1. Contribute to greater moisture retention for longer apparent freshness and keeping quality
2. Improved appearance and crust colour and absence of greasiness.
3. Improved flavour, richness and taste appeal.
4. Improved nutritional value.
5. It increases loaf volume, retards staling, increases absorption and dough strengthening.

Minor Ingredients

Malt Products

These are obtained from cereal grains usually barley. Greatest consumption of malt is in beverage industries but considerable quantities are used in milling and baking. It is classified as malt flour, malt syrups and dried malt syrup. Each of, which is further, classified as non-diastatic malt and diastatic malt.

Non-diastatic Malt

It is used principally to impart flavour and colour to baked products. They also have some effects on texture and supply fermentable carbohydrates and other nutrients to yeast. These are high in sugars.

Diastatic Malt

Have considerable enzyme activity. Malted grain from which these products are derived, is a veritable storehouse of enzymes which convert starch to reducing substances.

Flavourings

It helps the baker to add uniqueness to his product. These are natural- honey, molasses, malt syrup, cocoa, chocolate, lemon oil, vanilla extract, etc.

Classification

1. *Non-alcoholic flavour*: reduces vaporization *e.g.* glycerin, propylene, glycol, etc
2. *Alcoholic flavour*: used for icing and fillings, very volatile *e.g.* ethyl alcohol, etc
3. *Emulsifiers*: used in maintaining stability during baking, *e.g.* gum
4. *Powdered flavourings*: used in powder form *e.g.* heavy gum

Cocoa Products

Cocoa is a chocolate from which a substantial proportion of fatty material has been removed. It imparts flavour and colour changes.

Dough Improver

It is usually mixture of several inorganic salts together with starch or flour as an extender. Gluten oxidizing agents such as potassium bromate, potassium iodate or calcium peroxide. Calcium salts usually phosphate or sulphate which corrects any lack of hardness in dough water and provide buffering action to partially offset alkaline condition of water. Ammonium salts supply nitrogen which can be used by yeast for protein building.

Oxidizing Agents

Proper use of oxidizing agents results in larger volume, brighter crumb, better texture and improved appearance of finished loaf, *e.g.* Potassium bromate, calcium oxide and potassium iodate.

Yeast Foods

Use of ammonium salts, phosphates, and sulphate in dough improvers and yeast foods improves the fermentation capacity of yeast in dough.

Spices

These act as aromatic agents, *e.g.*

1. Cinnamon
2. Nutmeg (produce 7-15 per cent volatile oil)
3. Mace (produce 7-14 per cent volatile oil)
4. Cloves (contain 14-21 per cent non-volatile penetrating oil)
5. Ginger (provide 1-3 per cent volatile oil)
6. Allspice (provide 3-4.5 per cent volatile oil)
7. Cardamom seeds (3.5-8 per cent of oil of the seed weight provide flavour)
8. Caraway seed (used in making rye bread, corn muffins, cheese rolls, compatible with flavour of sugar, apple, peach, apricot and rye.)
9. Anise seed (provide 2-3 per cent essential oil, used in icings and fillings for cakes and sweet rolls.

Chapter 14
Bread Making

Bread has played a key role in the development of mankind and is one of the principal sources of nutrition. The history of bread is lengthy and largely obscure. Clearly, bread was being consumed long before recorded history. The purpose of bread making is to present cereal flours to the consumer in an attractive, palatable and digestive form. At its simplest this is achieved by baking portions of a kneaded mixture of crushed grain and water, usually with salt added to enhance flavour and cereals are still consumed in this form in many communities.

As wheat is predominantly milled for bread making, the general term baking quality usually refers to the specific properties required for the production of leavened bread. Bread is made by different procedures which depend upon many factors including tradition, cost, type of energy available, the type and consistency of the flour available, the type of bread desired and the time between baking and eating.

Ingredients

Bread making ingredients can be divided into two categories:

Essential

Flour, water, yeast, salt. If any one of these ingredients is missing, the product is not bread.

Optional

Sugar, fat, milk and milk products, oxidants, various enzyme preparations including malted grain, surfactants and additives to protect against molds.

Wheat Flour

Flour is the major ingredient of bread and is obtained through the milling process in which bran and germ part of the wheat grains are removed as far as possible. This is done to get the flour of desirable composition from baking point of view. The major components of flour are moisture (14 per cent), starch (70 per cent), protein (11.5 per cent), ash (4 per cent), sugar (1 per cent) and fat (1 per cent).

The baker should use the flour of following characteristics for the production of quality bread:

1. Colour
2. Strength
3. Tolerance
4. High absorption
5. Uniformity

Colour

Flour should have a creamy white appearance, free from bran fragments otherwise the bread will have a dead white crumb. Bleaching of flour contributes towards the control of degree of creaminess.

Strength

It is often said that the flour is strong or the flour is weak. Such statements refer to the strength of flour which is capable of producing a bold, large volumed and well risen upstanding loaf. For the production of quality bread, strong flours need a longer fermentation it will stand. Bread flour should have sufficient strength so that the dough made from it retains its shape after being moulded.

Tolerance

The ability of flour to withstand the fermentation process and to produce a satisfactory loaf over a period of time, in excess of what normally is required to bring the correct degree of ripeness for that practical process, means tolerance.

High Absorption

This refers to the ability of flour to take on and hold the maximum amount of moisture without additional mixing for full development of dough. If the dough is not given the required mixing time because of limited mixing capacity, or for other reasons, the baked product will lack volume and have a dry crumb and inferior eating and keeping qualities.

In considering bread-making flour, generally we think of hard wheat with a relatively high protein content. Hardness does not appear to be an absolute requirement but protein-content requirement does appear to be more absolute. It is impossible to make a good quality loaf of bread from flour containing low amount of protein (8 per cent or so). If a flour has higher quantity and better quality gluten, it is called as strong flour. Dough prepared from such a flour has better gas retention capacity. To be more precise, both the quantity and quality of protein is needed in the wheat flour to produce a quality loaf.

Gas production is another very important aspect of bread making process. For this purpose, the flour should have sufficient diastatic activity which depends upon the diastase enzyme. This enzyme converts flour starch into sugar.

Water

It is an essential ingredient because without water, dough cannot be prepared. Water has several functions in bread making. It is essential for the formulation of gluten. Gluten as such does not exist in flour. Only when flour proteins are hydrated, gluten is formed. Water helps in controlling the temperature of dough and its consistency. It dissolves salts, sugars and suspends other non-flour materials uniformly in dough. Water wets and swells starch and renders it digestible. Water is also required for activating enzymes. It makes the bread palatable. Water keeps the bread palatable longer if sufficient water is allowed to remain in the finished loaf.

The water used should be fit to drink and free from contamination and disease forming bacteria. Since water is a powerful solvent, it has some dissolved minerals in it. These minerals have a beneficial effect on gas production as yeast requires them for vigorous gas production. However, hard waters which have high content of minerals may not be used as they have tightening effect on the gluten and it retards fermentation. On the other hand, if soft water is used then the gas production and gas retention of the dough is poor. So medium hard water yields excellent result in the bread production.

Salt

Salt is mainly added to impart taste to the bread. It also brings about the taste of other ingredients and helps to improve the flavour and characteristics of the bread. It has controlling effect on the activity of yeast and thus has a check on the rate of gas production. Salt also aids in preventing the formation and growth of undesirable bacteria in yeast-raised doughs. Salt makes the dough stronger and acts as a toughner. It has a tightening effect on the gluten proteins. So it improves the gas retention power of the dough. Due to its strengthening effect, it improves the grain and texture of bread crumb.

Salt is hygroscopic in nature, due to this property it tries to keep the bread moist and fresh for longer time. Salt also indirectly affects the colour of bread due to its regulatory action on yeast activity. If salt is less, yeast activity will be more, more sugar will be used for fermentation and lesser sugar will be left at the time of baking for caramalization. This will produce a bread of poorer crust colour and vice-versa. Salt is generally used at levels of about 1-2 per cent based on flour weight.

Sugar

It is used in bread production as nutrient for the yeast. It is the source of energy for yeast activity which produces carbon dioxide gas that raises the dough fabric and is essential for imparting proper volume to the bread. It enhances the flavour of bread. Due to its hygroscopic nature, helps in the moisture retention in bread. It imparts golden brown colour to the crust of bread. The texture and grain become smoother and finer with added sugar. The basis for this is not well understood. It may be related to the action of sugars on delaying the gelatinization of starch and the denaturation of protein.

The sugar added in the formula is consumed in very short time by the yeast. The requirements of sugar then are met through the activity of diastase enzyme. The presence of sugar in sufficient amount is essential for the vigorous and sustained gas production in the bread making process. Hence, the flour must have sufficient amylase (diastase) activity. This is also essential for good oven rise during baking process.

Fat

In bread that is to be stored for any significant period of time after baking, fat is an important ingredient. Bread containing fat in the formula stays soft and more palatable for a longer period of time than does the bread prepared without shortening. Besides antistaling properties, the added fat has a lubricating effect on gluten structure. This improves the extensibility of the dough which helps in improving the bread volume. It improves the softness of bread and improves its sliceability. Fat should be added only during the last stages of mixing as at earlier stage it adversely affects the water absorption power of the flour.

Glycerol-monostearate (GMS)

It is an emulsifying agent and acts as surfactant. Sometimes the quantity of fat is reduced in the formula by adding some emulsifiers like GMS. If GMS is to be used, it should added alongwith fat.

GMS is an excellent flour strengthener, enhancing gluten. It increases absorption and dispersion of water, thus ensuring more loaves per batch. It improves texture of bread by ensuring a fine and more uniform crumb structure. It keeps the bread fresh and soft.

Milk

Milk may be used in bread formations in liquid or dry solid forms. In liquid form, milk consists of two parts *i.e.* water (87.75 per cent) and total solids (12.25 per cent). Total solids consist of fat (3.5 per cent), proteins (3.25 per cent), ash (0.75 per cent) and lactose (4.75 per cent). While using liquid milk, the water content should be taken into consideration for adjusting the formula. The moisture of the milk is neither a toughner nor a tenderizer, but when combined with other ingredients may contribute to both toughness and tenderness in the products. The milk solids have a binding effect on the flour protein, creating a toughening effect. They also contain lactose which helps to regulate crust colour. They improve the flavour and are important moisture retaining agents.

There are various advantages of adding milk solids in the bread dough. These are:

Increased Absorption and Dough Strengthening

The skim milk solids have strengthening effect on flour proteins particularly if the flour is of medium or weak strength.

Increased Mixing Tolerance

The doughs having milk solids have better mixing tolerance and resist overmixing. They recover more rapidly before reaching pan stage.

Longer Fermentation

Due to buffering action of milk, the non-fat dry milk solids will normally slow down the enzymatic activity especially the diastatic activity during the entire fermentation time. Therefore, tolerance to longer fermentation time helps in the production of a satisfactory loaf of a bread. Non-fat dry milk solids and diastatic malt added in the dough improve baking performance when low diastatic activity flour is used.

Better Crust Colour

The lactose, caseins and whey proteins in the non-fat dry milk contribute to a golden crust colour and also improve the toasting qualities.

Better Grain and Texture

The soft velvety texture and grain of uniform cells are the characteristics that are found in the crumb of a milk bread. These characteristics improve the sliceability of the loaf.

Increased Loaf Volume

There are various ways of raising the loaf volume and one of them is addition of milk in the dough.

Better Keeping Quality

Since the addition of milk permits high moisture content, it allows the bread to remain soft for a longer period.

Better Nutrition

The milk breads are nutritionally better because they contain more minerals, protein and vitamins. Milk also improves flavour and eating quality of bread.

Yeast

Yeast is one of the fundamental ingredients. Its major function in bread making is to lighten the dough and impart to it characteristic aroma and flavour. Yeast (*Saccharomyces cerevisiae*) is a source of several enzymes like zymase, lipase, protease, invertase, maltase etc. Yeast utilizes the fermentable sugars in the fermentation process to produce carbon dioxide gas through the action of enzymes. During fermentation process, alcohol and some acids are also produced which help in mellowing gluten which adds to the easy stretchability. The acids also add peculiar flavour to bread. For efficient action of yeast, we need to provide sugars, nitrogen, minerals and vitamins.

The yeast could be used in the form of compressed yeast or dried yeast. Compressed yeast has 30 per cent solids and can be stored for about 4 weeks under refrigeration *i.e.* 20°C (35°F).

Improvers

Besides the above ingredients, sometimes improvers like potassium bromate, potassium iodate, ascorbic acid and calcium peroxide are added at levels of parts per million. It is a common knowledge that the bread making properties of flour are increased if the flour is aged for sometime. This improvement is brought by the action of oxygen of air on the flour protein and the proteins form a better gluten. Similarly, the improvers add active oxygen to the dough, which improve the strength of gluten which is reflected in better bread quality.

Preservatives

Preservatives like calcium propionate and acetic acid are used to inhibit the growth of fungi or mold. They improve the keeping quality of bread.

Formula Construction

There are many different formulae for bread and yeast-raised products. Some of these formulae contain little or no enriching ingredients like eggs, fat and sugar and would be called 'lean'. Others have high percentage of these enriching ingredients and referred to as 'rich'. There are many formulas between these two extremes.

If the baker is to produce a certain amount of bread or sweet dough, he will have to know how to determine the desired weight of each ingredient to produce the desired amount of finished product. Formulas are written on a per cent basis, using the weight of flour as 100 per cent. Flour is the base of formula and each other ingredient will represent a certain per cent of the weight of the flour.

For example: If the per cent of sugar in the formula is 3 per cent and the weight of the flour is 50 kg, the weight of the sugar would represent 3 per cent of 50 kg ($0.03 \times 50 = 1.5$ kg of sugar).

The total per cent of the formula is the total of all the ingredient percentages or the per cent of yield based on the flour.

For example: The per cent of flour is 100 per cent and if the total percentages of all the other ingredients total 60 per cent, the total per cent of the formula would be 160 per cent or the total yield of the formula would be 160 per cent of the weight of the flour.

A dough formula can be increased or decreased. One has to simply increase or decrease the weight of each ingredient so that the total weight will be the desired weight and the proportion of ingredients or percentage of ingredients will remain the same. The four factors that must be available to base the solution on are as given below:

1. Weight of dough (bread, rolls or sweet rolls)
2. Total per cent formula to use
3. Amount of loss (2 per cent normal fermentation loss)
4. Scaling weight of dough pieces

Example Problem

Construct a formula that will produce 261 loaves of bread scaled at 450 g (The finished loaf will yield 400 g).

Ingredients	*Per cent*
Flour	100.0
Water	60.0
Salt	2.0
Yeast	1.0
Sugar	2.0
Shortening	1.5
Milk (Non-fat dry milk)	0.5
Total	167.0

There are four steps that must be determined to complete the increasing or decreasing of the formula which are as follows:

Step I

Determine the amount of dough needed to produce the desired number of loaves or amount of product.

$$\left[\begin{array}{c}\text{(Number of units}\\ \text{scaling weight)}\end{array}\right] \times \begin{array}{c}\text{1.02 fermentation}\\ \text{loss}\end{array} = \begin{array}{c}\text{Dough}\\ \text{Weight}\end{array}$$

$$(261 \times 0.450) \times 1.02 = 119.80 \text{ or } 120 \text{ kg dough}$$

Step II

Determine the amount of flour needed to produce the desired dough.

$$\frac{\text{Total dough weight}}{\text{Total formula per cent}} \times 100 \text{ kgs of flour}$$

$$\frac{120}{167} \times 100 = 71.89 \text{ kgs of flour or } 72 \text{ kgs of flour}$$

Step III

Determine the weight of each ingredient for the new formula by multiplying the per cent of each ingredient times the weight of the flour in the new formula (Step II).

Determine the weight of each ingredient based on the weight of the flour. Multiply the per cent of each ingredient times the weight of the flour:

Flour	100 per cent	=	72.00 kgs
Water	60 per cent × 72	=	43.20 kgs
Salt	2 per cent × 72	=	1.44 kgs
Yeast	1 per cent × 72	=	0.72 kgs
Sugar	2 per cent × 72	=	1.44 kgs
Shortening	1.5 per cent × 72	=	1.08 kgs
Milk (dry)	0.5 per cent × 72	=	0.36 kgs

The per cent of the original formula = 167.0 kgs

Total weight of the new formula = 120.24 kgs

Processing Methods of Bread

There are two procedures of bread making:

1. Straight-dough process
2. Sponge-and-dough process

The flow diagrams of these processes are given in Fig. 14.1. The straight-dough process is the simplest one for bread making. In this method, all the formula ingredients are mixed into a developed dough that is then allowed to ferment. During fermentation, the dough is usually punched one or more times. After fermentation, it is divided into loaf-sized pieces, round molded into the loaf shape and placed into the baking pan. In sponge-and-dough process, part of the flour (approximately two thirds), part of the water and the yeast are mixed just enough to form a loose dough (sponge). The sponge is allowed to ferment for upto 5 hr. Then it is combined with the rest of the formula ingredients and mixed into a developed dough. After being mixed, dough is given an intermediate proof ('floor time') of 20-30 min. so that it can relax, and it is divided, molded and proofed as is done in the straight-dough procedure.

Basic Operations in Bread Making

The bread is a foamed structure made basically from four raw materials *viz*, flour, water, salt and yeast. The following are the major steps in bread making:

STRAIGHT DOUGH PROCESS	SPONGE DOUGH PROCESS
Preparation of ingredients	Preparation of ingredients
↓	↓
Weighing	Weighing
↓	↓
Sifting and blending flour	Sifting and blending flour
↓	↓
Tempering of water	Tempering of water
↓	↓
Preliminary mixing of yeast, dried milk etc.	Preliminary mixing of yeast
↓	↓
Dough mixed	Sponge mixed
↓	↓
Dough placed in trough	Sponge placed in trough
↓	↓
Dough allowed to rise, turned and folded	Sponge allowed to mature
↓	↓
Dough sent to bench or divider	Sponge placed in mixer
↓	↓
Dividing and scaling	Sponge broken up and mixed with dough ingredients
↓	↓
Rounding	Final dough placed in trough
↓	↓
Intermediate proof	Allowed to rise Sometimes turned and folded
↓	↓
Moulding	Dough sent to bench or divider
↓	↓
Panning	Dividing and scaling
↓	↓

Contd...

Fig. 14.1–Contd...

Pan proof → Baking → Cooling → Slicing

Rounding → Intermediate proof → Moulding → Panning → Pan proof → Baking → Cooling → Slicing

Fig. 14.1: Methods of Bread Making

Sieving

The flour is generally sieved before using in bread; to aerate the flour; to remove coarse particles and other impurities; and to make flour more homogenous.

Weighing

The next step is weighing of different ingredients as per recipe/ formula. Minor ingredients have to be weighed in a more precise manner.

Preparation of Different Solutions

Generally, yeast is dispersed in a part of water and the remaining parts of water are used to dissolve sugar and other additives like oxidants, yeast foods etc. Sequence of addition of ingredients also affects the dough characteristics. Generally, shortening and salt are added after the clean up stage to reduce the mixing time.

Mixing

Mixing is one of the most important steps in bread making. A dough is mixed to distribute as equitably as possible all the ingredients. The best way to accomplish this is to dissolve or suspend the ingredients in water as this will 'wet' all the flour. The main purpose of mixing a dough is to make and develop the gluten. Gluten is not in the flour. The flour contains proteins the majority of which when wetted, pulled, stretched and kneaded take the form of a substance called gluten. The secret of mixing is how long to continue the mixing for optimum gluten development and water absorption. Total water absorption is not obtained until the gluten has been fully developed.

Mechanical mixers are used for thorough incorporation of all the ingredients of bread, to develop the gluten and to make the dough more extensible. The straight dough coming out of the mixer should have a desirable temperature of 77 to 80°F (25°-26°C) and the sponge dough 73-78°F (23°-25°C). The different stages of mixing are:

1. Pick up stage
2. Clean-up stage
3. Development stage
4. Final stage
5. Let-down stage
5. Break-down stage

The mixing time varies with the type of flour, type of speed of mixer, design of the arms in the mixer and their speed, presence of salt or shortening, additive, particle size as well as damaged starch content of flour and kind of bread desired. During mixing, a three dimensional net work of proteins is formed due to the interchange of disulfide bonds. Oxygen/air also gets incorporated into the dough during mixing which helps in the oxidation of flour as well as in the formation of nuclei for the formation of gas cells.

A dough that has been mixed to a peak can be referred to by a number of terms *e.g.*, a mixed dough, a dough with minimum mobility, or an optimally mixed dough. All of these imply that an end point has been reached. This also means that this is the point to which a dough should be mixed for producing a loaf of bread.

Strong flours require longer mixing time than the weak flours. Length of mixing is an indication of flour strength. When longer mixing time is used, the temperature of the dough rises. This in most cases reduces yield due to low water absorption. In these situations, cold water should be used. For instance, a strong flour when mixed at 95°F or 35°C will absorb 5 to 8 per cent less water than when mixed at 78°F or 25°C.

Both overmixing and undermixing are undesirable. After reaching the optimum development, continued mixing produces a wet, sticky dough with an 'overmixed' sheen. This is generally called as the dough being broken-down. Gluten structure is broken down during overmixing. It also heats the dough and slows down the fermentation. Excessively overmixed doughs produce bread of inferior volume and the breads are crumbly from inside.

Undermixing makes a dough less elastic. The volume of bread will be low and at times the bread will collapse in proofing or in the oven as gluten will not have the proper extensibility to hold the gas in the dough.

Fermentation

Yeast brings about fermentation in the bread making. Yeast can ferment under either aerobic or anaerobic conditions. Bread fermentation is an anaerobic process. Thus, little growth of yeast occurs during dough fermentation. The process of fermentation starts just after mixing and it increases during interproofing and final proofing.

The most favourable temperature for action of yeast in bread doughs is between 75°F to 85°F or about 24°C to 30°C and humidity about 70-75 per cent. In order to ensure uniform results in the fermentation of doughs, it is necessary to hold the temperatures, and allow them to ferment in a place where the temperature is constant.

The quantity of yeast has an influence on the rate of fermentation. It is poor economy to use too small an amount of yeast and to employ a long fermentation as this results in poor flavour. Generally, two per cent of baker's compressed yeast based on the weight of the flour, with a normal fermentation time, will produce a dough having normal tolerance which will yield good bread of excellent flour.

$$\underset{\text{Glucose}}{C_6H_{12}O_6} + \text{Yeast} \rightarrow \underset{\text{Ethanol}}{2C_2H_5OH} + \underset{\text{Carbon dioxide}}{2CO_2}$$

During fermentation, there is an increase in the volume of dough due to the production of gas, increase in temperature, number of yeast cells and the change of consistency of dough. The enzymes of yeast act on the starch and sugars to form carbon dioxide gas. The evolution of this gas causes the dough to rise and conditions the dough, makes it soft, light, elastic as well as extensible. The pH of the dough comes down from 5.5 to 4.7 due to formation of acids like acetic acid. Maltose is also produced by the action of diastatic enzymes by their action on damaged starch. Gas production during fermentation is controlled by the enzymes present in the flour, yeast concentration, amount of sugar and malt, presence of yeast food and temperature of fermentation. Gas retention is influenced by the quality of flour proteins. Approximately, there is a fermentation loss of about 1 to 2 per cent.

Overfermented doughs are inclined to become soft and sticky. They yield less bread of unappetizing appearance as quite a bit of dusting flour must be used during scaling and make up. Underfermented doughs do not bake properly and the crumb is darkish and very close. They also tend to crumble easily. The dough has a tendency to flatten out which can be noticed during the intermediate proof time.

Knock-back

As fermentation proceeds, it is customary to punch or remix the dough, depending upon which baking system is being used. Punching of dough in between the fermentation periods increases gas retaining capacity of the dough. The knock-back has the objectives of equalizing dough temperature throughout the mass, reducing the retarding effect of excessive accumulation of carbon dioxide within the dough mass and introduces oxygen for the stimulation of yeast activity. The knock-back also aids in the mechanical development of gluten by stretching and folding action. Usually knock-back is done when 2/3 of the normal fermentation time is over.

Scaling or Dividing

After fermentation, the dough is divided into individual pieces of pre-determined uniform weight. Generally, 12 per cent extra dough is taken to compensate for the baking loss.

Rounding

Each piece is rounded either by hand or mechanically, to give a ball shape. The function of the rounding is to impart a continuous surface skin that will retain the gas and reduce the stickiness. During the scaling in pieces and rounding, most of the carbon dioxide that has been formed in the first fermentation period will be squeezed out of the dough.

Intermediate Proof

The loss of gas during scaling and rounding is compensated by submitting the dough pieces to an extra fermentation period of 5 to 30 minutes, referred to as 'intermediate proof'. It is done at a temperature of 80-85°F, 75 per cent RH for a time period of 5-30 minutes.

Moulding

The next step is to mould the dough pieces in order to give them the desired loaf shape. The moulding action consists of sheeting, curling and sealing. Moulder consists of three pairs of roller. These rollers convert the rounded dough in the form of sheet. Mechanical moulder curls the sheet into a cylinder which is dropped into mould pan in which the bread is baked. The pan should be greased with 0.1 to 0.2 per cent pan oil (groundnut, soybean, and cottonseed). The pan temperature is 90°F. The optimum panning should be carried out so that seam of the dough is placed on the bottom of the pan. Moulding is done for the removal of extra gas formed by the process of fermentation at the time of intermediate proof.

The steps involved in hand moulding are:

1. Take rounded pieces of dough and place on floured board with topside down.
2. Press out gas with palms of hands.
3. Pull dough lengthwise to shape into oblong piece the length of a finished loaf.

4. Shape loaf by folding lengthwise to the centre. Press firmly with fingers to seal.
5. Fold over ½ of the dough and press for a final seal.
6. Roll dough to complete sealing and moulding of the loaf.

Put the moulded loaf in the centre of the greased pan in such a way that the seam on the piece of dough is placed down. Pan should not be excessively greased as it can seriously affect the proofing and baking of the bread.

After the dough has been formed in size and shape of the product being made, it is desirable to hold the dough undisturbed for a time to permit the CO_2 to thoroughly expand.

Final Proof

Final proofing is done at a temperature of 95°F (30-35°C) at 85 per cent RH for 55-65 minutes. The objectives of final proofing are:

1. To relax the dough from the stress received during fermentation operation
2. To facilitate production of gas in order to give volume to the bread
3. To change tough bucky gluten to a good mellow extensible character.

To determine whether the loaf is properly proofed, touch the loaf lightly with one finger-tip and press in slightly. If the impression made by the tip of the finger remains, the loaf is proofed; if the imprint does not remain and fills out when the finger-tip is removed, the loaf is still too tight and compact and should be proofed more. Underproofing will produce bread of small volume. A times it will burst on sides and in as much as the volume is less, it will be, as a rule, underbaked. There are times when the oven temperature is low that the bread should go to the oven underproofed. The reason for this is that the lower heat will take longer to form a crust on the bread allowing it to expand more than usual. Overproofing to a certain degree is justified if the bread has to be baked in a hot oven, as the excessive heat will form a crust in a shorter time before it has time to expand.

Baking

At the end of the final proof, the risen dough is put into oven and baked for 15-45 minutes, depending on the size of dough pieces. Normally, bread is baked at a temperature of 245°-250°C for 30 minutes. During baking, the dough volume will continue to increase. The better the quality of dough, the more the dough will increase in volume. The crust of the loaf and the texture of the crumb will be fixed during the baking stage at 55-65°C by gelatinization of starch, which then binds part of the water.

The purpose of baking is to transform unpalatable dough into a light porous and readily digestible flavoured product. The duration of baking, humidity and temperature of the oven influence the quality of bread and they vary depending upon the following factors:

Size and Shape of Loaf

If the loaf is large, the temperature of the oven will have to be regulated so that surface of the loaf will not burn before the loaf is baked. If the loaf is small, the temperature of the oven will have to be raised so the loaf will brown off before the crumb of the loaf is overbaked.

Total Sugars in Dough at Baking Time

If the formula contains a great amount of sugars, the heat of the oven will have to be lowered so that the colour will not odour excessively. If the sugar content of the loaf is low, the temperature of the oven should be raised. Bread that has a thick, hard crust has a low percentage of sugar and fat, and requires a longer baking period and higher temperature than for the regular type bread.

Inside properly baked loaves, the following conditions should have taken place:

1. Cell walls are no longer sticky.
2. Enzymatic and yeast action is terminated.
3. Right amount of moisture is lost and loaf holds its shape.

If the temperature of the oven is low, it will tend to open the grain of the loaf and if too high temperature is used, the loaf may burst in a rather violent manner, usually along the sides and result in unsymmetrical loaves of minimum size.

Cooling and Slicing

After baking, the loaves have to cool down to room temperature so that they do not dry excessively. Conditions which cause the excessive drying are that air is too dry or warm in the cooling room or there is excessive air circulation in the cooling room. Other purposes of cooling before slicing and wrapping are to:

1. Facilitate slicing
2. Prevent condensation of moisture in the wrapper.

Desirable temperature of bread during slicing is 95°-105°F.

Packaging

The packaging requirements of bread demand a few characteristics in the packaging materials. The packaging material should be sealable, should have low water vapour transmission rate and should be economical. For bread wrapping, mostly wax paper is used, however, in the developed countries, plastic films like polypropylene are also extensively used.

Chapter 15

Quality Control of Bread Making

Quality control covers the activities which help to keep the production running smoothly and efficiently and ensure that the finished products are within the predetermined specifications. There are different sections for this activity:

1. Testing of raw materials
2. Testing of final finished products

Testing of Raw Materials

It mainly involves:

1. Tests for wheat flour
2. Tests for packaging material
3. Test for yeast

Tests for Wheat Flour

Colour Test (Pekar Colour Test)

Principle

This method is used to assess the colour of the flour by visual comparison. As the tint of colour observed varies depending on the factors such as thickness of the flour layer, pressure applied and the moisture content, it is necessary to apply the same technique to both the test and comparison sample.

Procedure

Take about 15 g flour and pack it on one side of one of the glass/wooden/steel strip. Press it. Dip it in a water tub or pan slowly. After 10-15 minutes, take it out and check the colour of the flour. Compare with 15 g of the standard flour processed in the same way as the given sample. Check for the presence of bran or dust particles, if any.

Water Absorption Percentage

Strong flour with higher gluten content has a higher water absorption capacity which in turn results in higher yield of bread. Flour with higher water absorption capacity gives softer breadcrumb with better eating and keeping quality. Ideally, the bread flour should have 62-64 per cent water absorption percentage.

Procedure

Take 25 g of flour sample in china dish. Add about 15 ml of water into the dish from a thoroughly cleaned burette. Mix the flour and water with a spatula, adding water in small portions until well-kneaded dough of medium soft consistency is obtained. The consistency of the final kneaded dough should be neither too stiff nor too soft. It should not be sticky to hand but manageable. Record the volume of water required.

$$\textbf{Water Absorption Power (\%)} = \frac{\text{Volume of water required (ml)}}{\text{Weight of flour sample taken}} \times 100$$

Moisture Content

Principle

The raw material/flour used in bakery is dried in hot air oven for sometime at a regulated temperature in weighed metal dish with lid, the moisture is evaporated and moisture content is calculated from the weight loss due to the evaporation of moisture.

Procedure

Weigh accurately about 5 to 10 g of the prepared sample in a moisture cup previously dried in the hot air oven and weighed. Place the moisture cup alongwith sample in the oven maintained at 105° ± 1°C for 3 to 4 hours or till constant weight is obtained. Carefully transfer in the desiccator for cooling and weighing. Repeat the process of drying, cooling and weighing at 30 minutes intervals until the difference between the consecutive weight is less than one milligram. Record the lowest weight.

Calculations

$$\textbf{Moisture (\%)} = \frac{100\,(W_1 - W_2)}{(W_1 - W)}$$

where,

W_1 = Weight in g, of the cup with material before drying

W_2 = Weight in g, of the cup with the material after drying to constant weight and

W = Weight in g, of the empty cup.

Gluten Content

Procedure

Weigh accurately into a dish about 25 g of sample. Add about 15 ml of water to the sample and make it into a firm dough ball. Keep the dough gently in a beaker filled with water and let it stand for 1 hour. Remove the dough and place it in a piece of silk cloth. Wash it with gentle stream of tap water till the water passing through the silk does not turn blue when a drop of iodine solution is added to it. Transfer the wet gluten in a dish, spread into a thin layer and cut into small pieces. Transfer any residue sticking to silk by means of a spatula into the dish. Place the dish in a hot air oven (130-133°C) for 2 hrs. Cool in the desiccator and weigh.

Calculations

$$\textbf{Gluten (on dry basis) per cent by Mass} = \frac{10{,}000\,(M_2 - M_1)}{(100 - M_3)\,M}$$

where.

M_2 = Mass in g of the dish with dry gluten

M_1 = Mass in g of the empty dish

M = Mass in g of the material taken for the test and

M_3 = Percentage of the moisture in the sample.

Total Ash Content

Ash content represents the mineral matter present in the flour. It is also usually high when the bran contamination in the flour is high. Normally maida with higher ash content has a dull colour and produces bread of poor quality. The total ash content for bread flour should be ideally around 0.4 to 0.5 per cent on dry weight basis.

Procedure

Weigh accurately 5 g of sample in the dish previously dried in hot air oven. Heat dish gently on a flame at first and then strongly in a muffle furnace at 550° ± 10°C for 4 to 5 hrs or until ash is formed. Cool the dish in the desiccator and weigh.

Calculation

$$\textbf{Total Ash (\%)} = \frac{100\,(W_2 - W)}{(W_1 - W)}$$

where,

W_2 = Weight in g of the dish with ash

W_1 = Weight in g of the dish with the sample material taken for the test and

W = Weight in g of the empty dish.

Alcoholic Acidity Test

Flour which has been stored for a long time gives higher values of alcoholic acidity and hence, it is an index of deterioration the flour has undergone during storage. Alcoholic acidity includes the combined acidity due to hydrolysis of fats by lipases to free fatty acids, hydrolysis of proteins to amino acids by proteolytic enzymes and the presence of certain acid salts etc.

Procedure

Weigh 5 g of the flour sample in a conical stoppered flask. Add 50 ml of neutral ethyl alcohol. Mix well and allow to stand for 24 h with occasional shaking. Filter the alcoholic extract through a dry filter paper. Titrate the combined alcoholic extract against 0.05N standard sodium hydroxide solution using phenol-phthalein as indicator. Calculate the per cent of alcoholic acidity as sulphuric acid.

Calculations

$$\text{Per cent Alcoholic Acidity (as } H_2SO_4) = \frac{24.52 \times \text{Normality of NaOH} \times A}{M}$$

where,

A = Volume in ml of standard NaOH solution used in titration

M = Mass in g of the material taken for the test.

Acid Insoluble Ash

It indicates the quantity of silica matter present in the flour. This is due to improper cleaning of wheat prior to milling. In bread flour, acid insoluble ash should not be more than 0.05 per cent.

Procedure

Ash about 5 g of sample as in the determination of total ash. To the ash, in the dish add 25 ml of dil. HCl, cover with watch glass and heat on a water bath for 10 min. Allow cooling and filtering the contents of the dish through a Whatman filter paper # 42. Wash the filter paper with distilled water until the washings are free from the acid and return them to the dish. Keep it in an oven maintained at 100 ± 2°C for about 3 hours. Ignite in a muffle furnace at 550 ± 10°C for 1 h. Cool the dish in a desiccator and weigh. Repeat the process of heating for 30 min. Cooling and weighing until the difference between two successive weighings is less than 1 mg. Record the lowest weight.

Calculation

$$\text{Acid Insoluble Ash (\%)} = \frac{100\,(W_2 - W)}{(W_1 - W)}$$

where,

W_2 = Weight in g of the dish with the acid insoluble ash

W = Weight in g of the empty dish

W_1 = Weight in g of the dish with the sample taken for the test.

Granularity Test

Take 10 g of flour in a strainer. Strain it well for 2 min. Brush the upper surface of the sieve and sieve again for 1 min. The material shall be deemed to have satisfied the requirement of the test, if no residue is left on the sieve. Collect the unstrained particles on a paper and weigh.

Calculation

Weight of Unstrained Particles (g) = Final weight – Initial weight of paper

$$\textbf{\% Granularity} = \frac{P \times 100}{10}$$

where,

P = Weight of unstrained particles.

Maltose Figure of Flour

Maltose Figure of Flour can be determined by using Rumsey method.

Testing of Packaging Material

Gramage Test for GSM Test or g/m² Test

Procedure

Cut the piece of wrapper from the sample by the help of 20/10 cm gramage steel plate and blade. Weigh the cutting pieces separately and find out the average weight.

Calculation

$$\text{Gramage} = \text{Average weight} \times 50$$

Average weight is multiplied by 50 because in 1 m^2 piece, there are 50 pieces of 20/10 cm

Wax Test

Procedure

Take a wrapper of 20/10 cm, weigh it. Now cut it in about 4-5 cm small pieces and put them in soxhlet apparatus containing carbon tetrachloride for 1 h. Take out the paper after 1 h and keep in oven for drying. After drying, keep the paper in desiccator for sometime and weigh.

Calculations

Weight of Wax = (Initial wt.–Final wt.) = X per 20/10 cm

Weight of Wax = X x 50 = y g per gramage (GSM)

Tests for Yeast

Dough Raising Capacity Test

Procedure

Take 100 g of flour in a bowl. Add 4 g yeast and 1.5 g sucrose. A suitable quantity of water (50-60 ml) is added to knead the dough. Knead well. Take a large diameter measuring cylinder and put the kneaded maida in it. Press it with wooden rod to the bottom of the cylinder and note down the initial reading. Keep the cylinder in water bath at 27-30°C for 1 h and note down the final reading.

Calculation

$$\text{Dough Raising Capacity (\%)} = \frac{\text{(Final reading – Original level reading)}}{\text{Original level reading}} \times 100$$

Pop Test

Yeast is usually tested by gas production method. A useful rapid test for yeast is as under:

Procedure

Fill a glass beaker with 10 per cent sugar solution (30 to 32°C). Temperature should remain the same in each case. Take 10 g of each yeast (compressed or dried) to be tested. Make it into a pellet and drop into the separate beakers containing 10 per cent sugar solutions. Measure the time taken for the yeast to raise upto the surface. The yeast with the fastest initial gassing power will rise most rapidly. This is not necessarily the best yeast for bakery. Any yeast with inadequate action will be spotted before it can give rise to trouble in the bakery. A satisfactory yeast should rise to the surface under the condition of this test within about 1 minute. First pop should be within 10 seconds.

Testing of Final Finished Product

It is highly essential to examine sample loaves of each batch produced to see if they are upto standard. These should be based upon the definite characteristics of bread such as the following:

1. External characteristics
2. Internal characteristics

Regular scoring of the bread on the basis of the following external and internal characteristics will help the baker to determine which of the characteristics are not upto the standard and what immediate steps may be taken to improve the quality of bread.

External Characteristics

Volume

Volume is an important consideration in consumer acceptance. The greater the volume of the bread, the softer the loaf appears when squeezed with hands. A loaf of excessive volume will generally have open grain and weak texture while the one with a low volume possesses rough grain and honey comb texture. The volume of the loaf can be described as satisfactory, too large or too small. Volume is influenced by many factors both from the ingredients and processing.

Colour of Crust

The colour of the crust is also termed as 'bloom'. The desired colour is one with an appetizing golden brown shade.

Crust colour is the result of caramalization of sugars and is also due to the browning reaction due to interaction of protein and reducing sugar. The colour of crust is mainly dependent on the amount of sugar present in the dough when baked and temperature at which the loaf is baked. Undesirable colours of crust may be designed as dark, reddish brown, greyish or pale straw colour.

Evenness of Bake

This means that the loaf has been made with a uniformity of bake on all sides. Factors like correct proofing, controlled oven conditions as well as the proper distance between the pans during baking affect evenness of bake.

Symmetry of Form

The shape or symmetry of the loaf influences the customers to a great extent.

Break and Shred

The break and shred of a loaf have an important bearing on the general appearance of the loaf. An even-shredded break is desirable on the sides and ends of open top bread. The break should not be excessive to the extent that the top crust separates from the sides of the loaf forming crust. Faulty bread may show any of these faults– wild break, lack of attractive shred, shell top, no break or insufficient break.

Character of Crust

The bread crust should be thin and crisp. It should not be thick, tough or rubbery.

Internal Characteristics

The most important internal characteristic of a loaf of bread is the crumb structure. This is broadly divided into grain and texture.

Grain

Cell structure of the loaf is known as grain. A fine silky grain is one in which cells are small and uniform, elongated, rather than round and the cell walls are thin. A coarse grain is one in which the cells are large and the cell walls are thick.

Texture

Texture is actually the feel of the surface of the interior of the loaf when cut and sliced. Thus, a desirable texture may be classified as velvety, silky, soft and elastic. An inferior texture is often described as rough, hard, doughy, crumbly and lumpy. The texture of a loaf is determined by pressing the fingers against and rubbing them across the cut surface of the loaf.

Colour of Crumb

The cell structure affects the colour by its effect on the refraction of the light. A coarse grain slice will appear darker in colour and a fine grain slice whiter even though both loaves were made with identical ingredients.

Thick heavy cell walls due to young dough give the crumb a little tan colour. Open grain causes shadows which give the crumb a greyish colour. The colour of the crumb should be bright without any dark patches.

Aroma

The aroma of a loaf is determined by carefully smelling it. The aroma may be described as wheaty, sweet, musty, rancid, moldy, sour or flat. The ideal loaf has a pleasant wheaty and fermentation aroma.

Taste

The aroma and taste of a loaf are closely allied characteristics. Taste is actually the taste of the loaf when eaten. It can be described as wheaty, sweet, sour, flat or rancid.

Bread Faults: Their Causes and Remedy

There are a number of factors which are responsible for creating faults in bread. Major factors which adversely influence the quality of bread are:

1. Inadequate gluten in flour
2. Misappropriate quantities and inferior quality of raw material
3. Poor diastatic activity of flour
4. Improper time and temperature of fermentation, proofing and baking
5. Wrong methods of manipulation of dough *i.e.* knocking-back, cutting and moulding
6. Inadequate cooling of bread
7. Improper storage of bread and
8. Lack of knowledge about the principles of hygiene.

A thorough knowledge about raw material and its functions, adequate understanding of bread making procedure, control of temperature and humidity at different stages of bread making and above all personal skill and experience of baker goes a long way in avoiding faults in bread.

Major Faults in White Bread

The following are some of the major faults in bread:

Volume

Volume of the bread is the outcome of adequate conditioning of gluten and sufficient gassing power of the dough at the time of baking. A small volume of bread may be due to:

1. Tight dough
2. Little yeast and fermentation time
3. Low temperature
4. Under proofing
5. Lack of diastatic activity
6. Bran contamination
7. Undermixing or overmixing
8. Very high temperature during baking
9. Too long intermediate proof
10. Addition of excess of salt
11. Use of weak flour
12. Use of less amount of shortening

Excess volume can be due to:

1. Overfermentation
2. Lack of salt in formula
3. Excessive yeast and proofing time
4. Loose moulding
5. Lack of temperature in oven or cool oven

Crust Colour

Crust colour will be too pale under following conditions:

1. Crust colour is controlled by the amount of sugar in dough. If sugar is less in the formula, crust colour will be too pale whereas too much sugar will darken the crust colour.

2. If yeast is added in excess, it will consume more of sugar and bread will be light and pale brown.
3. Insufficient temperature will cause lack of crust colour
4. Insufficient humidity during proofing
5. Under baking
6. Oven temperature is low
7. Poor diastatic activity of flour
8. Old dough

Crust colour shall be too dark due to:

1. Addition of more sugar in the formula
2. Addition of more milk in the formula
3. Overbaking
4. High oven temperature
5. Old dough (Excessively fermented and conditioned)

Leathery Crust

The crust of bread should be crisp and should easily break but if the crust becomes tough and is not easily pulled, it is leathery. It is due to insufficient conditioning of gluten or if crust absorbs lot of moisture.

Blisters Under the Crust

This can be due to:

1. Over proofing
2. Excessive steam or humidity in proof box
3. Improper handling during baking
4. If bread is baked in excessive humidity
5. Moulding under pressure or tight moulding

Under above situations, the moisture deposits on the surface of bread. Due to this increase in moisture content, the gluten of the affected spots acquires more stretchability and forms blisters under pressure of expanding gas during baking. Sometimes if moulding is under pressure or it is tight, some air bubbles will be entrapped under thin film of gluten. These air bubbles will expand during proofing and cause blisters during baking.

Very Thick Crust

Too thick crust can be because of:

1. Use of less amount of shortening in the formula
2. Less sugar in the formula
3. Less moisture during proofing
4. Low oven temperature
5. Overbaking

Flinty Crust or Shell Tops

Sometimes crust of bread is hard and breaks like an egg shell called as flinty crust. This is generally with strong wheats where the flour is insufficiently fermented. Other factors for this fault are stiff dough formation, too young dough, inadequate pan proof and excessive top heat in oven.

Wild Break

A smooth break shred is desirable. If the gluten is not adequately conditioned during fermentation, the top crust instead of rising gradually will burst open under pressure of expanding gas. Insufficient proofing of bread and excessive heat are likely to give wild break.

Sticky Crumb

It may be due to sprout damaged wheat flour if it is proved or baked in excessive humid conditions and underbaked. Rope disease also causes sticky crumb.

Crumbiness of the Crumb

When the dough is adequately fermented, it gives elasticity to bread crumb otherwise the breadcrumb will break into small fragments while slicing called crumbiness. It may be due to:

1. Too slack or tight dough
2. Excessive use of fat
3. Low salt content
4. Excessive use of mineral improvers.

Holes and Tunnels in Bread

If for any reason gluten strands break during proofing or baking, a chain reaction starts and neighbouring gluten strands will also break. It may be due to:

1. Use of weak flour
2. High yeast content in formula
3. Improper dispersion of ingredients
4. Too hot oven base
5. Undermixing or overmixing
6. Unbalanced formula
7. Young (insufficient fermentation and conditioning) or cold dough
8. Excessive dusting of flour
9. High temperature during proofing
10. Over proofing

Irregularity

Loose moulding or moulding with uneven pressure results in large air pockets in the folds and causes irregularity of shape. An even pressure and proper moulding is required.

Deficiency of Bloom

The most important factor for bloom is diastatic activity of flour. Sufficient sugar production and formation of dextrin during baking impart bloom. Malt can be added to improve bloom.

Colour Spots

It is due to carelessness on the part of baker, unclean moulds, handling of bread with unclean hands or baking gloves, unclean cooling racks, falling of soot from chimney into the oven etc. Pressure of undissolved sugar crystals or dry milk pellets cause colour spots in bread.

Poor Flavour and Taste

These can be due to:

1. Improper storage of raw ingredients used
2. Poor quality ingredients
3. Off-flavoured ingredients
4. Unfermented or overfermented dough

5. Use of excess of salt
6. Old dough (fermented and conditioned for too long)
7. Dirty moulds or pans
8. Underbaking or overbaking
9. Cooling of bread under unsanitary conditions.

Condensation Marks

If the bread is not allowed to cool properly before wrapping, some water vapours will deposit in the crumb causing dark patches. The bread should be thoroughly cooled before packing.

Poor Keeping Quality

This may be due to:

1. Poor quality ingredients
2. Improper storage of ingredients
3. Too lean formula
4. Stiff dough
5. Old dough (fermented and conditioned for too long)
6. Over proofing
7. Low oven temperature
8. Bread cooled too long before wrapping

Ropy Bread

If the dough gets contaminated with *B. mesentericus*, bread ropiness is caused. The spores of these bacteria are not killed by heat during baking. A sticky, gummy material which can be pulled into threads develops in the centre of the loaf 1 to 3 days after baking. The bread also develops an off-flavour.

An analysis of the various causes as mentioned above can help the baker to understand the reason of a particular fault. By the process of elimination, then he can rectify the defect.

Staling of Bread

If the bread is stored for a number of days, certain changes occur which cause staling of the bread. These are:

1. Crust staling
2. Crumb staling

Crust Staling

In the fresh stale, crust is relatively dry, crisp and brittle. Upon staling it shall become soft and leathery. It shall lose its original aroma and flavour. An off-flavour shall be developed. During crust staling, moisture from the crumb is transferred to the crust and due to hygroscopic properties, the crust absorbs moisture and becomes soft and leathery. The use of wax paper in wrapping favours the crust staling as it prevents moisture loss from the crust.

Crumb Staling

Due to loss of moisture, the crumb becomes hard and more crumbly. Flavour gets deteriorated. Staling is associated with the gradual and spontaneous aggregation of the amylopectin giving rise to crystalline structure. This aggregation of amylopectin is less firm than that involved in the retrogradation of amylose and can be reversed by warming the bread to about 50°C. Bread stored at low temperature (0°C) hardens to a greater extent than that stored at higher temperature (40-45°). But the bread stored at high temperature develops an off-flavour and the crumb turns brown.

Chapter 16
Baked Products from Soft Wheat

Unlike hard wheat flour, which is mainly used for bread making, soft wheat has more than one major use. The products made from soft wheat flour can be grouped into cookies, cakes, crackers and pastry confections. However, there is a wide variation within each of these groups (Fig. 16.1). The principal basis for most of these products is wheat flour but other cereal flours *viz.* oats, rye, rice, maize etc. alone or in combination with wheat flour can add to the variety of above mentioned products.

Cookies

Cookies are one of the best known quick snack products. Cookies are often referred to as small sweet cakes. They are characterized by a formula high in sugar and shortening and low in water. Similar products in our country are called biscuits. In UK, cookie means something softer and thicker baked good while biscuit refers to a flat and crisp baked good. In USA, cookie covers any flat, crisp, baked good. The biscuits made in USA are more accurately defined as chemically leavened bread.

The diversity of cookie products is quite wide, they vary not only

Type of mix		Hard dough		Short dough		Batter		
Product category		Crackers	Semisweet products	Pastry products	Short sweet products	Wafers	Crisp bread	Cakes
Usual ingredient proportions	Flour	100	100	100	100	100	100 (rye)	100
	Fat	5–20	12–22	45–75	20–60	0–4	0	0–80
	Sugar	0–2	20–35	0–10	20–75	0–2	0	100–170
	Egg	0	0	0	0–10	0–3	0	50–125
Examples		Cream crackers Water biscuits American soda crackers Snack crackers	Tea & coffee biscuits Petit beurre For cream sandwiches	Pie crusts Puff pastries Danish pastries	For cream sandwiches For halfcoating Shortbread and shortcakes Digestive American style cookies Gingersnaps	Ice cream cones Plain ice cream wafers For cream sand-wiches	Tradit-ional rye crisp bread	Plain & flavored sponges Victoria sandwich Madiera Swiss roll Angel cake Slab cake Traditional & celebration fruit cake

Fig. 16.1: Baked Product Classification

in formula but also in type of manufacture. Cookies are classified according to the mixing method and the recipe adopted. These may be divided into two categories.

Batter Type Cookies

These include drop cookies, snaps and short breads. The recipe of these cookies is similar to cake except less proportion of eggs, milk and water are included. This helps to mix the doughs to a desired consistency to retain the cookie shape when deposited on baking sheets.

Drop cookies are made by dropping the mixture from a spoon onto a baking tray and baked in an oven at 190°C for 10 to 15 min until nicely browned. These cookies are soft and moist when baked.

Stiff batter cookies or snaps contain less liquids *i.e.* egg, milk and water. Due to less moisture, crisp baked product is obtained. Rolled cookies are made from refrigerated stiff dough. The dough is rolled and cut into the desired shapes and baked.

Short bread cookies are similar to snaps, only they have more shortening which provides them a richer texture. Butter upto 50 per cent alongwith shortening can be used and it imparts characteristic flavour to the finished products.

Foam Type Cookies

These include meringue and sponge cookies. Meringue cookies are made with dough prepared by beating egg whites until stiff and adding sugar slowly. Other ingredients like dried nuts, desiccated coconut and flour are folded in and the batter dropped on a sheet and baked. Care should be taken in blending the other ingredients so as not to force air out of the mixture.

Sponge cookies are made like meringue cookies, using the whole egg rather than egg white.

On the basis of the way the dough is placed on the baking band, cookies are classified into 4 types (Fig. 16.2):

1. Rotary mold cookies
2. Cutting machine cookies
3. Wire cut cookies
4. Sugar wafers

Rotary Mold Cookies

For this type of cookie, the dough is forced into moulds as rotating roll (Fig. 16.3). As the roll completes half turn, the dough is extracted from the cavity and placed on the band for baking. The consistency of the dough must be such that it will feed into the cavity, but still be extracted from the cavity without being distorted. During baking the cookie should neither rise nor spread (it will distort the design embossed on the cookie).

In this sugar and shortening contents are high (Table 16.1). Total moisture is less than 20 per cent. The typical dough is crumbly, lumpy and stiff with no elasticity. During mixing the gluten in the dough should not develop.

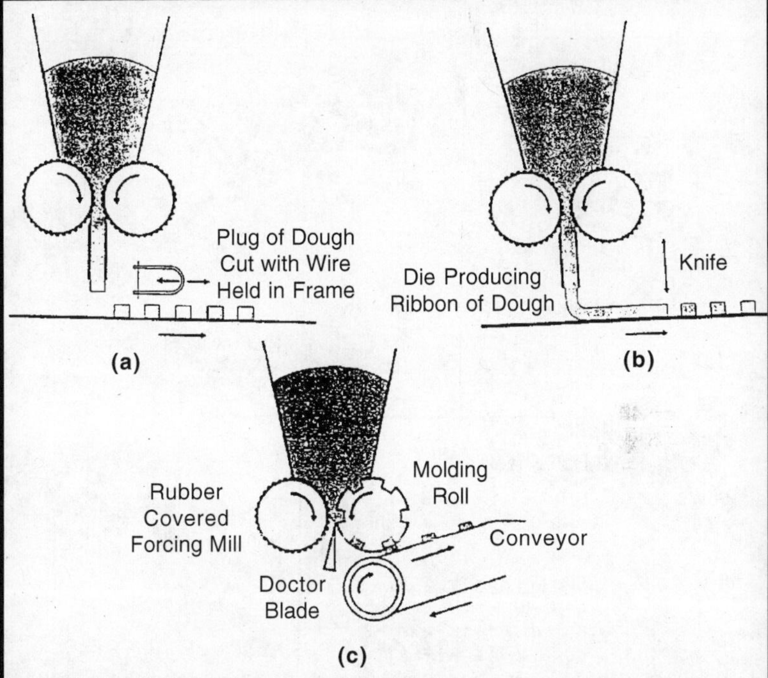

Fig. 16.2: (a) Wire Cut, (b) Rout Press, (c) Rotary Molder

Table 16.1: Typical Formula for Rotary-mold Cookies

Ingredients	*Parts**
Soft wheat flour	100
Sugar	20
Shortening	25
Acid cream (Cream of tartar)	0.5
Sodium bicarbonate	0.5
Salt	1.5
Condensed milk	6.0
Whole egg	3.5
Butter	1.2
Lecithin	0.3
Malt	1.4
Water (variable)	About 10.0

* Based on flour

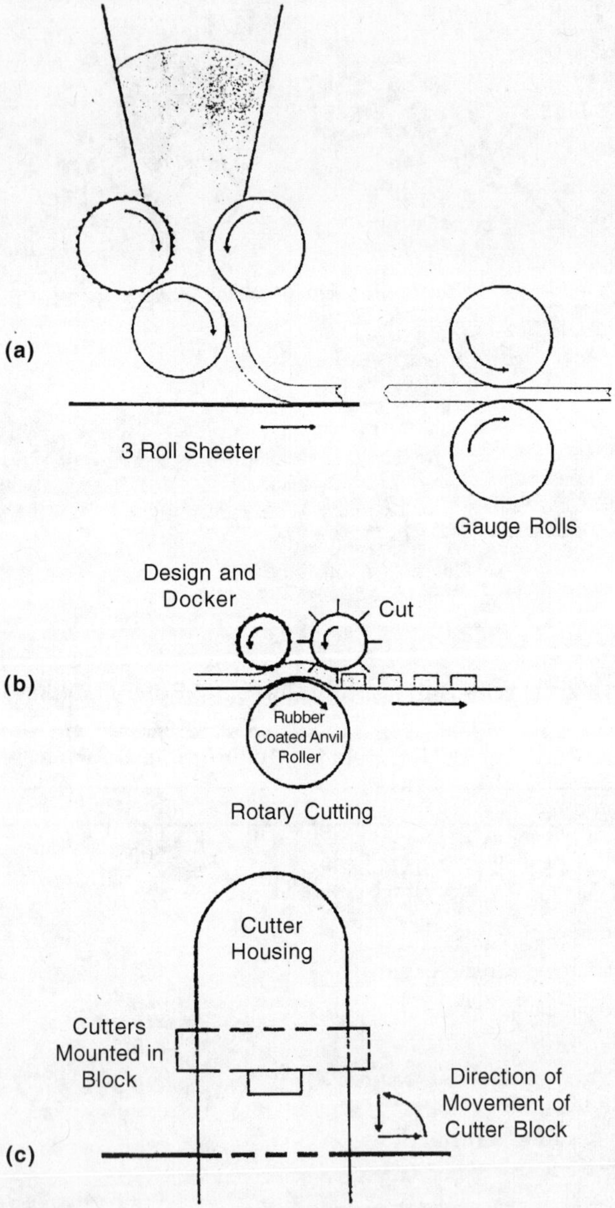

Fig. 16.3: (a) Sheeting and Gauging, (b) Rotary Cutting, (c) Reciprocating Cutting

Cutting Machine Cookie

The dough is made into a continuous sheet and the product is cut from it. Sugar is low. Gluten is developed so there is no spread and distortion during baking. Water content is more than in the formula used for a rotary mold.

Wire-Cut Cookies

A relatively soft dough is extruded through an orifice and cut to size, usually by wire. A typical formula may contain 50-75 per cent sugar, 50-60 per cent shortening and upto 15 per cent eggs. Wire-cut cookies rise and spread when they are baked. Final size is determined by formula and flour. A wide range of cookies can be made by using wire-cut mechanism.

Sugar Wafers

In real sense, these do not fit into the category of cookies, but it does not fit elsewhere. Ice cream cones and sugar wafers differ from other cookies. The formula contains no sugar, essentially no fat and an excess of water (Table 16.2).

Table 16.2: Typical Formula for Wafers or Ice Cream Cones

Ingredients	*Parts**
Flour	100
Water	135
Sodium bicarbonate	0.375
Salt	0.5
Lecithin	1.5
Coconut oil	1

* Based on flour

Cookie Ingredients

Flour

For cookies to be of premium quality, soft wheat flour containing 8 to 10 per cent protein and less than 0.4 per cent ash content is ideally suited. The colour of the flour may be a little darker but this type of flour will allow the cookies to have a better spread. Sifting of flour with other ingredients is necessary.

Sugar

A cookie with a higher percentage of the correct type of sugar will spread more than the one with a comparatively low amount of sugar. Powdered sugar does not give a cookie any appreciable spread. Even large sugar crystals will not appreciably melt during baking and consequently will not give the required spread to a cookie. A fine granulated sugar gives a cookie maximum spread during baking and retains its original granulation to a greater extent. Apart from causing the spreading action, the granulated sugar is generally used to promote cracked surface on the cookie. Sugar alone cannot produce the desired crispness but when combined with the shortening will give a cookie the desired crispness and shortness (desirable tenderness and pleasing eating quality).

Shortening

Regular hydrogenated fat with a bland flavour gives good result. Straight mixture of butter and vegetable shortening imparts better paste to the cookies. Fat due to its shortening or mellowing action on gluten also helps in promoting the spread.

Eggs

If added, give structure, impart flavour and taste. If used in large amounts, will result in giving cookie a rise rather than spread. Egg yolks produce a tender cookie than whole eggs, but care should be taken to supplement with little extra moisture from either water or milk or both.

Milk Solids

Milk solids have a binding action on the flour proteins. When milk solids are used in large amount, they cause less spread of the cookies.

Chemical Leavening Agents

Baking powder is widely used for leavening of the cookie mixture. It controls the spread and imparts lightness to the product. If sodium bicarbonate (baking soda) is used as a leavening agent, care should be taken not to use in excess as it will impart alkaline flavour. Ammonium bicarbonate should be used in products which are quite dry after baking, otherwise ammonia odour will be retained if the product is moist.

Suggestions in Cookie Making

1. Cookie dough should be mixed just enough to blend the ingredients homogenously. When the dough is slightly over-mixed, gluten tends to develop which will retard the spread of the cookies. Improper mixing of ingredients will produce cookies that are spotted.
2. Proper mixing of sugar and shortening is very important for optimum cookie spread. If sugar and shortening are creamed too much, this will reduce the size of sugar crystals which will then dissolve by greater extent. The finer (smaller) crystals or dissolved sugar checks spreading, resulting in smaller and compact cookies.
3. Cookies should be placed far enough apart on the pans to avoid sticking during baking. Sticking produces ragged edges and excess breakage and appearance is spoiled.
4. If the cookie dough is cut thick, the finished cookie will lose the appearance and the flavour also.
5. When the pans are greased, the cookie will spread more. To retard spreading, dust the pans with flour after they are greased.
6. Pans used for cookies should be cool as warm pans will melt the fat in the cookies resulting in inferior products.
7. If cookie dough is made up ahead of time and stored in a cool place, then these doughs should be made little softer as these will tighten up during storage. Such doughs can be handled more easily giving the finished products more tenderness.
8. In order to obtain the best results, cookies should be removed from the oven while they are still soft as they will continue to bake on hot pans.
9. To avoid chances of breakage, cookies should be removed from the pans when they are still little warm.
10. If raisins and currants are used for toppings, they should be soaked in malt solution (1 part malt + 10 parts water). This will help prevent them from being burnt.

Problems in Cookie Making

Cookie Dough Crumbles When Handled and Rolled

This occurs when formula is not balanced and large percentage of fat is not properly distributed during mixing. When fat is overcreamed, it will cause softness and tenderness. Dough can be refrigerated to overcome this.

Cookie Dough is Soft and Sticky

Overcreaming can result in this when flour is folded, all fat particles are not covered by flour. So added mixing is required. An excess of liquid also makes sticky dough. Dough mixed at high speed also results in overmixing.

Cookie Dough is Tough and Resists Rolling Out

This is due to overmixing and gluten development. If protein is high, 20 per cent cornstarch can be added.

Cookies Shrink After Cutting

Fat and sugar are low and liquid content is high. Allow the dough to relax before shrinkage.

Cookies Spread Too Much During Baking

Due to excess sugar in the cookie formula.

Cookies Have Uneven Colour and May Have Spots

This is due to improper mixing which fails to distribute sugar and syrup evenly.

Cookies Vary in Size and Shape

It is due to improper mixing.

Crackers

Cracker is a term used for biscuits of low sugar and fat content, frequently bland or savory. They are usually made from a strong flour and developed dough. They generally contain 100 per cent flour, 5-20 per cent fat and 0-2 per cent sugar. The doughs generally contain low levels of water (20-30 per cent). The leavening agent is either water vapour or a chemical leavening. Crackers and crisp breads are used as bread substitutes usually topped with savory foods like cheese, meat preparations and/or salad items.

Saltine crackers are distinguished by their long fermentation time and their particularly light and flaky texture. They are made by a sponge and dough process using a formula given in Table 16.3.

Table 16.3: Typical Saltine Cracker Formula[a b]

Ingredients	*Sponge (%)*	*Dough (%)*
Flour	65.0	35.0
Water	25.0	—
Yeast	0.4	—
Lard	—	11.0
Salt	—	1.8
Soda	—	0.45

a Ingredients based on flour weight.

b A 'buffer' is often added to the sponge to inoculate the system.

The sponge fermentation is carried out for 16 hrs and during this fermentation, pH is dropped from about 6.0 to about 4.0. An inoculum called 'buffer' which is an old sponge, is used to obtain the pH drop. The quality of saltine crackers varies widely depending upon the activity and amount of buffer used. Much of the texture and desirability of saltine crackers is because of their low moisture content. They generally contain about 2 per cent moisture fresh from the oven.

As compared to saltine crackers, snack crackers contain more shortening and much higher levels of flavouring materials. They generally do not contain yeast and are not given an extended fermentation period. They are chemically leavened. The doughs are mixed once with the ingredients, allowed to rest, sheeted and laminated, and cut and docked. The texture of snack crackers is denser than that of saltinery.

Biscuits

This is one processed wheat product which has found acceptability in rural areas in our country. The raw materials for biscuits are flour, sugar and shortening. For protein enriched biscuits, soy flour or peanut flour or protein isolate can be added at 15-25 per cent levels to provide 10 per cent extra protein. Other ingredients include leavening agents, vitamins, minerals and flavours. In sweet biscuits, cane sugar is added while in salty biscuits, sodium chloride (0.5-0.1 per cent) is added. Formulae for sweet and salty biscuits are given in Table 16.4.

Table 16.4: Formulae for Sweet, Salty and Protein Enriched Biscuits

Ingredients	*Sweet (Parts)*	*Salt (Parts)*	*Protein Enriched (Parts)*
Soft wheat flour	100	100	100
Shortening	10	10	10
Cane sugar	20	5	20
Salt	—	0.6	—
Skim milk powder/Soybean flour or peanut flour	—	—	30
Sodium bicarbonate	0.4	0.4	0.4
Ammonium carbonate	0.2	0.2	0.2
Flavour	0.1	0.2	1.2
Calcium phosphate	—	—	0.5
Vitamin premix	—	—	1.2

In the manufacturing of biscuits on commercial scale, ammonium carbonate or bicarbonate or sodium bicarbonate are used. Other leavening agents include baking powder containing sodium bicarbonate and acid salts.

The steps involved in biscuit making are:

Mixing and Kneading

In a mechanical mixer, weighed amount of sifted flour, sugar, shortening and flavouring agents are added and mixed. Water and baking powder are added and mixed continuously to obtain a dough of desired consistency. Optimum kneading (10-20 min) produces biscuits with fine structure, smooth crust and better appearance; overkneading produces a compact toughened product. Under-kneaded doughs give biscuits that are very tender, coarse in texture, small in volume and having a rough crust.

Sheeting and Shaping

The dough is rolled into sheets of desired thickness by passing through pairs of rolls. The rolled dough sheet is cut by mechanically worked stamped divider fitted with dies.

Baking and Cooling

The cut biscuits move forward on a continuous belt from which they are automatically transferred to a continuous plate sheet or wire mesh bands travelling through the ovens. The length of ovens depends upon the production capacity. The biscuits are baked at 450°F for 15 min and cooled after baking.

Packaging

The biscuits should be packaged in moisture and grease proof cellophane or metal foil laminated packaging.

Cakes and Pastries

Cakes are characterized by high level of sugar in the formula in which starch gelatinizes during baking. Cakes set when baked giving a light product.

Cake Types

There are 2 types of cakes:

Shortened

Those containing shortening or butter as an essential ingredient. They are leavened with baking powder. Examples are chocolate cake, pound cake etc.

Unshortened Cake

Those which do not contain fat as a basic ingredient. They are leavened by air or steam. Example is sponge cake.

Cake Making Ingredients

They are generally classified as:

Essential Ingredients

Flour, sugar, shortening and eggs.

Optional Ingredients

Baking powder, milk, fruits etc.

Above ingredients are also classified according to function which they perform in cake making. This classification is as under:

Structure Builders

They provide the structures and texture to the cake *e.g.* flour, eggs and milk.

Tenderizers

They provide softness and shortness in the cake *e.g.* fat, sugar and baking powder.

Moisteners

They provide moisture and keeping quality *e.g.* milk, water, eggs, syrup.

Driers

They absorb and retain moisture and provide the body to the cake. They are flour, milk solids and starches.

Flavours

They provide natural flavours. They are cocoa, chocolate, eggs and other natural flavour bearing ingredients.

Individual ingredients to be used in cake making are discussed as under:

Flour

Flour builds structure of cake and holds other ingredients together in an evenly distributed condition in the cake. Flour for cake making should have protein content of 7 to 9 per cent. Short patent flour made from soft wheat is ideally suited for cake making. Flour should have fine granulation which has the beneficial effect on the fineness of the grain structure of cake. Cake flours are bleached to a greater degree in order to brighten its colour. This extra bleaching has also a modifying action on gluten forming proteins as well as the pH of the flour which is lowered to approximately 5.2. At low pH, starch gelatinizes faster.

Sugar

Sucrose is most commonly used sweetening agent in cake making. Sugar used for all types of cakes should be of fine granulation to ensure an even grain and soft texture in cakes. This type of sugar dissolves very readily and produces a smooth creamy mass. Large sugar crystals produce a coarse texture. Sugar has a tenderizing action on flour proteins and makes the cakes tender. It helps to retain moisture in cakes and improve its shelf life. The golden crust colour of cakes is due to caramalization of sugar. Sugars lower the caramalization point of the batter, allowing the cake crust to colour at a lower temperature.

Shortening

Shortening for cakes should have good creaming properties, a neutral flavour and odour. It should have excellent emulsifying properties and should be white in colour. It should be elastic when used at temperatures between 70 and 75°F.

Fats have a tenderizing action on flour proteins and thus make the cake tender. It is the fat part of the batter which holds innumerable air cells incorporated during creaming operation. These air cells have a tenderizing influence on cakes. As a moisture retainer, fat helps to keep the cake moist and thus improves the shelf life of cakes. Fat used in cake making should be of plastic nature which could incorporate and hold minute air cells during creaming operation. Granular fats do not fulfil this function and should be avoided. Fat should be able to maintain its plasticity. Too hard fats will not cream up well while too soft fats will not be able to retain the aeration. For cakes to retain their moist eating quality for longer time, emulsifiers can be added in the fat *e.g.* GMS, sorbitol, polysorbate, lecithin, either singly or in combination.

Butter is considered to be best of all baking shortenings from a flavour standpoint. The creaming quality of butter is rather poor. Cakes made with butter are generally lower in volume and have coarser grain than those made with a high quality shortening with good quality creaming characteristics. Therefore, some bakers use a combination of butter and shortening in the cake formula.

Eggs

Eggs and flour form a skeleton to support the framework of a cake. Eggs by themselves during mixing perform this function. They provide moisture to cakes. Lecithin of egg yolk acts as emulsifier and later add to colour. Eggs improve the taste, flavour and nutritional value.

Milk

Milk when used as dry milk solids adds richness and structure to the cake. Milk proteins have a binding action on flour proteins which creates toughness in cakes. Lactose present in milk improves the crust colour and moisture retention capacity of cakes. Milk serves to improve the flavour and nutritive value of cake and is also a good moisture retaining agent.

Water

Water whether added as such or in the form of liquid milk hydrates flour proteins forming gluten which builds up the structure of cakes. Formation of gluten, release of CO_2 gas from baking powder and formation of vapor pressure are made possible by presence of water. These factors are important in regulating the volume of cakes. Water regulates the consistency of batter which affects the volume and texture of cakes. Shelf life of cakes is determined by the amount of moisture retained in cake which eventually depends upon the amount of water used in the formula.

Salt

Salt enhances the natural flavour of other ingredients used in cake making and thus improves the overall flavour of the cakes. It also improves the crust colour of cakes by lowering the caramalization temperature of sugar. Salt helps to cut down the sweetness of the cakes. Salt being hygroscopic helps in retention of considered complementary to each other. It may be used @ 0.7 to 1.2 per cent depending on flavour.

Leavening Agents

Cakes are leavened by three ways:

Mechanical Aeration

When fat is whipped with sugar, the mixture is filled with minute air cells which expand under the action of heat giving volume to the product.

Chemical Aeration

Baking powders of various types, when moistened with water and heated, evolve CO_2 gas which expands during baking and imparts volume to cakes.

Vapour Pressure

Water which is evenly distributed in the batter, forms vapor under the action of heat. This water vapor exerts pressure as a result of which the cakes are leavened.

The manner of leavening depends upon the type of cake being made in regards to richness of formula, consistency of batter and baking temperature.

Flavour

It is good to use a small amount of good flavour in cakes. Type of flavour varies with the cake. In general, flavouring ingredients are of three basic types: spices, extracts and emulsions. The spices are granular powders of roots, bark, seeds and blossoms of aromatic plants. Extracts are alcoholic solutions containing aromatic flavours. Emulsions are colloidal systems of volatile, essential oils dispersed with water and stabilized by gum plants.

Cake Making Methods

Following methods are used for making cakes:

1. Sugar-batter method
2. Flour-batter method
3. Blending method
4. Boiled method
5. Sugar-water method
6. All in process

Sugar-batter Method

In this method, all the fat and sugar is creamed together. Shortenings used for cake making should be plastic in nature. Granular fats should be avoided which have very poor whipping quality. Very often a combination of fats like hydrogenated shortening, butter or margarine is used in order to acquire specific characteristics in cakes. Fats should be at room temperature. Very hard shortening will not cream up well, while too soft shortening will not be able to retain aeration. Shortening used for cake making should not melt by heat produced due to friction during creaming process.

Fat should be first creamed together (either by machine or by hand) in order to blend them thoroughly. Then sugar is added gradually containing the creaming process. All the sugar should not be added to fat at a time as this will adversely affect the aeration process and it may take extra time to achieve the desired result. When adequate aeration is achieved, the mixture becomes very light and brighter in the appearance.

Next flour is added in the mixture. Flour should be sifted with baking powder, corn flour, calcium propionate for thorough dispersal. This is important stage. Slight mishandling of mixture will spoil the cake. There should be minimum possible mixing action in order to avoid toughening of gluten. Flour should not be added at once, but demanded in two or three portions and each portion should be added at a time with just necessary movement of hand. If mixer is used, flours should be mixed in batter at low speed.

When all the mixture flour is mixed, the remaining liquid is added. This liquid brings the batter to a definite level of fluidity which is necessary for even and gradual rise of cake during baking operation. Liquid helps to reduce toughening of gluten. The batter is now ready for panning and baking.

Flour-Batter Method

In this method, fat and quantity of flour not exceeding the weight of fat is creamed together. Fat should be in smooth and plastic state and the flour should be added gradually. The whole mass is whipped till it becomes light and fluffy. Eggs and an equal quantity of sugar is whipped to a stiff froth. This is added to the concerned mixture of fat and flour. Although there is less risk of curdling of batter, still the egg mixture should be added in small portions at a time and after each addition, mixed thoroughly. Then remaining sugar is dissolved in milk or water and added to the mixture. Any colour or flavour is also added along with this liquid. Lastly, remaining flour sifted with baking powder is added and mixed gently. Vigorous mixing will knock out the air cells and cake will be of poor volume.

Advantages

As a major portion of flour is coated with fat before any liquid is added, the development of gluten is avoided. This fact makes it possible to use slightly strong flour which otherwise, are unsuitable for cake making. Very small quantity of flour remains to be added at the last stage of mixing which avoids possibly of much gluten development. Egg and sugar are whisked to a stiff consistency and fat and flour is creamed to a light and fluffy consistency. Flour-batter method is specially suited for making lean cakes which do not contain much fat or egg and most of aeration is achieved through baking powder.

Blending Method

This method is suitable for making high ratio cakes in which quantity of sugar is more than quantity of flour. Emulsified shortening, flour, baking powder and salt are whipped together to a very light and fluffy consistency. Sugar, milk or any other liquid colour and flavours are mixed together and added to previous mixture. Eggs are added and the whole mass is mixed to a smooth batter (High ratio cakes).

Boiled Method

Butter or margarine is placed in a bowl and heated till it melts. Remove from heat and add 2/3 (or less) flour and mix thoroughly. Egg and sugar is whisked to a stiff sponge. Colour and flavour may be added while whisking the sponge. This sponge is added to the fat-flour mixture in about 4-5 equal parts. After each addition of sponge, it should be mixed thoroughly. Remaining flour can be added at this stage. When batter is smooth, put it in moulds and bake.

Sugar-Water Method

In this method, all the sugar and approximately half the quantity of water is agitated in the bowl till all sugar is dissolved, then the remaining ingredients except eggs are added and the mixture is well agitated to acquire aeration. Lastly egg is added and mixture is cleared. Due to more aeration and better emulsification the cakes have better texture and longer shelf life.

All in Process

In this process, all the ingredients are put into the mixing bowl together. Aeration of the mixture is achieved by controlling the speed of mixture as well as the mixing time. Wire whip is used for this operation. One should use emulsified type of shortening and special cake flours (fine granulation and low pH). After adding all the ingredients, the mixing is carried out as follows:

Half a Minute at Low Speed

This is done so that all the dry ingredients are moistened without flying off from the bowl.

Two Minute at Fast Speed

All the ingredients break and are incorporated evenly throughout the mass. The batter is also well aerated.

Two Minutes at Medium Speed

Aeration achieved during the second stage is not evenly disturbed in the batter. By mixing at medium speed the large air cells break up into smaller cells and the aeration of the mixture becomes even.

One Minute at Slow Speed

This is done in order eliminate any possible large air pockets and still finer breaking down of air cells.

Panning of Cake Batter

In greased pan, put the batter carefully so that no air is trapped. Only 2/3 height of moulds should be filled. Level the batter and load in oven as soon as possible.

Baking

Bake richer formula at low temperature and the lean formula at high temperature (375-400°F for 25-30 minutes).

Baking and Cooling Losses

About 12 per cent.

Characteristics of Cakes

Chief characteristics of cakes are as follows:

	External		*Internal*
1.	Volume	1.	Grain
2.	Colour of crust	2.	Colour of crumb
3.	Symmetry of form	3.	Aroma
4.	Character of crust	4.	Taste
		5.	Texture

External Characteristics

Volume

Volume of cakes is according to consumer preference. Cake should be well risen with slight convex top surface. Cake should not appear too small or too large for its weight.

Colour of Crust

Pleasing golden brown colour is desirable. Too dark or too light or dull colour is not desirable. Crust must have a uniform colour, free from dark streaks or sugar spots or grease spots.

Symmetry of Form

Cakes should have symmetrical appearance. Peaking, crack on top surface, low sides, sunken or high centre, burst, caved in bottom or uneven top are undesirable characteristics of cakes.

Character of Crust

Crust should be thin and tender. It should not be rubbery, sticky or overmoist, too tender, tough or bustry crust is indicative of poor quality of cakes.

Internal Characteristics

Grain

The grain is the structure formed by the extended gluten strands including the area they surround. Grain will vary according to type of cake. Uniformity of the size of cells and thin cell walls are desirable qualities. Coarseness, thick cell wall, uneven size of grains, large holes and tunnels are indicative of poor grain. Grains should not be too open or too close.

Colour of Crumb

It should be lively, lusterous and uniform colour. It should be free from any streaks or dark patches. Grey, non uniform, dark, light or dull colour crumb will be undesirable.

Aroma

Aroma should be pleasant, rich, sweet and natural. It is not desirable to have any foreign aroma–*i.e.* aroma not produced by normal ingredients of cake. Flat, misty, strong or sharp aroma is indicative of poor quality of cake.

Taste

It should be pleasant, sweet and satisfying (no after taste or foreign taste) salt and soda in excessive amounts affect the taste adversely.

Texture

Texture denotes the pliability and smoothness of the crumb as felt by sense of touch. It depends on the physical condition of crumb and type of grain. A good texture is soft and velvety without weakness and should not be crumby. Rough, harsh, too compact, lumpy or too loose texture is not desired.

Cake Faults and Remedies

Reasons for faults in cake are due to:

1. Wrong quality of raw material
2. Improper balancing of formula
3. Operational mistakes

Wrong Quality of Raw Material

If strong flour is used–gluten will develop. This results in:

1. Small volume
2. Peaked top
3. Unslightly crack
4. Uneven texture
5. Cake will dry easily and stale rapidly

Mixing operation time should be minimized; 5 to 10 per cent corn flour can be used to dilute the gluten.

If flour is too weak

1. It will not be able to carry sugar and fat and cake will be poor in volume. Unable to carry normal amount of liquid.
2. Crumb at the base will be compact. Fruits will sink at bottom.
3. Crumbly texture will result.

Sugar

Very large crystals of sugar will not dissolve during mixing and cake will have harsh crumb, poor eating quality and rapid staling. There must be sufficient water in the formula to dissolve the sugar. Other defect like white speck occurs on top crust which spoils the appearance of cakes. Too large or too small crystals of sugar are not desirable as they do not cream up well and texture and volume are not good.

Shortening

Shortening must be smooth and plastic. It should cream up well and hold the air cells which are incorporated during creaming. Granular shortening will not cream up and are not capable of holding air cells. Cake will be poor in volume and have coarse texture. If shortening melts during mixing operation aeration will be lost, affecting the volume and texture adversely.

Eggs

Weak and watery eggs have poor wrapping quality and curdle the batter and result in poor volume and texture.

Baking Powder

Baking powder should be stored in cool, dry place in air tight containers.

Fruits

Wash and dry before adding because dirty fruits discolour the cake. Fruits must be properly prepared.

Improperly Balanced Formula

Excessive sugar may cause excessive volume with open texture and cake are too tender to cut. Too little sugar will produce a very close grain and texture. Top crust sets earlier than the inner portions. So when inner portion expands, it will cause an ugly crack in the top crust and cake will have pale brown crust colour.

Lack of egg will make cakes too tender to cut specially high ratio cake. Lack of egg results in less air incorporation and reduced volume of cakes. Grain will be closed and compact. Heat penetration will be poor, crust will be light coloured, thin and sticky. Excessive eggs impart abnormal volume to the cake. The crust will be dark, thick and will peel off as a flake. Grain will be open and coarse. Texture will be rough and dry. Excess volume will cause moisture evaporation and thus making cake dry.

Baking Powder

Lack of baking powder will produce cakes having less volume and flat on top. There will be poor heat which results in penetration of light colour, tough, thick and sticky crust. Grain will be like solid unbaked mass. Excess baking powder produces excessive gas. So in the end, cake will collapse. Cake will have dark colour, it will be very tender and have dry crust. Grains are open and coarse. Texture is crumbly and fruit, if added, will sink down.

Operational Mistakes

1. Flour, baking powder and any other ingredients should be sifted sufficiently in order to ensure even blending. Uneven blending will result in substandard shape and texture.
2. While creaming, gradual addition of sugar in folds in small portion will ensure better and faster aeration.
3. Creaming operation should be carried till mixture is light and fluffy.
4. Eggs should be added gradually in small portions otherwise curdling results and aeration is lost.
5. After adding flour, minimum mixing. No gluten should develop.
6. While flour is added, simultaneously liquid should be added, otherwise gluten will develop.
7. A fruit cake batter should not be aerated much, fruits will sink down.
8. When batter is ready, stir it gently. Large air pockets will cause holes and tunnels in the cake.
9. After weighing load in oven immediately.
10. Avoid movement in oven till structure sets otherwise cake will collapse.
11. To make moist cake, put water in oven at least 15 minutes prior to baking.

Types of Cakes

Cakes are the most highly enriched members of the baked products family, with high proportions of sugar, egg and fat relative to flour (Table 16.5). This gives the cake its sweet taste and short, tender, moist texture. There are two broad categories of cakes:

1. The cakes which are higher in fat and whose structure depends on the fat-liquid emulsion created during batter mixing, for example fruit slab and ginger cakes.
2. The cakes with less fat or even none at all, but rich in egg that can aerate to a foam during mixing and give a characteristic spongy crumb to products such as angel food cake, sponge cake etc.

Table 16.5: Formula for Sponge Cake and Angel Cake

Ingredients	*Sponge cake*	*Angel cake*
Cake flour	100 g	90 g
Sugar	200 g	250 g
Egg	300 g	–
Egg white	–	–
Lemon juice	15 g	250 g
Water	30 g	30 g
Lemon rind (grated)	1 tbsp	–
Cream of tartar	–	4 g
Salt	1 g	1 g

Sponge Cake

Sponge cakes do not contain any added fat or shortening. Whole egg is used in sponge cake. Sponge cakes depend mainly upon the whipping of eggs for their lightness or aeration. Eggs are therefore, the most important ingredients in the sponge cakes. There are two types of sponge cakes:

Straight Sponge

These contain eggs, sugar, flour, salt and flavour.

Short Sponge

These contain the ingredients of a straight sponge and milk, shortening, water, leavening etc.

Soft bleached flour produced from soft wheat is generally used for making of sponge cakes. The flour used should be of good quality. To avoid flour pellets in the cake, it is best to sift the flour just before adding it to the beaten egg-sugar mixture.

Sugar has a tenderizing effect upon the cell structure of the cake and when too high a percentage is used, the cakes will sag in the centre or fall. Granulated sugar produces the best results. Equal parts of egg and sugar should be used for beating purposes. Any excess sugar should be either dissolved in the liquid or may be replaced by powdered sugar and sifted with the flour.

The formula for sponge cake is given in Table 16.5. Beat the whole egg. Add the sugar and beat again. Add salt, lemon juice, water and mix well. Add flour in small quantities and mix well. Add the flour in small quantities and mix well, till a smooth batter is obtained. Transfer the batter to cake pans and bake at 190°C for 30 minutes.

Angel Cake

It is a foam type cake which depends mainly on egg white protein for the bulk of the structure of the finished volume. It is a cake without shortening. The formula is given in Table 16.5.

The basic ingredients for angel cake are flour, sugar and egg. The other ingredients are salt, flavourings and cream of tartar or an acid. The flour used is weak and is often diluted with wheat starch. Flour alongwith egg whites provide the structure to the cake. Flour which is highly bleached, gives the cake finest grain, texture and whitest colour. Egg white gives best results when used at 60° to 65°F. They should be free from fats and yolk in order to give a good volume to the finished cake. Cream of tartar has a strengthening effect on egg whites. It is generally added before beating the egg whites. It also helps to retain the freshness of cake. Cream of tartar can be replaced by citric or tartaric acids. Granulated sugar gives good results. Salt is used for flavouring mainly but also gives strength to egg white.

Method involves the beating together of egg white, salt, cream of tartar and 60 per cent to 70 per cent of sugar which is added gradually. Continue beating till the desired stiffness is attained. Overbeating results in low volume owing to the rupture of overextended cell walls during baking process. The flavour is then added. The balance of the sugar which is thoroughly sifted with the flour is added lastly. The mixture is gently mixed until it is free from lumps. Transfer the batter to a baking cake tin and bake at 190°C for 30 minutes. A variety of angel cakes can be made by adding fruits and nuts. Fruits should be mixed with the flour before it is added to the mix as this helps to distribute the fruit thoroughly.

Pound Cake

It is a shortened cake with fat as an essential ingredient. Air is used for leavening purpose. The original formula for a pound cake was one pound each of flour, butter, eggs and sugar. This made a very heavy, rich and expensive cake.

Butter cake, chocolate, fruit cake etc. are generally shortened cakes leavened by carbon dioxide from baking powder. A good shortened cake has fine grain cells of uniform size, thin cell walls and a crumb that is more elastic than crumbly.

Other Baked Products

Other products made and sold alongside cakes are not in fact true cakes at all. These sweet dough products include swiss rolls, Danish pastry, doughnuts etc. They are generally yeast leavened and frequently contain fruit, nuts, syrups and jams.

Pastry

Pastry is characterized by a high fat and low water proportion, relative to flour, and little or no sugar. As with other short dough products, the objective is to prevent, as far as possible, flour protein from developing gluten and thus making a tough-textured product.

In most pastries, the first step is always the same *i.e.* rubbing some or all of the fat into the flour. This gives flour particles a waterproof coat, helping protect them from hydration later. Water can then be added, together with any other ingredients to bind the mixture to a paste. Variations on this main theme are many *e.g.* Danish pastry, puff pastry, flaked pastry, pie doughs etc.

Danish Pastry

The basic formula for Danish pastry is as under:

Ingredients	*Gms*	*Per cent*	*Remarks*
Yeast dried	30	3	Suspend yeast in water (if dried yeast is used) and dissolve. Dissolve yeast in warm water (110°F).
Yeast compressed	60	6	
Water	200	20	Dissolve milk, powder, sugar, salt and egg in water.
Milk powder	50	5	
Sugar	100	10	
Salt	15	1.5	
Egg	120	12	
Water (variable)	250	25	
Flour	1000	100	Sieve the flour and rub in the fat.
Shortening	50	5	Add the yeast ferment and the water in which milk powder sugar, salt and eggs have been dissolved to the flour. Mix well to develop a smooth dough. Keep the dough covered and allow for a short rest for 20-30 minutes.
Shortening	600	60	Cream it till it has a plastic consistency.

The further processing involves rolling out the dough after a short rest into a rectangular shape (1/4″ thick). Distribute one portion of the roll-in shortening evenly over two-thirds of the dough. Fold the uncovered portion of the dough to the centre of the shortening covered portion. Brush the excess dusting flour from the top portion of dough and fold the remaining shortening covered portion over the dough, similar to puff pastry. The dough is given time to relax. Again the dough is rolled out into a rectangular shape about ¼″ thick. Another portion of the roll-in fat is distributed over 2/3 of the dough. Folding of the dough is redone as mentioned above. After a short rest, the dough is to be rolled again to ¼″ thickness to distribute the remaining portion of the shortening. Folding of the dough has to be done on the same pattern. After a short rest the dough is ready to shape. Out of this dough, a variety of Danish pastries can be made. Filling can be of cake crumbs (130 g), icing sugar (50 g), whole egg (20 g), cinnamon powder (to taste) and milk (as required to give a spreading consistency).

Step 1

Roll out the oblong piece of as prepared above dough to a rectangular shape (approximately 8 ½″ × 12″).

Step 2

Spread the above mentioned filling over2/3 of the surface.

Step 3

Fold 1 over 2. After folding, brush top of 1 with egg wash. When washed, fold 3 over 1.

Step 4

After folding 3 over 1 and 2, place sealed side down and flatten slightly into a uniform strip.

Step 5

Now place on sheet pan in a horse shoe shape and cut.

Step 6

Bake at 450°F for 20-25 minutes.

Puff Pastry

Puff pastry is a rolled pastry in which layers of shortening are interleaved between layers and flaky layers are formed. The main ingredients used are flour (100 per cent), shortening (50 per cent), salt (1 per cent) and water (60 per cent). The method involves:

1. Mix a dough consisting of bread flour, salt and water.
2. Shape the dough into rectangular form and keep it in the refrigerator for some time. After cooling, roll the dough into one third inch thickness retaining the rectangular shape.
3. Cover the two thirds of rolled dough by spreading shortening and fold it over so that three layers of dough are separated by two layers of shortening. Roll the dough again to one third inch thickness and fold similarly into three layers.
4. Return the dough to the refrigerator and allow it to rest for about an hour. Always cover the dough from drying over.

Repeat the process of sheeting and folding and once again refrigerate the dough. Repeat the process once or twice.

5. After cooling down the dough, roll it and cut into desired shape. Bake at 400°F for 10 to 20 minutes.

Bread flour is generally used. To get best results, flour and shortening should be of same consistency. A melted or a soft shortening will not produce good results due to absorption of oil by the flour. Salt has a toughening effect upon gluten in the dough. Too much salt deteriorates the taste and lowers the volume of the product. Addition of lemon juice or vinegar during mixing helps to mellow the gluten. This facilitates the dough to roll out without difficulty and also makes the dough shorter.

Too much pressure during rolling should be avoided. The puff pastry should not be rolled too thin between foldings. The dough should always be given sufficient rest between the rollings for the gluten to relax. Care should be taken to roll the dough evenly. Too much of dusting flour should not be used. Excess flour should be brushed off the dough before folding which will help the folds to stick together. Sharp cutters and knives should be used while cutting the dough into desired shapes otherwise edges of the dough will be sealed with blunt tools, resulting in low volume product having uneven rise and tipping of flaky layers. The baking sheet should be dampened with cold water prior to deposition in the oven. This will prevent the product from shrinking during baking. If warm baking trays are used, shortening in the dough will melt before the products go into the oven, resulting in inferior product.

Short Pastry

Short pastry, like other pastries, is made from flour and fat mainly, some water and sometimes a little sugar. It forms the basis of many different confections, both savory and sweet, but best known are the tarts and pies. Fillings that set well, such as custards and jam in jam tarts, only require a single bottom crust, whereas more liquid fillings, like fruits and cooked meat in gravy, need both top and bottom crusts.

Short pastry is just that–short in texture and so not easily stretched or bent. It does not have a firm structure during baking, so it may often need the support of a tin or foil tray in the oven.

Hot Process Pie Paste

In hot process pie paste, sometimes known as 'stand-up' pastry, more water is used than with the other pastry types and it is added boiling hot. This has the effect of gelatinizing some of the starch in the flour and converting fat in the recipe to an oil. As the paste cools, the fat sets more, firmly than it was originally and so assists in maintaining shape and preventing collapse of the pies during filling and then baking. The gelatinized starch also aids the support function both by giving greater plasticity to the paste and by enabling pies to be raised more easily.

Wafers

The wafer is a thin, crisp and light textured product made by the very rapid baking, not of a dough but of a batter consisting of a liquid blend of flour, water and raising agent and sometimes small quantities of other ingredients.

The flour is usually of a short extraction and is generally from a white wheat. If the flour is too strong, the wafers are hard and flinty. The mixing of a wafer batter is usually a single-stage process or whisking action rather than the folding and kneading action required for most types of cookie dough. The objective of mixing is to evenly distribute flour particles and other ingredients into water without converting flour protein to gluten in the process. After mixing, batter is pumped to the wafer oven. This machine is different from the oven used for cakes and cookies or crackers (Fig. 16.4). The bake takes about 2 minutes. Cooling of a wafer sheet is done carefully so that both sides of the wafer lose their heat evenly, keeping the sheet flat and preventing warping. For wafers to be used for ice cream, the cooled sheets are stacked in groups and cut by being pushed through a set of stationary blades. For cream filled products, cream is applied to the surface of the whole sheet and a multilayered set of alternating cream and wafer is built up which can then go to the cutting machine.

Crisp Bread

Traditional crisp bread is usually made from rye flour. Of all the non-wheat cereals, rye most nearly resembles wheat. The grain size is similar, and protein in the endosperm can produce gluten of a sort, although without the strength associated with wheat. Traditional crisp bread is made from rye flour (whole flour) and

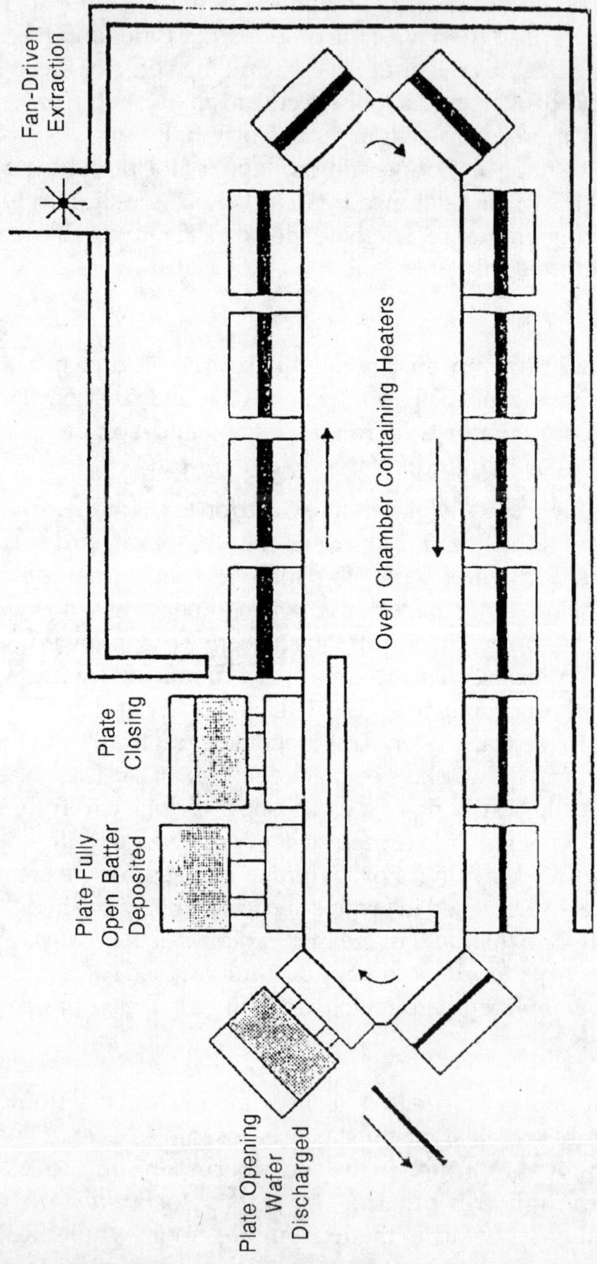

Fig. 16.4: Wafer Oven

water with salt and sometimes a little milk. Like wafers, water is the major ingredient, consisting of 55 per cent of the recipe. The product is neither fermented nor chemically raised and relies on expansion of air trapped in the dough and on the liberation of steam, which both occur during baking. Rapid mixing of the dough with aeration is the method used, and water is kept very cold so that it will hold more air in the dissolved form. It has a crisp texture derived from very rapid expansion during baking. The characteristic nutty, salty and slightly sour flavour of crisp bread makes it a very popular snack, usually as a carrier for savoury toppings.

Chapter 17

Macaroni Products

Macaroni products are also known as pasta products (alimentary pastes). They include:

1. Macaroni
2. Spaghetti
3. Noodles
4. Vermicelli

Macaroni products originated in the orient many years ago were taken to Italy in Middle ages. Macaroni products are widely consumed and manufactured in Italy and other European countries, USA, Canada and Australia. The common form of macaroni product consumed in India is vermicelli. Other macaroni products are not very popular in India.

The alimentary pastes are made by mixing wheat semolina (preferably derived from 100 per cent *Triticum durum* wheat) with the minimum water to form an unleavened dough. In areas where wheat is not available, the local cereal or other starchy foods are used instead. The traditional types of long pastas *e.g.* spaghetti are made with durum wheat in Italy but with local cereals such as rice in Asia. Alimentary pastes may also contain eggs, salt and other minor ingredients. They differ from bakery dough in that alimentary pastes are not leavened.

Method of Manufacture

Raw material for macaroni products is durum semolina. The grain of durum wheat is physically very hard, much harder than the hard common wheats. This wheat can be milled to give good yields of semolina, which is purified middling from durum wheat. This wheat is so hard that it is difficult to reduce to a flour fineness. The optimum size for the semolina particles for pasta is about 150 microns.

Water is added to semolina to obtain 28 to 30 per cent moisture (w/w). The semolina and water are introduced into the mixing chamber. Other ingredients *viz.* eggs, spinach powder, tomato powder, groundnut meal, soy flour, cassava flour, vitamins and minerals etc. can also be added. The blend is then mixed together until it forms a stiff dough, which when squeezed by hand, just holds together as a solid lump. Mixing should not develop the gluten. It is better to mix the dough under vacuum to protect the appearance and mechanical strength of the finished pasta. Air is determined for two reasons:

1. If air is trapped as tiny bubbles during mixing, it gives chalky appearance to the pasta.
2. All flour contain some lipoxygenase activity. The grain also contains free fatty acids. In the presence of oxygen, the enzyme bleaches the yellow carotenoid pigment. This oxidative action is limited when the air is removed. Best pastas are known to have yellow colour appearance.

After mixing, the dough is then either rolled into sheets, cut into flat noodles and then dried or extruded at high pressure through appropriate dies to make products of different shapes. An excessive increase in the temperature of pasta during extrusion irreversibly denatures the protein, and the pasta has very poor cooking characteristics. The barrel and die temperature is, therefore, maintained at around 45°C and extrusion is best carried out at intermediate speeds (25 rpm). Finally, the product is dried (10-12 per cent moisture) at controlled temperature and humidity and cut into desired lengths.

Noodles

Noodles are thought to have origin in China. They are a type of pasta that is generally made from flour rather than semolina and contain salt in addition to flour and water. In USA, noodles must contain less than 13 per cent moisture and more than 5.5 per cent egg solids. But the oriental noodles do not contain egg.

Method of Preparation

Noodles are made from relatively strong flours, so that they can be handled in wet form. This gives the cooked noodles a chewy texture. Noodle making is relatively simple. The dry flour is placed in the mixer and the water and salt are added. The amount of water is usually less than 35 per cent based on the flour weight. Mixing is done for 5-10 minutes basically to uniformly distribute water. After mixing, the dough is allowed to rest for 10-15 minutes, which helps again to distribute water evenly throughout the flour particles. The crumbly dough is then pressed between two large-diameter rolls to produce a dough sheet about 1 cm thick. The dough sheet is rolled thinner by seven to ten successive passes through reduction rolls. After reaching the desired thickness of 1-2 mm, it is passed through a pair of cutting rolls. Freshly cut noodles are dried over wooden dowels. The purpose is to obtain white, uniformly shaped noodles. Steamed noodles are produced to give instant products.

Different Types of Noodles

Dry noodles are not precooked but are formed at a moisture content of about 35 per cent and then dried to 8-10 per cent moisture. The drying is traditionally done in the sun but can be done under controlled low humidity. Instant noodles or ramen noodles or quick-cooking noodles, are made by steaming the cut and waved noodles dough for precooking and then frying (5-8 per cent moisture). Frying removes moisture and the noodles are not further oven dried. They are usually packaged with seasonings. Steamed noodles are precooked with low pressure steam, shaped and then dried to about 10 per cent moisture in the sun or oven. Such noodles have a good shelf life.

Alternative Raw Materials for Macaroni Products

Cereals other than wheat semolina, legumes or other food crops can be used for pasta making to have products of better nutritional quality than durum wheat pastas. Durum wheat dough has been substituted successfully with, for example, maize flour at 20 per cent, and 40 per cent w/w levels. Products from semolina-maize flour mixtures can successfully be supplemented with either 8 per cent defatted soy flour or 0.3 per cent l-lysine. Amaranth, spinach, eggs, peanut flour, cassava flour, pea flour (33 per cent), pea protein concentrates (20 per cent), rice, tapioca, fish protein concentrate etc. be added to improve the nutritional quality of pasta.

Chapter 18
Storage of Bakery Ingredients

The proper storage of bakery ingredients is important for the availability and uniform production. The ingredients should be stored properly at adequate temperature for a specified period to have good quality products.

Storage of Flour

A baker may store flour for several reasons *i.e.* (1) economic considerations. The flour is purchased at a time when the flour prices are favourable; (2) in order to have stocks in hand in case of failures or delay in arrival of flour of additional orders for products (3) in order to allow flour to improve in colour; and (4) in order to allow the flour to mature or become aged until ready for use. If the maturing agents like potassium bromate are not used at the mills the flour may take months to mature by natural processes during storage. Proper flour aging may require longer periods, but for that suitable storage space is required. There are the possibilities of flour getting infested. There is also the possibility of uneven maturing of flour in the bags.

It is, therefore, recommended that storage of flour for two to three weeks from the time the flour is milled, would be beneficial in certain cases for allowing the flour to complete these few biological changes. These changes result in improved baking characteristics of the flour.

The following points should be borne in mind when flour is stored:

Ventilation

The flour storage room should be well ventilated to allow free circulation of air around the piles of bags. It should also be ensured, that in the the storage room the moisture does not come through the floor and walls. The flour bags should be stacked in such a way to have passage between the stacks of bags for the circulation of air and also for the movement of personnel. Direct sunlight on the bags should also be avoided.

Humidity

The flours have a tendency to lose or gain moisture from the surroundings depending upon the humidity in which the particular flour is stored. The ideal relative humidity for storage of flour for long periods is from 55 per cent to 65 per cent particularly, when the flour with 12.5 per cent moisture is being stored. Whereas a 75 per cent relative humidity would be required to keep constantly a flour with 13.5 per cent moisture level in storage.

The flours having a moisture content as low as 11 per cent can be used without detrimental results. In these cases the addition of the proper amount of water would be required during mixing. If the flour is stored near the oven the moisture in flour decreases to low level and, the flour will never have the same baking performance.

It has been recommended that under normal conditions the water absorption of flour could be increased by 1.85 per cent for each 1 per cent decrease of original moisture content of flour. The water absorption of flour would decrease by 1.85 per cent for each 1 per cent increase of moisture content of flour. The bakers, therefore, should keep this factor in mind when flour is ordered because the moisture content of flour will affect the water absorption properties during mixing.

Temperature

At higher temperatures the flours get matured in shorter period and at lower temperature the flours take longer time for maturing. Flour stored at high temperatures loses certain characteristics and thus may have a poor baking performance. Flour stored at lower temperatures takes time to get to the desired temperature of proper aging.

The flour may be stored for long periods at a temperature of 65° to 75°F or 19° to 24°C.

Foreign Odours

Flour absorbs foreign odours much more quickly than any other bakery ingredients. Therefore the flour should be stored away from the ingredients which throw off undersirable odours. Materials such as oils, spices, onions and kerosene have off odours. If the flour is kept near these materials, the flour will absorb the odour from these materials and the odours of these materials will be noticeable in the finished product.

Storage of Yeast

When handling baker's yeast one should always remember that the baker's yeast consists of a mass of delicate small living cells and any negligence in handling baker's yeast could possibly ruin a portion or whole of the yeast. It is therefore suggested that yeast should be obtained as fresh as possible because old yeast has the tendency to lose its dough fermenting properties.

Baker's active dried or compressed yeast should be used in rotation so that older stocks are used before the new stocks. The yeast should not be subjected to extremes of heat even for the shortest period of time. The baker's dried yeast should always be stored at a cool place preferably at a temperature between 35°-50°F or 1° to 10°C. However, when using compressed yeast, which had been kept in the freezer, it should be thawed out slowly, because if there is an abrupt change in the temperature the yeast cells could easily be ruptured.

While using dried yeast, the lid of the tin containing yeast must be replaced soon after use and should not be kept open for longer periods.

The baker active compressed yeast is a perishable commodity. The compressed yeast loses little fermenting power during refrigeration at 35°F if it is stored for a period of four to five weeks. However, the compressed yeast can be stored for months in the frozen state. Since the compressed yeast is of perishable nature the packages containing it should never be exposed to humid conditions.

The compressed yeast should not be stored in warm atmosphere because in the warm surroundings certain harmful micro-organisms will grow at a tremendous rate in the yeast and certain changes will also occur in the yeast itself. These changes would be noticeable from an off odour of the yeast. Moreover the gassing quality of the yeast will also deteriorate.

When ready for use, the active dried yeast should not be dispersed in water with a temperature above 95°F or 35°C, because high temperatures prevent yeast from working at its optimum. The high temperatures, say 140°F or 60°C or over, will completely kill the yeast cells and thus render them useless for fermentation purposes.

Storage of Fat

Fat and oils should be stored in cool, dark, clean places, away from ingredients that have strong flavous, since fats readily absorb the smell and odor of spices and other material having strong, individual characteristic odours. Perisheable fats such as butter, should be refrigerated.

Storage of Baking Powder

Baking powder tin should always be tightly closed when not in use to avoid possible losses due to spillage and absorption of moisture from the atmosphere.

Storage of Sugar

Sugar stored at room temperature if packed properly should not be stored in damp room as sugar is hydroscopic.

Critical Storage Temperatures and Norms Form Inventory of Raw Materials

The best storage temperatures for sundry, raw material which production personnels and store keeper are likely to handle are given in Table 18.1. Especially for long time storage, the material should be stored at adequate temperature to maintain the quality.

Table 18.1: Adequate Temperature for Storage of Material Used in Bakery

Material	*Degree (°F)*
Flour and meals	38-40
Bread	60-65
Fruit and dried fruits	40
Liquid egg and egg albumen	5-15
Shell eggs	33-40
Compressed yeast	37-40
Vitamin premix, honey, malt extract, glucose, syrup	45
Butter and sweetened condensed milk/ fresh milk	33-39
Wax paper bread wrappers	50-60

It is fairly well established that bread depreciates and stales rapidly in very hot weather. The temperatures between 60 and 65°F have been found to be most suitable storage temperatures as maximum flavour is retained and staling is minimum at this temperature.

Hydroscopic substance like malt extract and substances which depreciate on exposure to air, such as milk, butter and baking powder should be stored in airtight containers with tight-fitting side.

Strong smelling aromatic substances should never be brought near the raw materials. Things such as kerosene, petrol, soap, paraffin etc. should be stored away from food material.

Table 18.2 depicts the recommended storage period, packing material and racking size for bakery ingredients.

Table 18.2: Recommended Storage Period Packing Material and Racking Size for Bakery Ingredients

Ingredients	*Normal Packing Recommended*		
	Material	*Pack Size (kg)*	*Storage Period*
1. **Ingredients Requiring Cold Storage Below 9°C (33-40°F) Conditions and RH 50 ± 5 per cent**			
Compressed yeast	Waxed wrapped	0.5	5 days
Dried yeast (Active)	Tins (packed under inert gas	15.0	3 months
Vitamin Premix	Fibre/M.S. Drum/Box	20.0	3 months
Tutti Fruit/candied fruits	Tins	15.0	2 weeks
Malt extract	Galvanised MS drum	30.3	1 month
2. **Ingredients Stored at Room Temperature**			
Wheat Flour	Gunny Bags (Jute)	90.0	3 weeks
Atta	Gunny Bags (Jute)	90.0	2 weeks
Salt	Gunny Bags preferably with polyethylene liners	75.0	1 month
Sugar	Gunny Bags (Jute)	100.0	1 month
Vegetable Oil	M.S. Drum (Galvanised) or Tins	180.15	1 month
H.V. Bakery fat Vanaspati	Tins A-Twill	16.0	1 month
GMS Powder	Polylined Gunny bags	25.0	3 month
Potassium Bromate	Plastic bottles or flexible packed in tin packed in cardboard box	0.5/10	12 months
Calcium propionate	Polylined-A Twill Gunny Bags	20.0	12 months
Acetic Acid	Plastic Carboys	30.0 lt	1 month
Tapioca Flour	Gunny bags Jute B-Twill	90	1 month
Defatted Soya Flour	Polyethylene bags	50	3 months
Liquid Paraffin	Galvanised MS Drums	205.0 lt	3 months
Bread wrapper	Reel	100 yds 12" dia	2 months
LLDP/HMHDP/PP/ LDP Guesseted or wicketed pouches	Gusseted/Wicketed pouches	1	2 months

Note: (1) When refrigeration facility is not available immediately, in such cases temperatures for storage will be 25-30°C and RH 65-85 per cent.

Chapter 19
Bakery Norms and Setting of Bakery Unit

In the production and merchandising of bakery products there are a number of norms that are quite common. All of these norms would not be found in any business. Any one of the norms listed below might be a very important factor in establishing whether a business is successful or not.

Some of the more common norms are:

Ingredients

Purchasing cheap or inferior ingredients due to a lower price is wrong. It must be kept in mind that a good product cannot be made from them. So always purchase a good quality ingredient.

Storing of Ingredients

Ingredients should be properly stored for adequate duration.

Sanitation

Sanitation is an important phase of baking industry. So, sanitation in bakery should be maintained.

Book-keeping-Costs-Selling Price

The baker must know his costs, not only of his material but also production, sales, packaging, overhead expenses etc. A set of book must be kept. If unable to do this himself, help must be obtained to do this very important work.

Scales

Inaccurate scales can be a costly piece of equipment not only through ingredient losses but also lack of uniformity in the finished product. Good scale should be purchased and checked periodically.

Lighting and Ventilation

There should be good lighting and ventilation for better working conditions.

Scaling

Scaling of ingredients of doughs and batters must be done carefully. Careless weighing either over or under, will produce non-uniform products.

Equipments

Equipments should be efficient and in good working condition to require a minimum time and expense to operate properly. Worn out equipment may cause problems in production.

Use of Sanitizer

Baker should know about use of various sanitizers and follow the manufacturer's recommended instruction before application and dilution rate. Degradable sanitizers should be used.

Knowledge

The baker should have a good knowledge of ingredients, equipments, process and trade. The baker has three important functions to perform; these are purchasing, producing or manufacturing and selling time, effort and money which must be expended in order to become efficient in any one or all these three.

Standard Norms for Handling Losses of Raw Material

Some standard norms for handling losses of raw materials due to loading, unloading spillage, evaporation during storage and left overs in containers are given in Table 19.1.

Table 19.1: Standard Norms for Handling Losses to the Stock of Ingredients Received

Ingredients	*Allowed Percentage of Handling Loss*
Wheat Flour/*Atta*	0.50
Salt	1.00
Sugar	0.20
Milk powder	0.50
Condensed milk sweetened	0.50
Compressed yeast	0.50
Dried yeast	1.00
Vitamin premix	0.50
Vegetable oil/Fat	0.50
Malt extract	1.00
Ammonium chloride	0.10
Potassium bromate	0.20
G.M.S. powder	0.50
Acetic acid	1.00
Calcium propionate	0.50
Wrapping paper	1.50
PP/LLDP/LDP/HMHDP Pouches	1.50
Liquid paraffin	0.50
Mixed fruits	2.00
Defatted soya flour	0.50
Tapioca flour	0.50
Curcumin powder	0.20
Vanilla flavour	1.00

Dusting Flour

Dusting flour is used in sparing amounts to prevent dough from sticking and dogging in the rounder and moulder. Norms for dusting flour are given in Table 19. 2.

Table 19.2: Some Standard Norms for Dusting Flour, Greasing and Lubrication

Ingredients	*Slow Speed Twin Arm/ Single Arm Mixer*		*High Speed Horizontal or Charleywood Mixer*	
	400g Bread % of Flour Weight	*800g Bread % of Flour Weight*	*400g Bread % of Flour Weight*	*800g Bread % of Flour Weight*
Dusting flour	1.0	1.0	2.0	2.0
Refined groundnut oil for greasing baking tins and dough bowls	0.5	0.5	0.5	0.5
Liquid paraffin for divider	0.3	0.3	0.3	0.3

Dough Divider Lubrication

For efficient operation of the dough divider, white mineral oil is applied to the pockets, hopper, knives and other metal parts to prevent adhesion of dough and inhibit rusting of parts. Animal or vegetable oil can not be substituted as these become rancid and develop off-flavour.

Proper selection of mineral oil is therefore very essential and has to be done keeping following in mind.

1. It must easily spread to a thin film on the metal surface.
2. It should not impart colour, odour or taste to the dough on long standing.

Pan Greasing

A light uniform greasing of the pans is essential to prevent loaves from sticking to the pan.

Setting of Bakery Unit

Baking is not an indigenous method of cooking. Yet baked products are finding their way into our diet. The demand of baked products is increasing day by day. Due to the present demand of baked products, there is an increased need for setting of bakery units. When we set a bakery unit we need information about bakery units like size, layout and equipments of bakery unit. And also needed the information about the relationship of laboratory to production, to the sale department to management and routines of laboratories and personnel requirements.

Successful laboratories are operating with one man and with 100 men, therefore the requirements of the bakery are one factor and amount of money they can be allocated to the laboratory each month is another factor. For a laboratory to produce its best results, capable personnel are necessary. For this reason, laboratory monthly costs must be calculated realistically with an exploration of the definite salary requirements of capable personnel.

Tests Essential in Baking

Some tests are essential for baking. These are as under:

1. Ingredient testing
2. Finished product testing
3. Testing of new products

The test necessary in a bakery laboratory will vary depending on the type of products manufactured *e.g.* in case of cookies and crackers would require a different testing programme than yeast raised products.

Some common ingredients' test essential to maintain uniformity of product should be carefully considered. The ingredients to be used should be checked for their specification.

Layout of Bakery Unit

Location

A small laboratory should allow approximately twice the space it will use initially. A long and narrow room will provide greater efficiency. Wall workbenches and center workbenches are the work areas. The aisles between these should be wide enough for workers to pass each other but no wider before any attempt to plan laboratory layout is undertaken. It is necessary to consider appropriate light, ventilator, plumbing, gas and electricity.

Equipment Requirements

A bakery laboratory should consist of equipments *viz.*, balance, dough mixer, electric egg beater, refrigerators, temperature and humidity control cabinet, dough molder, proof cabinet, bake oven and other small equipments such as scales, burettes, troughs, pans, trays, cutter etc.

For quality testing chemical laboratory in bakery would require some other equipment such as protein digester and estimation apparatus, furnace, viscometer, oven, soxhlet apparatus, pH meter, farinograph, amylograph, analytic balance, viscometer, autoclave, microscope, centrifuge and variety of glassware, moisture dishes etc. The chemical laboratory should be added to the bake shop equipment to facilitate quality analysis of ingredients received and to maintain uniform quality of products.

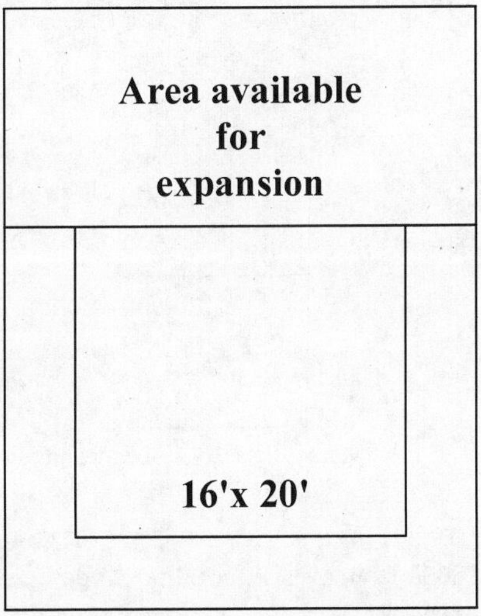

320 sq. ft. of floor space.

52 ft. of bench space plus 11 ft. center table

Established Bakery Unit (Cost and Profits)

		Amount (Rs.)
1.	**Fixed Assets**	
A.	Land and building	Rented house
B.	Equipments: Oven, dough mixture, bread slicer, cutters, cake tins, bread tins, heaters, cooking racks, muffin trays, spatula, mixing bowls, wooden spoons, dough cutter etc.	1,15,000

Contd...

Established Bakery Unit (Cost and Profits)–Contd...

		Amount (Rs.)
C.	Furniture (1 table and 4-6 chairs)	5,000
		1,20,000
	Interest on fixed assets @ 16 per cent p.a.	19,200
	TOTAL	**1,39,200**
2.	**Recurring expenses (per month)**	
	a) Rent of the building	1,200
	b) Electricity	2,500
	c) Water	200
	d) Raw materials	25,000
	e) Packaging material	600
	f) Maintenance	500
		30,000 /month
		3,60,000 /year
	Interest @ 16 per cent for 3 months	14,400
	TOTAL	**3,74,500 /year**
3.	**Salaries and wages (per year)**	
	Skilled worker (1) @ Rs.2500/month	30,000 /year
	Helpers (2) @ Rs.2000/month	24,000 /year
	TOTAL	**54,000 /year**
4.	**Income**	
	Products/day (300 days) 250 breads of 400 g = Rs.25000 per day at the cost of Rs.10 per bread (bread was taken as an example for calculating the gross income)	7,50,000 /year
Expenses		
	1. Fixed assets	1,39,200
	2. Recurring expenses	3,74,400

Contd...

Established Bakery Unit (Cost and Profits)–Contd...

	Amount (Rs.)
3. Salaries and wages	54,000
10 per cent depreciation of fixed assets	12,000
TOTAL	**5,79,600**

Profit = Gross income–Total expenses

Rs. 7,50,000 – 5,79,000	=	Rs. 1,70,400 /year
	=	Rs. 14,200 /month

Chapter 20

Specification for Raw Material Used in Bakery

Almost 60 per cent of an individual's income goes to food materials purchase and since the food materials that we consume have a direct connection to the health of the human population, we must be very cautious to produce good quality products and present the same to the consumer in a very hygienic way.

To manufacture products of better quality apart from baker's skill and the expert mind we need good quality raw materials. The bakers are mostly dependent on large scale manufacturers for their raw materials. The Government of India has brought in regulations on these raw materials. The Prevention of Food Adulteration Act during 1954 gave powers to the local health authorities to draw samples and analyze the same and to take action in case of any discrepancies.

As buyers of raw materials, we must also be aware of the quality of the material that we purchase, so that we get what we want to manufacture *i.e.* the products of our desired standards. The main raw materials that are purchased regularly by bakers are:

1. Maida
2. Sugar
3. Vanaspathi
4. Liquid Glucose
5. Butter
6. Salt
7. Yeast
8. Desiccated coconut
9. Cornflour
10. Milkpowder
11. Baking powder
12. Cocoa powder
13. Calcium propionate

In India, these raw materials are needed to meet the specifications laid down by Prevention of Food Adulteration Act 1954 and in specified cases the specifications laid down by Bureau of Indian Standards.

Maida

Maida (wheat flour) means the fine product made by milling or grinding wheat and bolting or dressing the resulting wheat meal. The material shall be free flowing, dry to touch, should not pack when squeezed, creamy in colour, free from bran particles, with a characteristic taste and smell, free of extraneous matter.

Table 20.1: Standards

Characteristics Code	*PFA. 1954 A.18.02*	*ISI IS.1009-1979*
Moisture % by mass	14.8	13.0
Total ash on dry basis % by mass, max.	1.0	0.7
Acid insoluble ash (on dry basis) % by mass, max.	0.1	0.05
Gluten on dry basis % by mass (min.)	7.5	7.5
Alcoholic acidity as H_2SO_4 in 90% alcohol % by mass, max.	0.12	0.1
Granularity test	To satisfy the test	
Uric acid mg/100 gm, max.		10
Rodent hairs and excreta	5 pieces per kg.	

Wheat Flour

Flour shall be the product obtained by milling, cleaned hard or soft wheat or blends thereof in a roller flour mill and bolting. Flour should be free flowing, dry to touch, shall not paste when squeezed.

Table 20.2: Standards

Characteristics Code	*ISI IS.9194-1979*
Moisture % by mass	13.0
Total ash (ODB) % by mass, max.	0.7
Acid insoluble ash (ODB) % by mass, max.	0.05
Gluten (ODB) % by mass	7.9
Alcoholic acidity as (H_2SO_4) in 60% alcohol % by mass, mix.	0.1
Granularity	To satisfy the test
Uric acid mg/100 gm, (max.)	10

Sugar (Cane Sugar)

Cane sugar is the crystallized sugar obtained from sugarcane/ beetroot etc.

Table 20.3: Standard

		0.7.01 PFA.684p.
Ash	:	Not more than 0.7 per cent
Water	:	Not more than 1.5 per cent
Sucrose	:	Not less than 96.5 per cent

Vanaspathi

Vanaspathi means any refined edible vegetable oil or oils subjected to a process of hydrogenation in any form. It shall be prepared by hydrogenation from groundnut oil, seasame oil or mixtures thereof or any other harmless vegetable oils.

Standards (19PFA.719p.)

1. It shall not contain any harmful colouring, flavouring or any other matter deleterious to health.
2. No colour shall be added.

3. If any flavour is used it shall be distinct from ghee.
4. It shall not have moisture exceeding 0.25 per cent.
5. The melting point as determined by the capillary slip method shall be from 31°C to 37°C both inclusive.
6. The Butyro refractometer reading at 40°C shall not be less than 48.
7. It shall not have unsaponifiable matter exceeding 1.25 per cent.
8. It shall not have free fatty acids (as Oleic acid) exceeding 0.25 per cent.
9. The product on melting shall be clear in appearance. Free from staleness or rancidity and pleasant to taste and smell.
10. It shall contain raw or refined seasame oil not less than 5 per cent by weight but sufficient so that when vanaspathi is mixed with refined groundnut oil in the proportion of 20:80. The colour produced by the Baudoin test shall not be lighter than 2.0 Red units in a 1 cm cell on a Loviband scale.
11. It shall contain not less than 25 IU of synthetic Vitamin, 'A' per gm.
12. No anti-oxidant, synergist or emulsifier must be added.

Glucose (Liquid)

Liquid Glucose is extensively used in confectionery, biscuit and food catering industries manufactured by 'Acid Hydrolysis' of starch. Liquid glucose or glucose syrup shall mean a refined and concentrated non crystallizable aqueous solution of d-glucose, maltose, and other polymers of d-glucose.

Table 20.4

Grades	*Dextrose Equivalent (DE)*
Low conversion (LC)	28 to 37
Regular conversion (RC)	38 to 47
Intermediate conversion (IC)	48 to 57
High conversion (HC)	58 to 67
Extra high conversion (EHC)	68 and above

Table 20.5: Standards

Characteristics Code	*ISI (IS.873-1974)*
Total solids, % by mass, min.	80
Ash, % by mass, max.	0.3
pH	4.8 to 5.5
Sulphur di-oxide, ppm, max.	400
Arsenic, ppm, max.	1.0
Copper, ppm, max.	5.0
Lead ppm, max.	2.0

Salt

Salt is sodium chloride. Depending upon use different names are given.

Common Salt

Crystalline solid, moisture not more than 6.0 per cent.

Table Salt

White crystalline coated with free flowing agents, as Ca, CO_3, Ca_3, PO_4, MgCO, 0.5 per cent moisture, 99 per cent should pass through 212 Micron IS Sieve.

Dairy Salt

Crystalline white solid, 99 per cent pass through 850 Micron IS Sieve. Moisture 0.5 per cent.

Table 20.6: Standards

Characteristics Code	*ISI Common Salt*	*ISI Table Salt (IS.253-1970)*	*ISI Dairy Salt*
Water insoluble matter % by weight max.	1.0	2.2	0.03
Chloride content (as NaCl) % weight min.	96.0	97.0	99.6
Acid insoluble matter % by weight max.	–	1.5	–

Contd...

Table 20.6–Contd...

Characteristics Code	*ISI Common Salt*	*ISI Table Salt (IS.253-1970)*	*ISI Dairy Salt*
Matter insoluble in water other than NaCl, max.	3.0	–	–
Calcium (as Ca) water soluble % by weight max.	–	0.10	0.01
Magnesium (as Mg) water soluble % weight, max.	–	0.10	0.01
Sulphates (as SO_4) % by weight, max.	–	0.50	0.30
Alkalinity (as Na_2CO_3) % by weight, max.	–	0.20	0.1
Lead (as Pb) ppm, max.	–	2.0	2.0
Iron (as Fe) ppm, max.	–	50.0	10.0
Arsenic (as As) ppm, max.	–	1.0	1.0
Copper (as Cu) ppm, max.	–	–	2.0

Baker's Yeast

Baker's yeast is used for the leavening of baked goods. It consists of *Saccharomyces cerevisiae* and related species. It is available in the compressed or dried form.

Compressed Yeast

It shall be in the form of block, creamy white colour and odour characteristic of yeast and fine even texture. Shall not be slimy or mouldy. Free from starch, adulteration. Should break sharply on bending.

Dried Yeast

It shall be in the form of powder, small granules, pellets and flasks. It shall have odour of good baker's yeast and fine even texture. Starch of an edible quality may be in a quantity not exceeding 10 per cent by mass.

Table 20.7: Standards (ISI)

Characteristics Code	*Compressed yeast (IS 1320-1972)*	*Dried yeast*
Moisture by mass, max.	75	8
Dispersibility in water	To satisfy the tests	
Fermenting power min.	900	350
Bacterial Flora, other than yeast, (Millions/Gm.) (ODB) max.	1.5	8.0
Dough raising capacity	To satisfy the tests	

Coconut (Desiccated)

Desiccated coconut shall be processed essentially from fully mature, fresh coconuts, natural white colour-free from cheesy, mushy odour-fungal and insect infestation. Coliform count not more than 10/g and free from salmonella. It shall be crisp and sweet, natural taste of coconut and free from extraneous matter like coconut shell, testa starch, added sugar etc.

It is available in three grades *i.e.*, fine, medium and coarse based on particle size.

Table 20.8

Grade	*Particle Size*	*Proportion, Per cent*
Fine	425 to 850 Micron	70–75
	250 to 425 Micron	25–30
Medium	850 Micron to 2.0 mm	65–70
	425 to 850 Micron	30–35
Coarse	2.36 to 4.00 mm	75
	1.18 to 2.36 mm	25

Table 20.9: Standards

Characteristics Code	*ISI (IS. 966-1975)*
Moisture % by mass, max.	3.0
Fat, % by mass, min.	65.0
Fat acidity, as lauric acid, max.	0.3

Corn Flour

Corn flour (edible maize starch) means the starch obtained from maize (*Zea mays* L.). It shall contain no added sweetening, flavouring, colouring agents or any foreign matter. It shall be free from dirt, insects, impurities and rancidity.

Particle Size

Not more than 2 per cent by mass of the material shall be retained on 75 micron IS sieve and not more than 0.5 per cent by mass retained on a 150 micron sieve.

Table 20.10: Standards

Characteristics Code	*PFA-1954 A.18.08*	*ISI IS.1005-1976*
Moisture % by mass, max.	12.5	12.5
Total ash (ODB) % by mass, max.	0.5	0.3
Acid insoluble ash (ODB) % by mass, max.	0.1	0.1
Starch (ODB) % by mass, min.	–	98.0
Protein (ODB) % by mass max.	–	0.5
pH of aqueous extract	–	4.5-7.0
Free acidity (as ml of 0.1 N.NaoH/100 g max.)	–	40.0

Milk Powder (Whole and Skim)

Powder obtained from milk which is dried either by 'Roller Drying Process' or the 'Spray Drying Process'. The milk powder shall be white or white with greenish tinge or light cream in colour. Free from lumps or caking practically free from scorched particles.

Whole Milk or standardized milk obtained from cow or buffalo or a mixture dried either by roller drying or spray drying is called as whole milk powder.

Skim Milk Powder–prepared by spray drying or roller drying of fresh milk of cow or buffalo or a mixture from which fat has been substantially removed.

Table 20.11: Standards

Characteristics Code	*PFA 1954 Whole*	*ISI Skim IS.1165-1967*
Flavour and odour	Good	Good
Moisture % by wt. max.	4.0	5.0
Total milk solids % by wt. min.	96.0	95.0
Solubility index max.	15.0 (RD)	15.0 ml RD
	2.0 ml (SD)	2.0 ml (SD)
Solubility % wt. min.	85.0 RD	85.0 RD
Total ash (ODB) % by wt. max.	7.3	9.3
Fat % by weight	Not less than	Not more than
	2.6	1.5
Titratable acidity % by wt. (Lactic acid) max.	1.2	1.5
Bacterial count/gm max.	50,000	50,000
Coliform count/gm, max.	90	90

RD: Roller Dried

SD: Spray Dried

Baking Powder

Baking powder finds widespread use as a chemical leavener of dough for baking products. The constituents of baking powder are (a) Sodium bicarbonate, (b) edible starch, (c) acid reacting components. The product shall be in the form of free flowing, whitish powder and free from any off odour.

Table 20.12: Standards

Characteristics Code	*ISI (IS.1159-1981)*
Available CO_2 % by mass, min.	12.0
Arsenic mg/kg max.	1.1
Heavy metals as (Pb) mg/kg max.	10.0

Cocoa Powder

Cocoa powder shall be the material obtained by mechanical transformation into powder of cocoa press cake resulting from partial removal of fat from the ground nib of sound and wholesome roasted beans of *Theobroma Cocoa* should be free flowing powder, having colour and flavour.

Particle Size

Not less than 98 per cent pass through 150 Micron IS sieve.

Table 20.13: Standards

Characteristics Code	*ISI (IS.1164-1980)*
Moisture % by mass, max.	7.0
Cocoa butter (on moisture free basis) % by mass, min.	
a) for breakfast cocoa powder	20.0
b) for low fat cocoa powder	10.0
Total ash (on moisture free and fat free basis) % by mass max.	14.0
Acid insoluble ash (OMF and FFB) % by mass, max.	0.20
Alkalinity of total ash as K_2O (OMF and FFB) % by mass, max.	5.5
Crude fibre (OMF and FFB) % by mass, max.	7.0

Chapter 21

Losses in Baking

There are many bakery losses which can be checked through proper control and efficient management but can't be completely eliminated. The losses are:

Invisible Loss

Invisible loss of material is the difference between the amount of material actually received and that accounted for during baking processes. Invisible Loss in percentage can be calculated as:

$$\textbf{Per cent Invisible Loss} = \frac{\text{Loss in weight (Kgs)} \times 100}{\text{Amount of material received}}$$

Sources of invisible loss include spillage of material, theft of material, absence of store records of materials used, inaccurate weighing of ingredients for the dough batches etc. The above losses look very insignificant but the sum total of these will be considerable over a period of time. These losses can be controlled by calculating at the end of each week / month depending upon the daily turnover of the shop. The total invisible loss should be about 1 per cent and should not exceed 2 per cent.

Mixing Loss

The mixing loss represents the total amount of ingredients dumped for kneading either by machine or hand and the finished dough out. This loss may be unimportant in terms of money but it serves to make the mixing personnel more efficient. The total loss should be calculated at the end of an entire's shift. Mixing loss in terms of per cent can be calculated as:

$$\textbf{Per cent Mixing Loss} = \frac{\text{Mixing Loss (Kgs)} \times 100}{\text{Formula weight}}$$

Fermentation Losses

Fermentation loss affects the baker in two ways. Firstly is the economic loss due to less yields, and secondly it affects the quality of the finished products. The total fermentation time of the doughs and the humidity of the dough room will have a definite bearing over the range of total fermentation loss. The longer the fermentation time, the more will be the fermentation loss as compared to the no-time, doughs which have practically no fermentation loss. If the humidity is low, there is a loss of moisture which in turn allows the formation of dry crust on the dough surface. This is the main cause of streaks and lumps in the finished product. Even if the proper humidity is maintained there is bound to be little fermentation loss due to the conversion of the sugars into carbon dioxide and alcohol. Normal fermentation loss should average about 0.75 per cent provided the baking operations are controlled; the uncontrolled operations would increase the loss and may go as high 3.5 per cent. Finished dough temperature is one of the other factors to be watched to avoid excessive fermentation loss due to conversion of sugars. The fermentation loss in per cent can be calculated as:

$$\textbf{Per cent Fermentation Loss} = \frac{\text{Fermentation loss in Kgs} \times 100}{\text{Weight of dough after finishing mixing}}$$

Trough Grease Losses

Avoid excessive use of shortening or oil for greasing the troughs or mixing-table tops, before the dough is allowed to rest for initial fermentation. The careless and inefficient workers will use an excessive amount so that the dough will turn easily as well as slide out without much effort. This factor should be controlled not only from the economic point of view but also it affects the quality of final finished product. When used in excess, shortening or oil will cause holes and streaks in the finished product. Care should be taken only to use sufficient quantity to prevent the dough from sticking. This is also true in case of bread pan greasing. Excessive amount will cause somewhat of porous crust on the finished product.

Dusting Flour Losses

This factor should also be controlled for the same reasons given above. This leads to:

1. Additional cost due to excessive dusting.
2. Too much dusting causing streaks, dark circles, lumps and a harsh texture in the finished product.

So, use a sufficient amount to prevent the dough from sticking. Dusting flour which remains unused after the dividing and moulding operations should be reused after sieving. The amount of dusting flour used should not exceed one per cent. Use the following formula to obtain the dusting flour percentage;

$$\textbf{Per cent Dusting Flour} = \frac{\text{Dusting flour used in Kgs} \times 10}{\text{Wt. of dough for dividing and moulding}}$$

Divider Loss or Gain

The shops which are using dough dividers should be very careful about their operation. The profitable operation will depend upon accurate uniform scaling with correct yields. Overscaling will result in a net loss; while underscaling of the dough will not only be a violation of the law but that shop will lose the much needed customer's confidence if the facts become known. The normal divider loss should not exceed 0.25 per cent. Doughs coming out of the divider should often be checked manually to ensure the uniform scaling operation. To obtain loss or gain in scaling, use the following formula:

$$\textbf{Loss or Gain Percentage in Scaling} = \frac{\text{Divider loss or gain in Kgs} \times 100}{\text{Weight of dough divider}}$$

Divider Efficiency

The following formula to be used in determining the divider efficiency:

Step 1

$$\textbf{Number of Possible Units} = \frac{\text{Wt. of dough to divider}}{\text{Scaling weight per unit}}$$

Step 2

$$\textbf{Per cent Divider Efficiency} = \frac{\text{Actual unit} \times 100}{\text{Possible units}}$$

Cripples

Dough loaves are sometime crippled in the moulding machine or during panning and also in a similar way during dividing and scaling if due caution is not exercised. If the humidity of the proof box is excessive there is a deposition of moisture on the top of dough loaves. The condensation of water causes unsightly spots and air bubbles, resulting in cripples. Loaves are often crippled during baking either by excessive heat which results in burnt loaves or by wild irregular bursts in the oven which result in deformed, unsymmetrical loaves, which are unsaleable except for animal feed. Oven cripples can be avoided by proper regulation of the oven temperature and steam and also by maintaining correct conditions during pan proofing.

Finished loaves also get damaged in the slicing machine. Improper, loose and careless packing may also result in cripples. Unsaleable cripples result in a total loss of material as well as manufacturing costs. Proper care and steps should be taken to prevent the continuance of such cripples.

To obtain the percentage of dough cripples the following formula should be used:

$$\textbf{Per cent Cripples} = \frac{\text{Total number of cripples} \times 100}{\text{Number of Units Produced (after dividing and moulding)}}$$

Calculation of the Number of Individual Dough to be Secured from a Given Dough Batch

On an average the losses are 10 to 12 per cent. So, the exact number of pieces of dough which should be obtained from any particular batch of dough can be calculated as follows:

Divide the total weight of the dough batch, expressed in grams at the time it is sent to the divider, by the scaling weight of each individual piece of dough as delivered from the divider. The resulting figure will be the number of individual dough loaves which should be expected.

$$\textbf{Scaling Weight} = \frac{\text{Weight of the loaf}}{\text{(10-12\% losses in baking, cooling and scaling)}} \times 100$$

Chapter 22
Packaging and Sale of Baked Products

The packaging of food is one of the prime requisites to improve and monitor the producer–to–consumer food production systems. It forms an integral part of the food manufacturing process providing the link between the processor and the consumer. In fact, it plays a dominant role in the total food manufacturing activity and in the marketing sector. Bakery products have to be packed in attractive packing so as to give an impression of wholesomeness and freshness of the product to increase sales appeal. The packaging should be hygienic.

The term packaging encompasses both the direct or primary packaging around the food product itself and the secondary and tertiary packaging, the over packaging such as cartons, overwraps, and crates etc. The need for packaging can be directly linked to the progress of the society *i.e.* consumers drive awareness and the requirements to preserve perishable for longer periods of time for consumption at places distant from the production centres.

Need for Packaging

Packaging is essential part of processing and distributing food. It may be emphasized that preservation of food in a safe condition is the major role of packaging. In addition, there are several other functions for packaging which should be kept in mind by the food manufacturer:

1. Packaging must protect against a variety of assaults including physical changes, chemical attack and contamination from biological vectors including microorganisms, insects and rodents.
2. Packaging is expected to protect food from oxygen and moisture which will spoil the food if they are allowed to enter and come in contact with food.
3. Packaging helps distribution against any physical damage that may occur during the distribution of foods, particularly from long distances.
4. Good standard packaging aids in storage of food.
5. Packaging provides information on the ingredients, nutritional content and other pertinent information to the consumer. Such information is required by the food laws of a country.

Characteristics of Packing Material

The packaging material suitable for bakery products should have the following desirable properties/characteristics:

1. The package must contribute to the dimensional stability of the product.
2. The film should be capable of being handled by wrapping machines.
3. The film should protect the product from drying and no moisture should reach the product from outside.
4. The film protects the product from dirt, bacteria etc.
5. The packaging should have sale appeal. For certain uses the film should be transparent while in other cases it may not be so.
6. The packaging material should be easy to print.
7. The packaging material should be non-toxic.
8. The packaging material should be easily dispersible.
9. The packaging material should have low cost and be compatible with the food.

10. The packaging material should be easy to open, should have dispersing and resealing features.

Packing Materials for Bakery Products

Some of the important packaging materials for bakery products are:

Waxed Paper

Waxed paper is an ideal packaging material for sliced bread. It gives as impression of softness and freshness. It has moisture proof barrier.

Grease Proof and Glassine Paper

Grease proof and glassine paper is suitable for biscuits, pastries etc. It protects against transmission of off odour or flavour. It is good for packaging of fatty materials.

Disadvantages

1. Not quite moisture proof.
2. Papers can't be heat sealed so coated with wax or lacquer.

Polythene Film

Polythene is low in cost and can be printed by rotogranure process but the best process is the flexographic process for decorative printing. Polythene film has excellent resistance to water vapour and flavour transmission.

It is of 3 types:

(i) Low Density Polythene (LD Polythene)

LD polythene is used in bag form. It is not stiff to be used in a machine. Bags of LD polythene are taken and filled with the product by hand.

(ii) Medium Density Polythene (MD Polythene)

It has good heat sealibility and stiffness.

(iii) High Density Polythene (HD Polythene)

It has better stiffness.

Polypropylene Film

It has better machinability, stiffness and toughness. Polypropylene film in 0.9 to 1mm thickness is used. It gives excellent end folds giving a neat packaging. It has higher sealing temperature and wider sealing range.

Cellulose Film

It has the advantage of transparency. It can be printed easily, cheap, heat sealed, excellent transparency and adds to the attractiveness of bakery products.

Foil Laminations

It is used for packaging of biscuits and similar bakery products. Laminated aluminium foils have moisture resistance. Its tear strength is improved by paper web.

18 Litre Tinplate Cans

Biscuits are packed in 18 litre tin plate cans and salty biscuits in one litre can.

Bleached Sulphite Paper

It is used for hard and crisp materials. They are glued, as heat sealing is not possible with them. Its desirable property is its low cost.

On the whole, the growth of food packaging during the next 5-10 years will increase at a faster rate in view of the changing food habits and life style of the people. More efficient biodegradable, reasonable and recyclable material should be developed. Excellent facilities should be established for the testing and quality control of the packed foods. Establishment of the packaging complexes closer to the production centers will reduce the losses.

Bakery Sales

With the gradual mechanization of the baking industry and free availability of the essential baking ingredients, the people have more inclination to buy more and more baking products bearing the brand names.

Bakery Sales Tips

In order to attract more customer's the retail baker shall keep in mind the following suggestions:

The retail bakeries should manufacture a variety of baked goods such as sweet dough goods, cake, pastries, cookies, etc. The retailers should manufacture sufficient quantities of best quality products which are in demand and with little imagination and the acquired skill bakers can formulate their own recipes and designs of the product. The product should be fresh and the quality, and price of the baked product should be according to the customers. The bakers should use metal tongs or tissue paper for packing up cakes, cookies. The bakery should have a cozy atmosphere and should not have any aromas other than that of fresh baked goods. Arrangements of the store displays should be appealing and eye-catching. Window should be dressed to seasonal specialties. No soiled paper doilies and dirty baking pans should be displayed in the show windows. Windowpanes should be brightly polished to give the perfect impression. The premises should be well lighted and the bakery goods should be price labelled which would help customers to budget their needs. The selling area should be free from flies, ants, cockroaches and other insects.

Floor and wall should be clean and nicely maintained. The packaging material should be properly stacked. Sales personnel should be equally efficient. They should be properly dressed and provided with appropriate clean uniform. The sales staff should have pleasant appearance and good manners. The staff should be properly oriented in relation to the make up method of merchandise.

It is necessary to find out the negative aspects of bakery sale. It has been observed that consumers quit buying at retail bakery because of following reasons:

General

1. No variety of baked goods.
2. Running out of certain baked goods, at an early hour.
3. Wrong management.
4. Prices too high, or quality too high for class of people served.
5. Quality too poor for class of people in neighborhood.

6. Goods being stale.
7. Out of date store.
8. Cooking flavour coming into store from kitchen or shop.
9. Odours, other than baked goods, such as paint etc.
10. Store too cold in winter time.
11. Store too hot in summer time.
12. Lack of advertising.

Bakery Shops

1. Poor arrangement of store.
2. Poor arrangement of windows.
3. Poor lighting
4. Flies, ants, cockroaches and other insects.
5. Floors being dirty.
6. Windows and glass soiled.
7. Soiled showcases and doilies.
8. Baking pans being dirty.
9. Owner's children or babies in store.
10. Newspapers and other rubbish lying around store.
11. Loss of interest, because windows are not changed often enough.

Sales Personnel

1. Soiled hands.
2. Soiled uniforms
3. Hair not dressed.
4. Haughtiness or superiority complex.
5. Indifference or lack of pleasant appearance.
6. Over insistence in selling additional items.
7. Lack of knowledge of merchandise.
8. Slow in serving customer.
9. Serving on customers out of turn.
10. Not using tissue paper for picking up cakes.

11. Packing up cakes after falling on floor and putting with others.
12. Carelessly wrapping packages.
13. Errors in making change.
14. Not thanking customers for purchases.
15. Substitution of goods.
16. Misrepresentation of goods.
17. Shop help going into store when not in presentable appearance.
18. Sale people reading books and papers.
19. Making remarks about customers' faults or appearance.

Successful Retail Salesmanship

The following points should be kept in mind to improve the sale.

1. Be Agreeable
2. Know the goods you are selling.
3. Don't argue
4. Tell the truth
5. Be dependable
6. Remember by name and face
7. Beware of egotism
8. Think success.
9. Be Human.

Chapter 23

Bakery Sanitation and Personal Hygiene

The word 'Sanitation' is derived from the Latin word 'Sanitas' which means 'health'. To further apply this word to the food industry sanitation is the creation and maintenance of hygiene and healthful conditions during processing, preparing and handling of food. Sanitation is the application of a science to provide wholesome food handled in a hygienic environment by healthy food handlers to prevent contamination with food-poisoning microorganisms and minimize contamination by food spoilage microorganisms. Effective sanitation refers to the mechanism which helps to accomplish these goals.

Food sanitation is an applied sanitary science related to the processing, preparation and handling of food. Sanitation application involves hygienic practices to maintain a clean and wholesome environment for food production, storage and preparation. Proper sanitation practices are important in maintaining food safety. Lack of hygienic practices can contribute to outbreaks of food borne illness.

Bakery sanitation can briefly be defined as the cleanliness of surroundings and machines and the hygiene of the persons and the way they handle things.

Utmost cleanliness and sanitation is not only an important factor but it is absolutely indispensable. This applies to the bakery products, delivery equipments, salesroom and of course all the employees. A quality product made in a clean atmosphere as well as handled in a sanitary manner will definitely have more customer appeal.

Personal Hygiene

The word 'hygiene' is used to describe a system of sanitary principles for the preservation of health. Personal hygiene refers to the cleanliness of a person's body. The health of workers plays an important part in food sanitation. People are potential sources of microorganisms that cause illness in others through transmission of viruses or through food poisoning. Every baker has a part to play in the hygiene practices which will minimize the possibilities of infection through the bakery food he prepares.

Employee Hygiene

The ill employee should not be in contact with food and with equipment and utensils used in processing, preparation and serving of food. Human illnesses that may be transmitted through food are diseases of the respiratory tract such as common cold, sore throat, pneumonia, scarlet fever, tuberculosis and trench mouth. Other transmissible diseases are intestinal disorders, dysentery, typhoid fever and infectious hepatitis. When employees become ill, their bacterial count and source of contamination increase dramatically. Even when evidence of illness passes some of the microorganisms that caused the illness may remain as source of recontamination. Diseases are transmitted directly and indirectly.

The following practices should be maintained:

1. Illness should be reported to the employer before working with food so that work adjustment can be made to protect food from the employee's illness or diseases.
2. Hygienic work habits should be developed to eliminate potential food contamination.

3. During the work shift, hands should be washed after using the toilet, handling garbage or other soiled materials, handling uncooked muscle foods, egg products or dairy products, handling money, smoking, coughing and sneezing.
4. Personal cleanliness should be maintained by daily bathing and use of deodourants, washing hair at least twice a week, cleaning finger nails daily, use a hat or hair net while handling food and swearing clean underclothing and uniforms.
5. Employee hands should not touch food service equipments and utensils. Disposable gloves should be used when contact is necessary.
6. Never return a tasting spoon to food without washing it and do not lick the finger.
7. Rules such as no smoking should be followed and other precautions related to potential contamination should be taken.
8. All staff reporting on duty must be fresh, well groomed and clean, not half asleep or unkempt in appearance.
9. They must be changed into fresh clean overalls and those working in kitchens and service area should wear head covering to protect from loose hair falling in it.
10. Infection is easily transferred from hair, nose and mouth therefore
    (*a*) comb should be kept out of kitchen.
    (*b*) spitting or smoking in kitchen or service area should strictly be prohibited.
11. When sneezing while handling food, the face should be away from food and handkerchief or tissue used.
12. In refilling cups or glasses, never allow the container from which the liquid is poured to touch rims.
13. Every bakery should have a first aid box in case of any accidental cuts or burns.
14. Periodic physical examinations of all employees will not only totally safeguard the health of the worker but will also protect the health of the customer.

Transmission of Food Borne Diseases and Spoilage Microorganisms

Chain of Infection

A chain of infection is a series of related events or factors that must exist to occur and be linked together before an infection will occur. These links can be identified as agent, source, and mode of transmission and host. The essential links in the infectious process must be included in such a chain. The causative factors that are necessary for the transmission of bacterial food borne disease involve the following:

1. Transmission of the causative agent from the environment, in which food is produced, processed or prepared to the food itself.
2. A source and reservoir of transmission for each agent.
3. Transmission of the agent from the source to a food.
4. Growth support of the microorganism through the food or host that has been contaminated.

Conditions such as required nutrients, moisture, pH, oxidation-reduction potential, lack of competitive microorganisms and lack of inhibitors must also exist so that the contaminants can survive and grow. Contaminated food must remain in a suitable temperature range for a sufficient time to permit growth to a level capable of causing infection or intoxication.

Sources of Contamination and Their Preventive Measures

One of the most viable contamination source is the food product itself. If raw products are not handled in a sanitary way they become contaminated and support microbial growth.

Contamination from Ingredients

Ingredients are potential vehicles of harmful or potentially harmful microorganisms and toxins. The amount and types of these agents vary with place and method of harvesting, type of food ingredients, processing technique and handling. The food plant management team should be aware of the hazards connected with the incoming ingredients and should limit procurement of such supplies and material to those that conform to recognized good practices in harvesting, processing and handling of these important materials. Raw materials especially those of animals origin *viz.* milk, cream, egg etc. are a major concern of all ingredients.

Milk

Factors affecting the sanitary quality of milk which may be reflected in its bacterial count include health of the cow, the health and hygiene of human handlers, barn and utensils sanitation, speed and degree of cooling, time of holding and pasteurization.

Egg

Cool storage of egg at all times reduces the chances of shell penetration. If shells are washed before breaking the hazard is small. Do not use stale egg or low quality eggs.

Equipment/Utensils

Equipment can be instrumented in the contamination of food. Contamination of equipment occurs during production as well as when the equipment is idle. Even with hygienic design features, equipment can collect microorganisms and other debris from the air as well as from employees and materials during productions. Reduction of the product contamination from equipment can be accomplished through improved hygienic design and effective cleaning of equipment.

Cleaning and Care of Pans/Baking Sheets

Bread pans or bun/roll baking sheets should always be kept clean and in good condition. After each usage, pans should be wiped clean with a dry cloth so as to remove all traces of grease, burned crumbs, sugar, oil etc. The pans should then be carefully stacked so as to avoid denting or exposure to any form of dirt or foreign matter.

At frequent intervals, it is highly desirable to wash the pans in a dilute solution of either detergent or 'Trisodium Phosphate' solution which is a mild alkaline salt and may be procured under certain brand names. In making up such a solution about 60 g should be used per 4 litres of hot water. The pans should be allowed to soak for one to two hours in the cleaning solution. Care should be taken to protect the hands and clothing from such solutions. Usually rubber gloves are used. After this treatment, the pans should be put through several rinsing with clean hot water so as to remove any traces of the washing solutions previously employed. After that the washing pans/baking sheets are to be dried and regreased before using. If the pans have become exceptionally dirty and sticky, a more vigorous washing and scrubbing is to be carried out if necessary.

Keeping all pans/baking sheets in a clean condition is an important factor in the production of uniform high quality bakery products. If pans or baking sheets are not cleaned from time to time the oil film coating on the inner-side and corners of the pans may become rancid due to oxidation. This undesirable condition results in imparting a very objectionable flavour and taste. When pans/baking sheets are not in use, these should be stored on raised pellets and pans should be upside down, thus preventing the inside pans from collecting dust and foreign matter.

If baking pans/sheets are to be stored away, temporarily out of use, they should be freed from all grease before use, otherwise old fat/oil film will give objectionable flavour and taste to product. Pan/baking sheets are to be stored in a dry place and where condensation of steam is not likely to occur.

Employees

Of all the viable sources of exposing microorganisms to food employees are the largest contamination source. Employees through unsanitary practices contaminate food with spoilage and pathogenic microorganisms that they come in contact with. Various parts of the body such as hands, hair, nose and mouth harbour microorganisms that can be transferred to the food during processing, packaging, preparation and service by touching, breathing, coughing or sneezing because of the warm temperature supplied by the human body; microorganisms rapidly proliferate on humans especially if hygienic practices are not conducted.

Air and Water

Although water serves as cleaning medium during the sanitation operation and is an ingredient added in the formulation of various processed foods. It can also serve as a source of contamination. To reduce water contamination, samples should be analysed for microbial contamination. If excessive contamination exists another wáter source should be obtained or water from existing source should be treated by chemicals or other methods. As with water, contamination can result from airborne microorganisms in food processing, packaging, storage and preparation areas.

Sewage

If raw sewage drains or flow into potable water lines, wells, rivers, lakes and ocean bays, the water and living organisms such as seafoods are contaminated. To prevent this kind of contamination, pipes and septic tanks should be sufficiently separated from wells, steams and other bodies of water. Provide adequately lighted and ventilated toilets and urinals separately for males and females with adequate arrangements for cleaning them out.

Insects and Rodents

Flies and cockroaches are associated with mankinds living quarters, eating establishments and food processing facilities as well as toilets, garbage and other filth. To stop contamination from these pests, eradication is necessary and food processing, preparation and service area should be protected against their entry. Rats and mice are rodents that can transmit filth and disease if they are not eradicated. The principal means of controlling rats and mice are:

1. Exclusion
2. Traps
3. Poisoned Baits
4. Poisonous gases or dusts.

Use of Sanitizers and Insecticides

Insecticides

There are two types of insecticides:

1. Non-residual and
2. Residual

Non-residual insecticides which exert their effects only at the time when treatment is generally applied such as space foggers or contact sprays. Natural or synthetic pyrethrins with a synergizer, can be applied in food areas when raw materials and finished products are covered during treatment, whereas the residual insecticides maintain their effects for several days or longer and are usually employed on walls, or cracks and crevices.

Cleaning and Sanitary Materials

Always follow manufacturer's recommended instructions before application and dilution rate. Never blend different types of detergents together, because as one may neutralize the function of another and its effective cleaning becomes almost nil. In market various types of detergents are available and are listed below for information.

Type	*Use*
Alkaline	Prevents mineral scale build-up in brew tanks, tempering tanks and water coolers.
Chlorinated caustic and alkaline	Enhances cleaning and decolourisation but can corrode equipment made from mild steel, aluminium or galvanized iron.
Neutral	Used where surface deterioration may occur.
Acid	Removes mineral scale build-up.
Solvent based	Removes accumulated grease due to fat but care should be taken to avoid taint contamination of the product.

As far as possible dry cleaning method may be followed rather than applying detergent solutions. This is because dry cleaning does not encourage the growth of molds and bacteria, whereas wet cleaning may allow micro-organisms to multiply and cause cross infestation and contamination.

Sanitizers

Selection of the appropriate sanitizers for a given situations be carried out with recommendation and advice of a leading manufacturer. Some of the common sanitizers which are used are listed below:

Type	*Advantage*	*Disadvantage*
Hypochlorites	Broad spectrum of activity, inexpensive and easy to use.	Corrosive, irritating to skin, noticeable odour.
De-sanitary ammonium	Non-corrosive, no flavour and non-irritating.	Non effective against certain bacteria.
Iodophores	Non-corrosive, non-irritating.	Fairly expensive, forms dark colour with starch.

The ideal sanitizer should have the following properties:

1. The ideal sanitizer should have microbial destruction properties. The effective sanitizer should be uniform, broad spectrum activity against vegetative bacteria, fungi and molds.
2. An ideal sanitizer should be effective in the presence of
   (*a*) Organic matter
   (*b*) Detergent and soak residues
   (*c*) Water hardness and pH
   (*d*) Good cleaning properties
   (*e*) Non toxic and non irritating
   (*f*) Water soluble in all proportions
   (*g*) Acceptable odour or no odour
   (*h*) Stable in concentrate and use dilution
   (*i*) Easy to use
   (*j*) Readily available
   (*k*) Inexpensive
   (*l*) Easily measured in use solution

Bakeshop Sanitation

Bakery proprietors should become familiar with the municipal laws dealing with the sanitary measures and should educate their staff in enforcing them. Every precaution should be taken to create perfect conditions of cleanliness.

Before work is commenced and after it is finished all the working tables and machines should be brushed and wiped down. Each person should be responsible for the cleanliness of the area he has been allotted. All the working tables and the utensils used, should be maintained in a clean and tidy condition, after each job is completed. The floor should also be kept clean, free from dusted flour and leftover pieces of dough.

The greasing of bread pans and the depanning of the bread should be carried out in such a way so as to minimize the possibilities of the floors getting greasy. After use, bread pans should be wiped clean and stacked in such a manner so as to avoid the dust depositing inside the pans.

Ingredients should not be stored in the bakery, but should be drawn from store as required and should be placed, weighed down for each mixing in suitable clean containers.

Perishable ingredients such as compressed yeast and milk should not be left in the bakery for long. Compressed yeast in case of spoilage should be dumped away to prevent the spread of obnoxious colour.

Bakery products are sterilized by the heat of the oven. To avoid the possibility of such goods being contaminated after they leave the oven, every precaution should be taken during handling of the products either in the bakery or in the course of delivery. Delivery equipment should be taken care of properly.

Advantage of Cleanliness

By maintaining of a clean, well lighted, ventilated bakery, the efficiency of operation will be increased. The bakery employees will be more careful about their work and will surely be proud of their profession. This will result in a reduction of waste, improvement in quality and quantity output.

Furthermore cleanliness is in itself an advertisement to boost up your sales. If your bakery is kept spotlessly clean, you should not hesitate to invite the housewives visit the bakery, and witness for herself the extreme care which is taken in making the baked goods which are available to her fresh daily. Nothing impresses the modern housewife more than thorough cleanliness and neatness. If she is assured that the bakery is operated with the same care that she employs in her own kitchen, she is sure to become your permanent customer. Moreover, she will be induced to buy more and more bakery products. But on the contrary, if the housewife witnesses that no cleanliness is maintained in the bakery, she represents a lot of customers whose trade it will be next to impossible to regain. The same condition applies to the bakery salesroom and the sales staff as it does for the bakery proper.

Many a time it is not economically possible to maintain a bakery with proper sanitation due to the surroundings and improper planning of the premises. Anyone proposing to shift or to set up a new business will naturally examine possible sites primarily from the point of view of the amount of rent and other overheads, the cost of conversion or equipping and the number of potential customers. But the consideration of hygiene should not be overlooked. Adequate lighting, ventilation and water supply should be regarded as essential.

The immediate neighbourhood should also be examined for the presence of noxious trade and practices, breeding grounds for rats, mice, flies or harmful insects.

Working Premises

Floors in the working quarters have to stand up to a good deal of traffic as well as the weight of the equipment and are liable to have water and grease spilt on them. The essential requirements are that they should be even and impervious, without cracks or open joints, smooth but not slippery, hard wearing and capable of being easily cleaned. The junctions of the wall should be covered. Walls should be substantially durable, smooth, impervious and washable in order to prevent the accumulation of unnoticed dirt, cobwebs, flour dust and to provide agreeable surroundings for the staff, they should be lightly coloured.

Adequate ventilation is essential. Natural ventilation is attractive because it is cheap. Windows provide good natural ventilation only if they are properly situated. Windows used for ventilation and entrance doors should be insect proof, since openings afford an entrance to dust, dirt, flies and other insects.

Good lighting is essential in the bakery and in all parts of the premises used for storage and bakery food preparation. This is required not only in order that the workers can see clearly what they are doing but also in order that dirt shall be evident and promptly cleared. In most establishments, therefore, artificial lighting will be required to supplement natural lighting even during day time, but careful planning will reduce the expense to the minimum.

Point to Keep in Mind

1. After the bakery premises (in and out) are swept, the garbage of the premises and Bake House shop should not be thrown on the passage area inside compound but to be deposited only in the garbage bins.
2. Outside bkery premises, do not allow children on the way to entrance of bakery or roadside places and lanes to avoid spread of disease.

3. Do not allow your pet/domestic animals inside the bakery for any reasons.
4. Do not throw banana peels/*beedi* or cigarette buts or wrapper pieces inside bakery.
5. Do not use water from taps for cleaning animals or for cleaning vehicles. Keep the surroundings of the bakery clean.
6. It is an offence to disfigure walls by either writing on them or pasting posters on them. Do not spoil their beauty.
7. Day-to-day Bake House should collect the garbage/fungus/ market returns in plastic covers and deposit them in the push carts of bakery, whenever bakery attendants arrive, throw them only in the garbage bins and burn in incinerator.
8. It is the primary duty of every employee of the unit to keep the unit clean and to preserve the beauty of bakery. Maintenance efforts alone are not sufficient, let all of us resolve to-day to maintain the beauty and cleanliness of our bakery.

Safety Measures

1. Fencing and covering of all dangerous parts of machinery while they are in motion of use; covering of all pits, pumps and openings which may be a source of danger, causing new machinery, encasing and guarding of every set of screw, bold, spindle, wheel or pinion, periodical examination of appliances and plant such as hoist, lifts, cranes, chains, pressure vessels, supply of safety appliances like goggles, safety boots, and gloves etc.; necessary precautions against fire, dangerous fumes, risk of injury to eyes, lifting of excessive weights and excessive speed of revolving machinery.
2. All hoists, lifts lifting machines chains, and ropes are to be of good mechanical construction, sound material and adequate strength. They are to be maintained properly and examined thoroughly by a competent person approved by the Government once in six months, and registers are to be kept for recording the particulars of each examination. They are not to be loaded beyond the safe working load

which is to be clearly marked thereon. Hoists and lifts are also to be sufficiently protected by enclosures fitted with gates.

3. Women and young persons and unskilled workmen are not to be allowed to clean, lubricate or adjust any part of engine or electric motor, of any transmission machinery when these are in motion, and work near. Such work is to be done by specially trained adult skilled male workers wearing tight fitting clothing.
4. Young persons are not to be allowed to work on any dangerous machines without adequate training and supervision.
5. Adequate number of fire extinguishers, water and sand buckets are to be provided inside the mixing, baking, packing and dispatching section. Handling of fire extinguishers are to be handled by taking adequate, training through National Safety Council. All fire extinguishers are to be inspected periodically and supervised from time to time.

Chapter 24
Prospects and Problems in Bakery

The bakery industry has an important role to play in the economic development of the country in fuller utilization of its wheat resources, and in building up the health of its people. Much attempt is being made to popularize bakery products among all because these products are considered easy, convenient and rather inexpensive means of taking foods in hygienically prepared ready to eat form.

Wheat is considered the major cereal crop of the world and is consumed mainly in the form of bakery products in most parts of the world. In India, wheat is consumed mainly in form of *chapatti*- an unleavened baked product. In recent years bakery products have become popular among different cross-sections of population due to increased demand for convenience products. Among the bakery products, particularly bread is the cheapest processed ready to eat product in the country. However, the per capita consumption of bread in India is only 0.8kg as compared to 50 to 150 kg in advanced countries. Hence, there is an unlimited scope for expansion of the bread industry in the country. This would help in the effective utilization of the surplus wheat produced in the country.

The policy of the government in promoting the growth of bakery industry only in the small sector since 1978 appears detrimental to the full realization of the potential of the bakery industry. Bakery products offer advantages of nutrition and convenience at relatively low costs. Bakery products in India are now in common use and are used by a common man so there is a vast scope for bakery industries.

Status of Bakery Industry in India

In India about 90 per cent of wheat is consumed in the form of *chapatis* and 10 per cent as bread, biscuits, buns and other bakery products. The bread and biscuit manufacturing in India is reserved for small scale sector. The production of bread in both organized and unorganized sectors is estimated to be 14 lakh tonnes and 10 lakhs, respectively. Out of total biscuits manufactured in India, nearly, one third is in organised sector and remaining two thirds in the small and unorganized sector.

The production of bakery products has increased by two-folds in the last five years indicating thereby, increasing popularity of these products. The production of bakery items in India in 1990, is estimated to be 19.5 lakh tons; whereas in 1993 the estimated growth of bakery products are 2.4 million tones.

About 6 million tonnes (MT) of wheat are milled in roller flourmills into 4.5 MT of flour, *maida*, *rawa* and bran. The bakeries producing about 1 MT bread, 1.9 MT biscuits and 1.4 MT other bakery products mostly use the *maida*. As high as 43 per cent of the total bakery products *i.e.* mainly biscuits produced in the country are consumed in rural areas.

It is estimated that there are over 54,000 bakery units in the country, out of which 54 are large scale units registered under DGTD, 35 units are producing biscuits and 19 units bread. There are over 4,133 other factory (bakery) units belonging to both medium and small-scale sectors. The number of bakery units in the small sector is estimated to be about 3328. A majority of bakery units numbering about 50,000 are household units.

Prospects in Bakery Industry

The demand for bakery products is bound to increase further in the country due to the following reasons:

Demand of Baked Products is Likely to Increase

Statewise, distribution of bakery products suggests that some states have large share in bakery products outlay as compared to their population than other states.

States	*Rural Sector*		*Urban Sector*	
	Share in Population (%)	*Share in Bakery (%)*	*Share in Population (%)*	*Share in Bakery (%)*
Andhra Pradesh	7.9	3.6	7.6	3.4
Assam	3.2	7.4	1.4	(*a*) 3.3
Bihar	11.7	7.3	5.5	(*b*) 3.6
Gujarat	4.4	4.2	6.6	(*c*) 5.2
Haryana	1.9	2.4	1.7	(*d*) 20
J and K	0.8	3.1	6.7	(*e*) 4.7
Kerala	4.0	8.0	3.5	(*f*) 3.9
Madhya Pradesh	7.8	4.4	5.9	(*g*) 3.3
Madras (T.N.)	6.4	10.7	10.5	(*h*) 7.9
Maharashtra	7.8	9.4	14.3	(*i*) 18.2
Karnataka	5.0	4.5	6.5	(*j*) 2.9
Orissa	4.5	2.7	1.5	(*k*) 1.1
Punjab	2.5	3.1	3.4	(*l*) 2.8
Rajasthan	5.0	1.2	4.1	(*m*) 2.1
Uttar Pradesh	17.8	11.6	11.5	(*n*) 9.5
West Bengal	7.5	11.4	10.8	(*o*) 18
Union Territories	1.8	5.0	4.4	(*p*) 7.1

Change in Eating Habits Gradually Increase in the Consumption of Bakery Products

Spread of industry and commerce and general change in eating habits shall gradually improve consumption in total market for bakery products. As at present approximately 80 per cent of the total population biscuit consumption is of only 38.2 per cent. The balance

61.8 per cent of the production of bread and biscuits is consumed in urban centers that accounts only for $1/5^{th}$ of the total population.

Increased Income

At current estimates, the production of bakery products is about 22 lakh tons of biscuits, bread and other bakery products. This will surely increase the income. Current data shows that in 1984 estimated growth of bakery products was 1.2 million tonnes whereas in 1993 estimated growth of bakery products was 2.4 million tonnes.

Increase in the Employment

Due to the increase in bakery units, there is increase in the number of employment of labour. As these products are manufactured in the large and small scale and cottage sectors of the industry, totaling to about 75000 units.

Utilises Agricultural Inputs

The bakery industries utilizes agricultural inputs such as wheat, flour, sugar, and vegetable oils and fats. The processing converts these short shelf life agriproducts into long shelf life bakery products, which are enjoyed by all age groups, who derive a part of their daily nutrition from it.

Migration of Population

With the migration of population from rural to urban areas, with gradual economic upliftment taking place in rural areas and with more children in India going to school so the demand of baked products is likely to increase.

Formation of Government Policy

The production of bakery products in small scale units will increase further, in view of the recent Government policy of permitting the further expansion of bakery industry only in small sector. The requirement of bakery products in 1990 was about 31-lakh tones. This increased requirement has to be met by small-scale industries. There is a good scope for starting a new small-scale bakery unit.

Increase Demand for Bakery Products

The demand for bakery products is bound to increase further in the country due to an increasing demand for convenience products, shift in eating habits and better transport and distribution method.

Unlimited Scope for Expansion of Bread Industry

In recent years bakery products have become popular among different cross sections of the population due to increased demand for convenience products. Among the bakery products, particularly bread is the cheapest processed ready to eat product in the country. However the per capita consumption of bread in India is only 0.8 kg as compared to 50 to 150 kg in advanced countries. Hence, there is an unlimited scope for expansion of the bread industry in the country.

Scope for the Development of Health Foods

Many healthful bakery items have been developed for specific health conditions *e.g.* sugarless bakery products are made for the diabetic patients. Many other baked dietetic foods are also prepared.

Problems of Bakery Industry

Bakery products can become one of the ready means to utilize the surplus wheat produced in the country. This calls for popularization of bakery products among different cross sections of the population. This would necessitate solving the following problems:

Quality of Raw Material

Major problem faced by the bakery industry is in respect of quality of raw material. Refined wheat flour is the main raw material for the preparation of bakery products, so the quality of *maida* used greatly influences the quality of baked good. For different types of bakery products specific variety of wheat is required, for hard wheat has less than 14 per cent protein whereas soft wheat contains about 8 per cent protein. Therefore, this needs a categorization and a proper selection of wheat.

Categorization of Wheat

Some variety of wheat grown in the country has been found to have good bread making potential. However, such type of wheat is not made available to the mills separately for processing into *maida*, as Food Corporation of India, which is the main supplier of wheat to the flour mill, does not either grade the wheat according to its functional characteristics, or store it separately. Hence, millers get wheat of different blends. Though of late government has permitted the millers to buy wheat from the open market, very few are making use of this facility due to higher price of wheat in the open market.

Therefore, it is essential that wheat during procurement from the farmers be graded according to the quality and stored separately. This would help the millers to process wheat of their choice and hence make available the different types of flour to the bakeries to suit the manufacture of various bakery products. This is all the more possible now in view of the surplus wheat produced in the country. Categorisation of wheat will also help in exporting wheat and earning foreign exchange.

Selection of Proper Streams

In a roller flour mill, refined flour is obtained by mixing different streams of flour coming from series of break rolls and reduction rolls. The quality of these streams varies considerably. The protein and ash contents in the break fractions increase with increase in the break passages and similar trend is observed in reduction passages also. Hence, flour with the desired level of protein/gluten or ash content can be obtained by blending the streams suitably.

There is no uniformity in the quality of raw materials required to prepare bakery products. There is a limited variety of bakery products *i.e.* bread and biscuits or introducing newer bakery items to suit the different life styles.

Duties and Taxes on Bakery Products

Taxes on processed foods are highest in India, which may discourage new entrants and result in low consumption as taxes increase the final price of product. Lack of skilled manpower, managerial expertise and low capacity utilization of units are major area of worry. The major cause of concern for the small scale units in industry may be the entry of multinational companies which on one hand will increase exports but on the other hand pose threat due to their financial and managerial power.

The duties and taxes on the bakery products add up to over 40 per cent. For an industry engaged in preserving the short shelf life agriproducts and providing nutrition to children, such high duties and taxes are unreasonable. If the duties and taxes are progressively brought down and eliminated completely, the industry's growth would be spectacular and more consumers would be able to afford to enjoy more quantities of bakery products.

By the policy of reservation applied to this industry, this latent growth is stifled. Because of a slow growth in the biscuit industry, the ancillary industries like bakery machinery and bakery additives like emulsifiers, flavors, leavening agents, enzymes and yeast are also not as well developed as in other countries.

It is an established fact that for being successful in the consumer food products market, the product must meet the quality consistently and the expectation of the consumers, be hygienically produced and be available in all parts of the country. This requires considerable expenditure in technological inputs, research and development into new products and packaging, efficiencies in production and distribution network and reach to far-flung markets in advertisement and promotion.

It is also a fact that small scale biscuit manufacturer's have not been able to provide these inputs in their business and hence they restrict themselves to small volumes and regional sales and find that they are unable to grow in volume and their cost of manufacture and distribution keeps going up.

Bakery Industry in India is not a very developed sector at present but its planned growth in future has a vast potential to fulfil many of the nation's requirements. With the growing population bakery industry can help into prevent the food from spoilage, in energy conservation and employment generation. So there is a vast scope in bakery industries.

Appendix I
Cake Faults

List of Common Faults and their Diagnoses

Fault: Cake Sinking in the Center

Causes

Too Much Aeration

This may be caused by:

1. Too much sugar used in the recipe. This can be detected by excessive crust color and a sticky seam running in the shape of a U.
2. Too much baking powder. Difficult to detect because it can be confused with (c).
3. Overbeating of fat/sugar/egg batter prior to adding flour

Undercooked

This can easily be detected by the presence of a wet seam just below the surface of the *top* crust.

Knocking in Oven Prior to Cakes Being Set

If during cooking when all the ingredients are in a fluid state, a cake gets a knock or disturbance (such as a draught of cold air) some collapse may take place which will result in the center of the cake caving in.

Too Much Liquid

This is easy to detect because, firstly the sides will tend to cave in as well as the top, and if the cake is cut a seam will be discovered immediately *above* the *bottom* crust. Cakes containing too much liquid do not show this fault until they are removed from the oven. During baking, the excess moisture is in the form of steam and actually contributes to the aeration of the cake. On cooling, this steam condenses into water which sinks to the bottom of the cake, collapsing the texture by so doing.

Fault: Peaked tops

Causes

Flour Used was Too Strong

For cake making, a weak flour with a low gluten (protein) content is required. If a strong flour is used, the cake will be tough, giving rise to a peaked top which looks unsightly.

Mixing was Toughened

The flour of a cake should be only just mixed in. Overmixing will cause the batter to become tough as the gluten of flour is being developed. Not only will a tough batter produce peaked tops but also a tough and coarse crumb, detracting from its eating qualities.

Too Hot an Oven with Insufficient Steam

The ideal baking condition for a cake is to have a quantity of steam present which will delay the formation of a crust until the cake has become fully aerated and set. If an overfull of cakes is baked, there is usually sufficient steam generated from the cakes themselves for this purpose, but for small quantities a tray of water should be inserted to get this required steam. A very hot oven will form a crust on the cake too soon and this will in turn cause the cake to rise in the center only, giving the characteristic peak.

Fault: Small Volume with Bound Appearance

Causes

This is caused by insufficient aeration due to:

1. Insufficient beating of the batter.
2. Insufficient sugar used in the recipe.
3. Insufficient baking powder used in the recipe. Such cakes will have a close crumb structure and be tough to eat.

Fault: Fruit Sinking in Fruit Cakes

Causes

1. Cake mixing is too soft to carry the weight of fruit. This may be due to:
   (*a*) Cake mixing being too light because of overbeating (fat/sugar/egg).
   (*b*) Excessive sugar used.
   (*c*) Excessive baking powder used.
   (*d*) Insufficient toughening of batter.
   (*e*) Too runny a mixture
2. Use of too weak a flour: Slight toughening of the batter is sometimes necessary to strengthen the crumb and thus make it possible to support the fruit.
3. Fruit was washed and insufficiently dried before being incorporated into the cake batter.
4. Baking temperature was too low.
5. Moving the cake in the oven before it is set

Fault: Cracked Top or a Peak

1. Cake pan may be too small
2. Cake is placed too high in the oven.
3. Oven may be too hot.

Fault: Burnt Crust

1. Thin cake pans
2. Too long a baking time
3. Too hot an oven
4. Insufficient outer protection of the tin *e.g.* brown paper used to protect

Fault: Badly Shaped/Uneven Rising

1. Uneven lining of the tin
2. Careless filling of the pans
3. Tilting the pan in the oven
4. Wrong consistency
5. Too slow an oven or under baking
6. Allowing cold air to enter oven or moving cake tin before cake is set
7. Excess raising agent resulting in over stretching and collapse of the gluten.

Fault: Heaviness

1. Insufficient amount of raising agent
2. Much too slow an oven
3. Far too much liquid

Fault: Dryness

1. Insufficient liquid
2. Too much chemical raising agent

Fact: One Should Know to Make and Serve Perfect Fruitcakes

1. Fine fruitcake tends to be more expensive to make, but is so delicious and has such wide appeal that most homemakers want to know how to make it. Several factors contribute to its success.
2. Choose a recipe with well-proportioned ingredients and clear-cut directions.

3. Bake fruitcakes for holidays or for special occasions at least 2-3 weeks beforehand. This enables the homemaker to work leisurely and carefully and allows time for cakes to ripen and mellow to their best flavour and texture.

3. Choose fresh ingredients–such as nuts, moist candied fruits, eggs, butters/margarine etc. Dried or rancid nuts

produce cake inferior in aroma and flavour. Likewise too many raisins and currants give the cake a bitter or scorched flavour.

4. When a high proportion of fruits is used, these should be chopped, as fruits which are round or cubed shaped give cake a texture that makes it difficult to cut into thin slices.
5. Line cake pans with half-inch of paper extending above the edge of pans all around to protect cakes from browning too fast on top and aids in removing cakes from pans. Grease pans and paper lightly.
6. Parchment or smooth brown unglazed wrapping paper is best for lining pans. Paper insulates the pans and protects the cake batter from scorching. Fruitcakes contain a high percentage of sugar and scorches very easily. Line pans with one layer of heavy parchment paper or smooth brown paper or two layer of typewriter paper. Fit closely into inside of greased pans to preserve pan-shape of cake.
7. Have ingredients at room temperature. Measure dry ingredients; remove lumps from sugar. If molasses or jelly is used stir in after the sugar. Add whole eggs and beat until smooth and fluffy: add flour in 4 or 5 portions (alternating with liquids such as fruit juice or wine).
8. After cake mixture is poured into the pans, rap pans on table 2 or 3 times to pack batter down evenly. Fill pans with batter to within 1/8 to ¼ inch of top.
9. As much as is possible, place cakes of same size and shape in the oven at any one time. Keep cakes at least ½ inch apart for heat circulation.
10. Cakes can be kept moist while baking by placing cake pans in a pan with water. Pour hot water into pan to a depth of ¼ inch. As water evaporates replace with boiling water. Alternatively, when pans are placed on oven rack, a pan of water may be placed directly on the oven rack to keep cakes moist.
11. When cakes are done, remove to racks to cool thoroughly in pans then lift items out with paper attached onto racks.
12. Trim off edges of lining paper and wrap cakes in moisture-proof wrap. Sealing air tight with scotch tape, or wrap in

waxed paper, then in aluminum foil and store in the refrigerator.

Baking Temperature for Cakes

The general rule is that cakes should be baked as quickly as possible consistent with their being properly cooked through without adverse discoloration of the crust. The following are the factors which affect the baking temperature of cakes.

Steam

Humid atmosphere is essential in order to achieve a flat top on a cake and to ensure that thorough baking is carried out with a pleasing crust color. A pan of water inserted in the oven is usually sufficient for this purpose.

Richness

The more sugar a cake contains, the cooler the oven temperature and the longer the cooking time that is required. This is because the richer the cake, the more crust color is formed.

Shape and Size

The overriding consideration to be given here is the penetration of heat into the cake mass. It follows from this that the smaller the cake the shorter the baking time, and then the higher the baking temperature. Conversely, large cakes require a lower baking temperature with a longer baking time. However, it is not always appreciated that shape plays an important part. Since it is the penetration of heat that counts, a thin slab of cake cooks very much more rapidly than the same weight but say, double the thickness. The range of temperatures over which cakes may be baked is very wide, ranging from 350°F (177°C) for wedding cakes to 450°C (232°C) for very small fairy cakes.

Additions

Substances like sugar or almonds added to the surface of a cake act as improving the richness of a cake, and baking temperature should be reduced by 10-20°F (5.5-11°C) to compensate.

Certain substances like glucose, invert sugar, and honey take on color at a much lower temperature than sugar. If such substances are added (for example, for their cake moistening properties), the baking temperature also needs to be lower.

Preparation of Dried Fruit for Fruit Cakes

The moist eating and keeping qualities of cake containing dried fruit depend to a large extent on the amount of moisture retained by the fruit in the cake. To achieve the maximum retention of moisture by the fruit, proper preparation is essential. The fruit should be sorted, washed, and well-drained before use.

Essences, fruit juices, spirits, etc. may be mixed into the fruit, preferably some time prior to their being used. The fruit is always added last after the flour has been mixed in.

Choice of Ingredients for Cake Making

Flour

Always use a soft flour but if this is not possible replace a proportion with corn flour.

Fat

Since the aeration of a good quality cake is partly achieved by the trapping of air by the action of beating the fat, one with good creaming qualities is essential. Unfortunately, both butter and normal lard (special processed lards with good creaming qualities are now available) suffer in this respect. In most recipes where butter is used a small quantity of shortening should be incorporated to help overcome this defect.

Sugar

Fine grain castor is best so that it will readily dissolve in the batter.

Cake Faults

The following table shows some common cake faults and their possible causes.

Poor keeping quality

Sugar content low
Too little moisture
Cake over-baked
Cake improperly cooled

Poor flavour

Too much artificial flavour
Too much pan grease
Baking pans dirty
Cake over-baked
Poor storage conditions
Incorrect levels of ingredients
Rancid ingredients

Holes near bottom crust

Damp pans
ingredients
Too much pan grease
Too much bottom heat

Tunnelling/uneven crumb

Too much flour
Poor dispersion of ingredients

Pale crust colour

Too much flour
Too much baking powder
Over temperature too low

Poor Volume

Formula not balanced
batter improperly mixed
Too much flour
Excessive egg
Insufficient baking powder
Wrong batter weight for size of pan
Time between mixing and backing to long
Incorrect oven temperature
Excessive moisture in oven

Coring/crumpeting of cake crumb

Too little flour, Too much water
Unbalanced formula
Too much water

Top crust peeling

Too much sugar
Cake improperly baked (flash heat, excessive top/bottom heat, moisture in oven)

Cake peaks in centre

Insufficient sugar
Excessive egg
Batter too stiff
Batter over mixed
Too little batter in pans
Pans too shallow
Oven too hot

Poor crust colour

Too many moisture-absorbing

Too much egg colour
Lack of alkalinity
Cake over-baked/under-baked

Texture too coarse

Too much leavening
Too much sugar
Batter

Texture too fine

Lean formulation
Not enough leavening
Under-whipped batter
Sugar too coarse
Flour too fine

Collapsing in oven

Too much leavening
Too much sugar
Not enough flour
Oven too cool
Oven too hot (post backing collapse)
Batter too hot
Batter over whipped

Excessive shrinking

Silicone contamination
Too much leavening
Batter over-mixed
Too much pan grease
Not enough batter weight

Glossary of Baking Terms

Absorption: A taking in or reception by molecular and or physical action. The property of flour to absorb and hold liquid.

Aeration: The treatment of dough or batter by charging with gas to produce a volume increase.

Ash: The incombustible residue left after burning matter.

Bake: To cook or roast by dry heat in a closed place such as an oven.

Baking powder: A chemical leavening agent composed of soda, dry acids and corn-starch (to absorb moisture); when wet and heated carbon dioxide is given off to raise the batter during baking.

Batter: A homogenous mixer of ingredients with liquid to make a mass that is of a soft plastic character.

Bleached flour: The terms refer to flour that has been treated by a chemical to remove its natural colour and make it white.

Bleeding: Term applied to dough that has been cut and left unsealed at the cut thus permitting the escape of leavening gas.

Blend: A mixture of several ingredients or grades of any ingredient.

Boil: To bubble, emitting vapour, when heat is applied. Boiling temperature for water is 212°F or 100°C at sea level.

Bolting: Sifting of ground grain to remove the bran and coarse particles.

Buttercream Frosting: Rich, uncooked frosting containing powdered sugar, butter and or other shortening and whipped to a plastic condition.

Butter Sponge: Cake made from sponge cake batter to which shortening has been added.

Butterscotch: A flavour produced by the use of butter and brown sugar.

Beat: To make mixture smooth or to introduce air by using a brisk, regular motion that lifts the mixture over and over.

Caramelized Sugar: Dry sugar heated with constant stirring until melted and dark in colour, used for flavouring and colour.

Carbohydrates: Sugars and starches derived chiefly from fruits and vegetable sources which contain set amounts of carbon, hydrogen and oxygen.

Carbon Dioxide: A colourless, tasteless, edible gas obtained during fermentation or from a combination of soda and acid.

Carbonated Ammonia: Leavening agent made of ammonia and carbonic acid.

Cardamom: Seed of a spice plant used for flavouring.

Casein: The principal nitrogenous or protein part of milk.

Cinnamon: The aromatic bark of certain trees of the laurel family, ground and used as a spice flavouring.

Citron: The sweetened rind of the fruit.

Clear Flour: Lower grade and higher ash content flour remaining after the patent flour has been separated.

Cocoa: A powder made from chocolate from which part of the cocoa butter has been extracted.

Coconut: The inside meat of the coconut, shredded or grated.

Colours: Shades produced by the use of dyes.

Compounds: In the baking industry, certain mixtures of fats and oils.

Congealing Point: Temperature at which a liquid changes to a plastic or a solid.

Corn Meal: A coarse meal made by grinding corn.

Cottage Cheese: The drained curd of soured or coagulated cream, pressed and mixed until smooth.

Cream: That fat portion of cow's milk; also a thickened cooked mass of sugar, egg, milk and a thickener used for pies and fillings.

Creaming: The process of mixing and ereating shortening and another solid such as sugar or flour.

Cream Pies: One crust pies having cream filling, usually topped with whipped cream or meringue.

Cream Puffs: Baked puffs of cream puff dough which are hollow, usually filled with whipped cream or cooked custard.

Crescent Rolls: Hard crusted rolls shaped into crescents, often with seeds on top.

Crusting: Formation of dry crust on surface of doughnuts due to evaporation of water from the surface.

Cupcakes: Small cakes of layer cake batter baked in muffin pans.

Currant: The acidulous berry of a shrub; usually dried.

Custard: A sweetened mixture of eggs and milk which is baked or cooked over hot water.

Danish Pastry: A flaky yeast dough having butter or shortening rolled into it.

Dates: The fruits of a species of palm.

Date Filling: A cooked blend of dates, water and sugar.

Diastase: An enzyme possessing the power to convert starches into dextrose and maltose.

Dissolved: To bring a solid into solution in a solvent.

Divider: A machine used to cut dough into a desired size or weight.

Dough: The thickened mass of combined ingredients for bread, rolls and biscuits, but usually applied to bread.

Dough Conditioner: A chemical product added to alter flour in its properties to hold gas.

Doughnut: A cake, frequently with a centre hole, made of yeast or baking powder dough and fried in deep fat.

Dry Yeast: A dehydrated form of yeast.

Dusting: Distributing a film of flour or starch on pans or work bench surfaces.

Dusting Flour: Flour used to sift on to dough handling equipment to prevent dough from sticking.

Eclair: A long thin shell of the paste as cream puffs.

Emulsification: The process of blending together fat and water solutions of ingredients to produce a stable mixture which will not separate on standing.

Enriched Bread: Bread made from enriched flour and containing prescribed amounts of vitamins and minerals.

Enzyme: A substance produced by living organisms which has the power to bring about changes in organic materials.

Evaporated Milk: Unsweetened canned milk from which water has been removed before canning.

Extract: Essence of fruits of spices used for flavouring.

Fat Absorption: Fat which is absorbed in food products as they are fried in deep fat.

Fermentation: The chemical changes of an organic compound due to action of living organisms (yeast or bacteria), usually producing a leavening gas.

Flavour: An extract, emulsion, or spice used to produce a pleasant taste.

Flour: Finely ground meal of grain.

Flour Extraction: A term referring to the proportion of the wheat that becomes flour. Commercial flour in the United States are 72 per cent extraction.

Fluff: A mass of beaten egg white, air and crusted fruit.

Foam: Mass of beaten egg and sugar as in a sponge cake before the flour is added.

Fold: To lap yeast dough over on to itself. With cake batter to lift and lap the batter on to itself to lightly incorporate ingredients.

Fondant: Low moisture content sugar syrup containing a small quantity of invert syrup which has been rapidly cooled so that the sugar crystals are small in size.

French Bread: An unsweetened crusty bread, baked in a narrow strip and containing little or no shortening.

Germ: That part of the seed from which the new plant grows.

Ginger: The spicy root of a tropical plant used for flavouring.

Glace: Sugar so treated as to resemble ice.

Gliadin: One of the two proteins comprising gluten which provides elasticity.

Glucose: A simple sugar made by action of acid on starch.

Gluten: The elastic protein mass that is formed when the protein material of the wheat flour is mixed with water.

Glutenin: One of the two proteins comprising gluten, which gives strength.

Graham Flour: Finely ground whole wheat flour.

Greasing: Spreading a film of fat on a surface.

Hardness of Water: A measure of mineral salts in greater amounts than is found in soft water.

Hearth: The heated baking surface of the floor of an oven.

Hot Cross Buns: Sweet, spicy, fruity buns with cross cut on top which is usually filled with a plain icing.

Hydrogenated Oil: A natural oil that has been treated with hydrogen to convert it to a hardened form.

Ice: To frost or put on an icing or frosting.

Incorporating: The act of mixing or blending one ingredients with another.

Ingredients: Food material blended to give palatable products.

Invert Sugar: A mixture of dextrose and levulose made by inverting sucrose with acid or enzymes.

Jelly: A combination of fruit juice and sugar, stiffened by the action of the pectin of the fruit, as a result of heating.

Lactose: The sugar of milk.

Leaven: To make food light by an agent such as yeast or baking powder.

Leavening: Raising or lightening by air, steam or gas (carbon dioxide). The agent for generating gas in a dough or batter is usually yeast or baking powder.

Levulose: A simple sugar found in honey and fruits.

Loaf Cake: Cake baked in bread pans or similar deep containers.

Malt Extract: A syrupy liquid obtained from malt mash; a product obtained as a result of converting the starch to sugar.

Melting Point: The temperature at which a solid becomes liquid.

Meringue: A white frothy mass of beaten egg white and sugar.

Middlings: Granular particles of endosperm of wheat made during grinding of the grain in the mills.

Mocha: A flavour combination of coffee and chocolate, but predominately that of coffee.

Molasses: Light to dark brown syrup obtained in making can sugar.

Muffins: Small, light, quick breads baked in muffin pans.

Pouring: To empty a liquid, out of vessel.

Quick Breads: Bread products baked from a lean chemically leavened batter.

Raisins: Dried sweet grapes may be dark or bleached.

Rocks: Small rought-surfaced fruited cookies made from a stiff batter.

Rounding or rounding up: Shaping of dough pieces into a ball to seal end and prevent bleeding and escape of gas.

Rub in: To combine fat and flour for pastry, plane cake etc. fat is first cut into small pieces and then rubbed into flour using the tips of fingers until the mixture looks like fine bread crumb.

Saturation: Absorption to the limit of the capacity.

Shortening: Fat or oil used to tenderize baked products or to fry products.

Sifting: Pass through fine sieve for effective blending and to remove foreign or oversize particles.

Solidifying point: Temperature at which a fluid changes to a solid.

Spices: Aromatic vegetable dry substance used for flavouring.

Steam: Vapour formed and given off from heated water.

Malt Extract: A form of sugar obtained by germinating cereal grain. Usually supplied as a syrup.

Unmould: To remove from container.

Wash: A liquid brushed on the surface of an unbaked product. May be water, milk, starch solution, thin syrup of egg.

Water Absorption: Water required to produce bread dough of desired consistency. Flours vary in ability to absorb water. This depends on the age of flour, moisture content, wheat from which it is milled, storage conditions and milling process.

Whip: A hand or mechanical beater of wire construction used to whip materials such as cream or egg whites to a frothy consistency.

Yeast: A microscopic plant which reproduces by budding and causes fermentation and the giving off carbon dioxide.

Young Doughs: Yeast dought which is under-fermented. This produces finished yeast goods which are light in colour, tight in grain and low in volume.

References

Altenburrow, G.E., Barnes, D.J., Davies, A.P. and Ingman, S.J. 1990. Rheological properties of gluten. Journal of Cereal Science. 12: 1-14.

Bloksma, A.H. 1990a. Dough structure, dough rheology, and baking quality. Cereal foods World. 35: 237-244.

Bloksma, A.H. 1990b. Rheology of the breadmaking process. Cereal Foods World. 35: 228-236.

Briggs, D.E. 2001. Barley. In Dendy, D.A.V. and Dobraszczyk, B.J., Cereals and Cereal Products: Chemistry and Technology. ASPEN Publishers, Inc. Gaithersburg, Maryland. pp 325-335.

Brockway, B.E. 2001. Maize. In Dendy, D.A.V. and Dobraszczyk, B.J., Cereals and Cereal Products: Chemistry and Technology. ASPEN Publishers, Inc. Gaithersburg, Maryland. pp 315-321.

Chasseray, P. 1994. Physical Characteristics of Grains and their by Products. In B. Godon and C. Willm (Eds.), Primary Cereal Processing a Comprehensive Sourcebook. VCH Publishing Inc. pp 85-141.

Dendy, D.A.V. Sorghum and the Millets. In Dendy, D.A.V. and Dobraszczyk, B.J., Cereal and Cereal Products: Chemistry and Technology. ASPEN Publishers, Inc. Gaithersburg, Maryland.

pp 325-345.

Dendy, D.A.V. 1995. Sorghum and millets, chemistry and technology. St. Paul, MN: American Association of Cereal Chemists.

Dendy, D.A.V. 2001. Rice. In Dendy, D.A.V. and Dobraszczyk, B.J., Cereals and Cereal Products: Chemistry and Technology. ASPEN Publishers, Inc. Gaituersburg, Maryland. pp 276-313.

Dendy, D.A.V. and Brockway, B.E. 2001. Introduction to Cereals. In Dendy, D.A.V. and Dobraszczyk, B.J, Cereals and cereal products: Chemistry and Technology. ASPEN Publishers, Inc. Gaithersburg, Maryland. pp 1-21.

Dendy, D.V.A. and Bogdom, J. Dobraszczyk, B.J. 2001. Cereal and Cereal Products: Chemistry and Technology. An SPEN Publishing Aspen Publishers, Inc.

Dubey, S.C. 2002. Basic Baking. Published by Society of Indian Bakers, F-1 Jyoti Building, 16A/19, Ajmer Khan road, Karol Bagh, New Delhi.

Hoseney, R.C. 1994. Principles of Cereal Science and Technology. Published by the American Association of Cereal Chemists, Inc. St. Paul, Minnesota, USA.

Hoseney, R.C. 1986. Wet milling: Production of starch, oil and protein. In Principles of Cereal Science and Technology (Sec. Ed.). American Association of Cereal Chemists, Inc. St. Paul, Minnesosta, USA. pp 147-158.

INABIM. 1996. Flour. Incorporated National Association of British and Irish Miller Ltd., London.

Juliano, B.O. 1985. Rice, chemistry and technology. St. Paul, MN: American Association of Cereal Chemists.

Khatker, B.S. and Schofield, J.D. 1997. Molecular and physico-chemical basis of breadmaking properties of wheat gluten properties: a critical appraisal. J. Food Sci. and Technol. Vol. 34: 1-85.

Kulp, K. and Joseph, G.P. 2000. Handbook of Cereal Science and Technology (2nd Edition). Revised and Expanded Edited. Marcel Dekker, Inc. New York.

MacMasters, M.M., Hinton, J.J.C. and Bradbury, D. 1971. Microscopic structure and composition of the wheat kernel, In

Wheat Chemistry and Technology, Y. Pomeranz, Ed., AACC, St. Paul, Minnesota, USA. pp 51.

Manley, D. 1991. Technology of Biscuits, Crackers and Cookies. Woodhead Publishing Ltd., Cambridge, UK.

McConnell, J.M. and Welch, R.W. 2001. Oats. In Dendy, D.A.V. and Dobraszczyk, B.J., Cereals and Cereal Products: Chemistry and Technology. ASPEN Publishers, Inc. Gaithersburg, Maryland. pp 367-385.

NIN. 1995. Nutritive Value of Indian Foods. NIN. Hyderabad, India.

Pomeranz, Y. and Williams, P.C. 1990. Wheat hardness: Its genetic, structural and biochemical background, measurement and significance. In Y. Pomeranz (ed.), Advances in Cereal Science and Technology. St.. Paul, MN: American Association of Cereal Chemists. Pp 471-547.

Schofield, J.D. 1994. Wheat Proteins: structure and functionality in milling and bread-making. In W. Bushunk and V. Rasper (Eds.), Wheat: Production, properties and role in human nutrition. Glasgow: Blackie Academic and Professional. pp 23-106.

Street, C.A. 1991. Flour confectionery manufacture. Chapman and Hall. London; Blackie.

Sugdan, T.D. and Osborne, B.G. 2001. Wheat flour milling. In, Dendy, D.A.V. and Dobraszczyk, B.J., Cereal and Cereal Products: Chemistry and Technology. ASPEN Publishers, Inc Gaithersburg Maryland. pp 140-168.

Townsend, G.M. 2001. Cookies, cakes and other flour confectionery. In Dendy, D.A.V. and Dobraszczyk, B.J., Cereals and Cereal Products: Chemistry and Technology. ASPEN Publishers, Inc. Gaithersburg, Maryland. pp 233-252.

Watson, S.A. and Ramsted, P.E. 1987. Corn, chemistry and technology. St. Paul, MN: American Association of Cereal Chemists.

Ziegler, E. and Greer, E.N. 1971. Principles of milling, in Wheat Chemistry and Technology, Y. Pomeranz, Ed., AACC, St. Paul, Minnesota, USA. p 115.

Sources

Chapter 1

Fig. 1.1: Dendy, D.A.V. and Brockway, B.E. (2001)

Chapter 3

Fig. 3.1: Dabraszsczyk, B.J. (2001)

Fig. 3.2: Salunkhe, D.K., Chavan, J.K. and Kadam, S.S. (1985)

Fig. 3.3: Dendy, D.A.V. (2001)

Fig. 3.4: Salunkhe, D.K., Chavan, J.K. and Kadam, S.S. (1985)

Fig. 3.5: Salunkhe, D.K., Chavan, J.K. and Kadam, S.S. (1985)

Chapter 4

Fig. 4.1: MacMasters, M.M., Hinton, J.J.C. and Bradbury, D. (1971)

Fig. 4.2: Sugdan, T.D. and Osborne, B.G. (2001)

Fig. 4.3: Ziegler, E. and Greer, E.N. (1971)

Chapter 5

Fig. 5.1: INABIM (1996)

Chapater-6

Fig. 6.1–6.7: Dendy, D.A.V. (2001)

Chapter 7

Fig. 7.1: Brockway, B.E. (2001)

Fig. 7.2: Hoseney, R.C. (1986)

Chapter 8

Fig. 8.1–8.2: Dendy, D.A.V. (2001)

Chapter 9

Fig. 9.1: Briggs, D.E. (2001)

Chapter 10

Fig. 10.1–10.2: Welch, R.W. and McConnell, J.M. (2001)

Chapter 11

Fig. 11.1–11.2 Dabraszczyk, B.J. (2001)

Fig. 11.3–11.7: INABIM (1996)

Fig. 11.8–11.14: Dabraszczyk, B.J. (2001)

Chapter 12

Fig. 12.1: Khatkar, B.S. and Schofidd, J.D. (1997)

Chapter 16

Fig. 16.1–16.4: Townsend, G.M. (2001)

Index

A

Ammonium carbonate of bicarbonate, 144

B

Baked products from soft wheat, 186-217
- baking and cooling, 197
- cake faults and remedies, 206-207
  - baking powder, 207
  - eggs, 207
  - fruits, 207
  - shortening, 207
  - sugar, 207
  - wrong quality of raw material, 206
- cake making ingredients, 197
- cake making methods, 201-204
  - advantages, 202-203
  - all in process, 203
  - baking and cooling losses, 204
  - baking, 204
  - blending methods, 203
  - boiled method, 203
  - flour batter method, 202
  - half a minute at low speed, 204
  - one minute at slow speed, 204
  - panning of cake batter, 204
  - sugar-better method, 20-202
  - sugar-water method, 203
  - two minute at fast speed, 204
  - two minutes at medium speed, 204
- cake types, 197
- cakes and pastries, 197
- characteristics of cakes, 204
- cookie ingredients, 191-192
  - chemical leavening agents, 192

eggs, 192
flour, 191
milk solids, 192
shortening, 192
sugar, 192
cookies, 186-187
crackers, 194-195
crisp bread, 215-217
cutting machine cookie, 191
biscuits, 195-196
driers, 198
eggs, 199
essential ingredients, 197
external characteristics, 205
character of crust, 205
colour of crust, 205
symmetry of form, 205
volume, 205
flavours, 198, 201
flour, 198
foam type cookies, 188
improperly balanced formula, 207-208
baking powder, 208
internal characteristics, 205-206
aroma 205
colour of crumb, 205
grain, 205
taste, 206
texture, 206
leavening agents, 200-201
chemical aeration, 200
mechanical aeration, 200
vapour pressure, 201
milk, 200
mixing and kneading, 196
moisteners, 198
operational mistakes, 208
other baked products, 211
Danish pastry, 212-213
hot process pie paste, 215
pastry, 211
puff pastry, 213-214
short pastry, 214
packaging, 197
problems in cookie making, 194
cookie dough crumbles when handled and rolled, 194
cookie dough is soft and stickly, 194
cookie dough is tough and resists rolling out, 194
cookies shrink after cutting, 194
cookies spread too much during baking, 194
cookies have uneven colour and may have spots, 194
cookies vary in size and shape, 194
rotary mold cookies, 188-190
salt, 200
sheeting and shaping, 197
shortened, 197
shortening, 199
structure builders, 198
sugar, 198-199

sugar wafers, 191
suggestions in cookie making, 193
tenderizers, 198
types of cakes, 209
angel cake, 210-211
pound cake, 211
short sponge, 210
unshortened cake, 197
wafers, 215
water, 200
wire-cut cookies, 191
Bakery norms and setting of bakery unit, 228-235
book keeping costs selling price, 229
dough divider lubrication, 231
dusting four, 230-231
equipments, 229
ingredients, 228
knowledge, 229
layout of bakery unit, 232
equipment requirements, 232-235
location, 232
lighting and ventilation, 229
pan greasing, 231
sanitation, 228
scales, 229
scaling, 229
setting of bakery unit, 231-232
standard norms for handling losses of raw material, 229-230
storing of ingredients, 228
tests essential in baking, 232
use of sanitizer, 229
Bakery sanitation and personal hygiene, 258-270
advantage of cleanliness, 267-268
bakeshop sanitation, 266-267
cleaning and sanitary materials, 265
employee hygiene, 259-260
personal hygiene, 259
point to keep in mind, 268-269
safety measures, 269-270
sanitizers, 265-266
sources of contamination, 261-264
contamination from ingredients, 261-262
milk, 262
egg, 262
equipment/utensils, 262
cleaning and care of pans/baking sheets, 262-263
employees, 262
air and water, 263-264
sewage, 264
insects and rodents, 264
transmission of food borne disease, 261
use of sanitizers and insecticides, 264
working premises, 268
Bread making, 151-169
baking, 168
basic operations in bread making, 160-162

basic operations in mixing, 163-164
basic operations in sieving, 162
basic operations in weighing, 162
colour, 152
cooling and slicing, 169
essential, 152
example problem, 158-159
fat, 155
fermentation, 164-165
final proof, 167
formula construction, 158-160
glycerol monostearate, 155
high absorption, 153
improvers, 157
ingredients, 151
intermediate proof, 166
knock-back, 165
milk, 155-157
better crust colour, 156
better grain and texture, 156
better keeping quality, 156
better nutrition, 157
increased absorption and dough strengthening, 156
increased loaf volume, 156
increased mixing tolerance, 156
longer fermentation, 156
moulding, 166-167
optional, 152
packaging, 169
preparation of different solutions, 162-163
preservatives, 157
processing methods of bread, 160
rounding, 166
salt, 154
scaling or dividing, 166
size and shape of loaf, 168
strength, 152
sugar, 154-155
tolerance, 153
total sugars in dough at baking time, 168
water, 153-154
wheat flour, 152
yeast, 157

C

Cake faults, 278-285
badly shaped/uneven rising, 281
baking temperature for cakes, 283
additions, 283-284
richness, 283
shape and size, 283
steam, 283
burnt crust, 280
cake faults, 284-285
cake sinking in the center, 278-279
causes, 279
knocking in oven prior to cakes being set, 278-279
too much aeration, 278

too much liquid, 279
undercooked, 278
choice of ingredients for cake making, 284
fat, 284
flour, 284
sugar, 284
cracked top or a peak, 280
dryness, 281
fruit sinking in fruit cakes, 280
heaviness, 281
peaked tops, 279
flour used was too strong, 279
mixing was toughened, 279
too hot an oven with insufficient steam, 279
preparation of dried fruit for fruit cakes, 284
should know to make and serve perfect fruitcakes, 281-283
small volume with bound appearance, 279-280
Cake making methods, 201-204
Cookie ingredients, 191-192
Cookies, 186-187

I

Importance of cereals, 1-9
carbohydrates, 6-7
cereal production and importance, 3-4
energy, 4-6
fat, 7
minerals, 7-8
protein, 6
utilization of cereals, 8-9
vitamins, 8
Importance of wheat gluten protein in baking, 126-132
bread making performance, 132
characterization of wheat gluten proteins, 127-128
charge density of gluten proteins, 130
gliadin glutenin ratio, 131
gliadins, 128
gluten protein, 126-127
glutenins, 128-130
importance of gluten proteins to bread making quality, 127
quality and quantity of gluten proteins, 130-131
structural properties of gluten proteins, 130
Ingredients, 133-150

L

Losses in baking, 246-250
cripples, 249-250
divider efficiency, 249
divider loss or gain, 248-249
dough to be secured form a given dough batch
dusting flour losses, 248
fermentation losses, 247
invisible loss, 246
mixing loss, 247
trough grease losses, 247-248

M

- Macaroni products, 218-221
  - alternative raw material for macaroni product, 220-221
  - different types of noodles, 220
  - method of manufacture, 219
  - methods of preparation, 220
  - noodles, 220
- Milling of wheat, 40-51
  - break system, 45-48
  - end products of milling and their application, 49
  - flour treatments bleaching, 50-51
  - flour treatments bleaching: maturing, 51
  - milling of soft wheat vas hard wheat, 50
  - milling of wheat, 41
  - milling process, 41
  - milling quality, 49-50
  - modern milling, 43
    - conditioning or tempering, 44
    - graining cleaning, 43-44
    - roller milling, 44-45
  - reduction system, 48-49
  - traditional milling, 42

N

- Nutrient composition of cereal grains, 10-25
  - barely, 20-22
    - carbohydrates, 21
    - lipids, 21
    - minerals, 22
    - protein, 21
    - vitamins, 22
  - corn, 19-20
    - carbohydrates, 19-20
    - lipids, 20
    - minerals, 20
    - protein, 19
    - vitamins, 20
  - pearl millet, 24-25
    - carbohydrates, 24-25
    - lipids, 24
    - minerals, 25
    - protein and amino acid, 24
    - vitamins, 25
  - rice, 16-18
    - carbohydrate, 18
    - enzymes, 18
    - minerals, 18
    - moisture, 17
    - pigments, 18
    - protein, 17-18
  - sorghum, 22-24
    - carbohydrates, 23
    - lipids, 23
    - protein, 23
    - vitamins and minerals, 23-24
  - wheat, 1116
    - amylase, 15-16
    - carbohydrates, 13-14
    - enzymes, 15
    - gluten, 12-13
    - lipase, 16
    - lipids, 13

lipoxidase, 16
minerals, 14-15
moisture, 11
phenol and aromatic amine oxidases, 16
proteases, 16
protein, 11-12
vitamins, 14

P

Packaging and sale of baked products, 251-257
bakery sales tips, 255
bakery shops, 256
general, 255-256
sales personnel, 256-257
successful retail salesmanship, 257
bakery sales, 254
characteristics of packing material, 252-253
need for packaging, 251-252
packing material for bakery products, 253
waxed paper, 253
grease proof and glassine paper, 253
disadvantages, 253
polythene film, 253
low density polythene, 253
medium density polythene, 253
high density polythene, 253
polypropylene film, 254
bleached sulphite paper, 254
cellulose film, 254
foil laminations, 254
litre tinplate cans, 254
Processing and parboiling of rice, 59-76
aging of rice, 69
baked rice products, 76
breakfast foods and snack foods, 74
by products of rice, 66-67
canned rice products, 73-74
cleaning, 59
dehusking, 59-61
engleberg paddy huller mill, 64
fermented rice products, 75
flaked rice, 74
hand pounding, 61-62
mechanical hullers, 62-63
milling, 64-66
noodles (rice pasta), 75
parboiling of rice, 69-72
parched extrusion paddy/ puffed rice from paddy, 74
precooked and instant rice, 73
processed rice products, 73
puffed rice from parboiled rice, 74
rice bran, 68-69
rice flours and starch, 75-76
rice hulls, 68
rice polishings, 69
rubber roll dehuller, 64
stone dehullers, 63-64
Processing of barley, 90-95
barely flake, 91

barely grit, 91
barley flour, 92
blocked and pearl barley, 91
dressing, 95
germination, 93-95
grain selection, 92
kilning, 95
malting, 92
milling, 90
preparation and storage, 92-93
steeping, 93
uses of barely malt, 95

Processing of maize, 77-83
dry milling, 77-78
maize products, 82-83
milling 80-81
screening centrifugation and washing, 81-82
steeping, 78-80
wet milling, 78

Processing of oats, 96-100
cleaning, 96-98
cutting grading and cleaning groats, 100
grading, 98
impact dehulling, 98
milling, 96
stabilization, 98-100
use of oat mill products, 100

Processing of sorghum, 84-89
cleaning and dehulling through hand pounding, 84-85
decortication or attrition milling, 85
dry milling, 86-87
grinding and pulverizing, 85-86
processed sorghum based products, 88-89
processing malted grains, 87-88
wet milling, 87

Prospects and problems in bakery, 271-277
duties and taxes on bakery products, 276-277
problems of bakery industry, 275
prospects in bakery industry, 273-275
change in eating habits, 273-274
demand of baked products is likely to increase, 273
formation of government policy, 274
increased income, 274
increase in the employment, 274
increase demand for bakery products, 274
migration of population, 274
scope for the development of health foods, 275
utilises agricultural inputs, 274
unlimited scope, 274
quality of raw material, 275-277
selection of proper stream, 276
status of bakery industry in India, 272

Q

Quality control of bread making, 170-185
- acid insoluble ash, 174-175
  - calculation, 174-175
  - procedure, 174
- alcoholic acidity test, 173
  - calculations, 174
  - procedure, 174
- aroma, 179
- bread faults, 179-180
- colour of crumb, 179
- colour test, 170-171
- external characteristics, 177-178
  - break and shred, 178
  - character of crust, 178
  - colour of crust, 177
  - evenness of bake, 278
  - symmetry of form, 178
  - volume, 177
- gluten content, 172
  - calculations, 172-173
  - procedure, 172
- grain, 178
- granularity test, 175
  - calculation, 175
  - weight of unstrained, 175
- internal characteristics, 178-179
- major faults in white bread, 180-184
  - blisters under the crust, 181
  - colour spots, 183
  - condensation marks, 184
  - crust colour, 180-181
  - crumbiness of the crumb, 182
  - crust staling, 185
  - crumb staling, 185
  - deficiency of bloom, 183
  - flinty crust or shell tops, 182
  - holes and tunnels in bread, 182-183
  - irregularity, 183
  - leathery crust, 181
  - poor flavour and taste, 184
  - poor keeping quality, 184
  - ropy bread, 184
  - staling of bread, 184
  - sticky crumb 182
  - very thick crust, 182
  - volume, 180
  - wild break, 182
- maltose figure of flour, 175
- moisture content, 171-172
- pop test, 176-177
  - procedure, 177-178
- taste, 179
- testing of final finished product, 177
- testing of packaging material, 175
- testing of raw materials, 170
- tests for wheat flour, 170
- tests for yeast, 176
- texture, 178
- total ash content, 173
- wax test, 176

Quality evaluation and functional properties 101-125

alpha-amylase activity and hagberg falling number, 112-114
alveograph, 120-122
amylograph, 122-123
appearance, 104
asha, 114
density, 107-109
DNA fingerprinting, 114
extensiograph, 120
farinograph, 116-117
flour quality testing, 114
hardness, 109
impurities: screenings, 105
mixograph, 117-120
moisture, 109-110
protein, 111-112
rhelogical tests, 115-116
sampling, 103
sedimentation value, 115
size and shape, 104-105
smell, 105-106
specific weight, 106-107
starch damage, 114-115
test baking, 123-125
thousand grain weight, 107
victoriously, 106

R

Raw material used in bakery, 236-245
Role of bakery ingredients, 133-150
ammonium carbonate of bicarbonate, 144
baking powder, 142
baking soda, 141
butter, 139
characters of yeast, 141
classification, 149
cocoa products, 149
colour, 135
commercial available sugars, 138-139
brown or soft sugar, 138
extra fine granulated sugar, 138
medium granulated sugar, 138
sanding sugar, 138
sugar, 138
composition, 136
diastatic malt, 149
different types of sugars, 138
double acting, 142-143
dough improver, 149
egg wheat, 145
egg yolk, 145
eggs, 144
fast acting, 142
flavourings, 149
flour, 134-135
functional classification of ingredients, 133-134
structure builders, 133
tenderizers, 133
moisteners, 133
structure builders, 133
tenderizers, 134
moisteners, 134
driers, 134

flavours, 134
functions of salt, 147
functions of water in baking, 146
hard wheat, 135
lard, 140
leavening agents, 140
malt products, 148
milk and milk derivatives, 147-148
minor ingredients, 148
mono-calcium phosphate, 143
non-diastatic malt, 148-149
oxidizing agents, 149
pH, 136
phosphates, 143
properties of shortening, 139
salt, 146-147
shortenings, 138-139
slow acting, 142
soft wheat, 135
spices, 150
strength, 135
sugar, 136-137
sulphates, 144
tartrates, 143
tolerance, 135-136
uniformity, 136
use of shortenings, 139
use of sugar, 137
water absorption, 136
water, 145-146
yeast, 140
yeast foods, 150

S

Specification for raw material used in bakery, 236-245
baker's yeast, 241
baking powder, 244
cocoa powder, 245
coconut, 242
common slat, 240
compressed yeast, 241
corn flour, 243
dairy salt, 240-241
dried yeast, 241-242
glucose, 239-240
maida, 237
milk powder, 243-244
particle size, 243
salt, 240
sugar (cane sugar), 238
table salt, 240
vanaspathi, 238-239
wheat flour, 238
Storage of bakery ingredients, 222-227
foreign odours, 224
humidity, 223-224
inventory of raw material, 226-227
storage of baking powder, 225
storage of fat, 225
storage of flour, 222-223
storage of sugar, 225
storage of yeast, 224-225
temperature, 224

ventilation, 223
Structure of cereal grains, 26-39
barley, 35-36
corn, 31-33
endosperm, 32-33
germ, 32
hull, 32
tip cap, 33
pearl millet, 39
endosperm, 39
germ, 39
pericarp, 39
rice, 33-35
aleurone layer, 34
endosperm, 34-35
germ, 35
hull, 33-34
sorghum, 36-38
aleurone layer, 38
endosperm, 38
pericarp and testa, 38
wheat, 27-31
aleurone layer, 29
bran layer, 27
central, 30-31
endosperm, 27
endosperm, 30
germ or embryo, 29-30
germ, 27
pericarp, 27-29
peripheral, 30
prismatic, 30
seed coat and nucellar epidermis, 29

T

Types and grades of flour, 52-58
biscuit flours, 54-55
bran, 58
brown flour, 53
cake flours, 55
clear flours, 58
composite and alternative flours, 55
germ enriched flour, 53
germ, 58
grades of flour, 57
multigrain flour, 54
organic flour, 54
patent flours 57-58
plain of self-raising flour, 55
quality for raw materials, 56
raw materials suitable for composite products, 55-56
red dog flours, 58
straight flour, 57
wheat shorts, 58
white flour, 52-53
whole meal flour, 53